ALL IS VANITY

ALL IS VANITY

Memoirs of a Hollywood operative

Michael Selsman

new world digital
entertainment

© Copyright 2009, Michael Selsman. All Rights Reserved

ALL IS VANITY
Copyright © 2009, Michael Selsman, All Rights Reserved.
Digitally authored and printed in the
United States of America. No part of this book may be used or reproduced in any
manner whatsoever without written permission except in compliance with
Fair Use provisions of U.S. copyright laws using brief quotations embodied
in critical articles, reviews and for journalistic purposes.

New World Digital Publishing
ALL IS VANITY

All rights reserved under United States and World copyright protection.
Published Worldwide by New World Digital Publishing
www.nwdigitalinc.com

Los Angeles, California, USA.

Copyright © 2009
ISBN 978-0-9825314-0-2

Acknowledgments

Lori Tierney, Ken Levine and Steve Brain were invaluable in bringing this memorabilia to new readers. I would also like to thank all the 'teachers' at all the movie companies, film studios, networks, and agencies, theatrical and advertising, and in the little towns across America where we made movies, for all I learned about people – what made them happy, what made them cry. And what allowed them to hope.

(*Although the incidents depicted are true, I've changed some of the names to protect the guilty.)

Dedications

To my kids, Jill and Alexandra, who may learn more about me from what follows than they might have wanted. And to my G-kids, Julianne and Jasper, for whom this might be their only intimate remembrance of me.

To the movies, and the movie stars – the real ones. The ones made from 1927, when sound came in, up to around 1970, when Hollywood was overtaken by the youth movement, and glamour, mystery, and stories disappeared. Those days are gone, and greatly missed by those of us who grew up believing in magic. Today we believe in special effects via blue/green screen and computer. Nothing wrong with that, but it brings the level of artifice down to the extent that only five year-olds are unaware of the Wizard of Oz, who famously said, "Pay no attention to that man behind the curtain."

ALL IS VANITY*

Memoirs of a Hollywood operative

By

Michael Selsman

An Unauthorized Autobiography

*Ecclesiastes 1:1-11

TABLE OF CONTENTS

5-	Prologue
5 -	Marilyn Monroe
9-	Beginning
9-	The Way Up
12-	Maurice Chevalier
12-	Cary Grant
14-	Robert Evans
15-	Russians in America
16-	Carol Lynley
21-	The Donald & I
21-	Hank, Jane & Peter
23-	Peter Sellers
24-	Young Hollywood 1961
25-	Another Unsolved Hollywood Murder Mystery
26-	This Superman Wasn't Faster Than a Speeding Bullet
29 -	Why You Never See Movie Stars on the Street
29-	Rock & Larry
30-	Phil Silvers
31-	Manipulating the Media
34-	Darryl Zanuck
35-	Why You Shouldn't Drink on the Job
36-	Marlene
37-	Judy
40-	Jimmy
41-	Why Warren Beatty Liked Me
42-	Bing
44-	Bing's Kids
45-	It Takes Talent to Be an Agent
47-	Fritz Was a Fucker
48-	Francis and Me
49-	The Real Reason Gen. Westmoreland Never Appeared On "Laugh In"
51-	Now I Am a Man?
51-	Mr. Lincoln, I Presume?
52-	Howard Hughes Calling
53-	How to Get Away With Murder in Hollywood
57-	Why Lew Wasserman Hated Me
58-	Sondra
59-	Swifty
63-	Ratman
63-	The Unfriendly Six
66-	Jack L.
68-	Brigitte, Claudia & the Maestro
70-	Kiss My Nanny

70-	Rita Hayworth
71-	Truheart
71-	The Chaplins
72-	Marilyn & Carol
74-	Dating In Hollywood
77-	The Mexican Connection
81-	Marilyn (One More Time)
88-	Orson
96-	How (Some) Films Are Financed
100-	Sound & Fury, Signifying Nothing
101-	How Some Other Films Are Financed
102-	Catch 22½
103-	Southern Comfort
106-	Flying So High with Playboy Models In the Sky
107-	Indians in America
110-	The Real Reason Films Are Made On Location
111-	The $6 Million Dollar Man & a Charlie's Angel
114-	Tom Cruise Can Cook
116-	Bill W.
119-	A Pork-A-Lips Now
120-	Stan & Cheryl, Freddie & David
126-	If it's Good, Steal it
127-	Judy & David
130-	Goldwynisms
132-	Napoleon's Retreat
133-	Jack H.
135-	007's Car
136-	Beauty Is As Beauty Does
138-	Sexual Addiction
146-	Sic Transit Gloria
153-	Lying For a Living
161-	How Much Does It Cost To Learn To Lie?
163-	Speaking of Lying to One's Self
165-	Hubris
166-	Ultimate Hubris
167-	Then there's Mel Brooks Hubris
168-	Greed
170-	Direct This
171-	More Rumors
172-	Career Suicide Is
173 -	Truth Revealed: God Is a TV Critic
174-	Jay Bernstein
176-	Donald T.
177-	Beauty Secrets
177-	Henry Miller Died Happy

178- How Far Would You Go To Get An Agent?
184- L.A. is a Factory Town –
185- The Cult of Celebrity
186- Philosophically Speaking
189- Go Have Kids

PROLOGUE

I've been a press agent, a theatrical agent, a personal manager, a studio executive, an independent producer, and a studio producer. I've also been in a couple of films, not that you'd recognize me - represented a bunch of movie stars, hired and fired writers, actors, and directors, married and had love affairs with a few above-and-below-the-line alpha women, and generally had a great time.

Press agents probably are as old as the Greek playwrights. I can see some guy in a soiled toga, in the middle of the night, stealthily gluing, if they had glue, posters on the columns of the Acropolis, pleading for citizens to support Euripides' "Trojan Women," before it closed Saturday night, a little earlier than planned.

Caesar too, most likely, had a shifty-eyed henchman racing toward Rome in a commandeered chariot, proclaiming he had defeated the Egyptians, not Marc Antony.

How did Bill Shakespeare get Londoners into the Old Globe? Twofers? Maybe, but I'd bet his hawkers did a better job. Even John Wilkes Booth wasn't above using his famous Uncle Edwin's flack to get his name in the papers. Of course, he figured out a better way, and it would have worked too – if only he hadn't broken his leg.

Who knows what a press agent, or an agent or a personal manager, or a producer does? The tabloids and TV entertainment shows try to describe these vocations, but unless you've done it, it's impossible to imagine. The business has changed over the years, but the goal has always been the same – visibility for a paying client, in a good light if possible, but not always necessarily. P.T. Barnum, who famously said, "There's a sucker born every minute," also said, "Without publicity, a terrible thing happens: nothing!" The entire process of making entertainment, especially films, has also changed, in my opinion, irrevocably for the worse. Read on.

MARILYN MONROE

There I was - standing outside the yellow police "Do Not Cross" tape." Dawn was breaking over the Hollywood hills. How was I going to handle this pack of hungry reporters? *"Mr. Selsman, can you tell us what happened?" "Mike, how did she die?" "Was it suicide?" "What time was the body discovered?" "Michael, Was anyone with her?"*

I was in front of the most famous bungalow at that moment in the world, 12305 5th Helena Drive, in Brentwood. It was the last house Marilyn Monroe ever lived in. And I am, by attrition, her last press agent. Her body had been wheeled, lifeless, covered with a sheet, into a coroner's van. "Mr. Selsman, Mr. Selsman," I could hear the reporters' questions echoing in my ears, the flash bulbs going off. I remembered back to the first time I ever met Marilyn Monroe.

I was a very young twenty-two in 1960, several years into my career as a publicist for 20th Century-Fox in New York. I had been assigned to cover the arrival of Yves Montand at Idyllwild Airport, now known as JFK, in Queens, New York. He was on his way, with a brief layover in New York, to Paris, having completed acting in his first Hollywood movie, "Let's Make Love," with Marilyn Monroe. His TWA 707 taxied towards the arrival gate at approximately 9 P.M. I arrived on the tarmac with a reporter, Vincent Canby, of Variety, and Murray, our staff photographer to interview him, as per orders from my boss. The plane screeched to a halt as stairs were wheeled toward the door of the plane. A large and hysterical woman, Marilyn Reiss, came running up to me, screaming in my face, "What the hell are you doing here?" "What do you think we're doing here?" I replied. "He's our actor, doing our movie. We're covering this for Harry Brand, the studio's publicity chief." "Well, you've got to get out of here right now. This has not been cleared."

Cleared, I wondered? By whom, other than the studio, did it need it to be cleared? Marilyn Reiss was an east coast press agent with the firm of Rogers & Cowan. I had invited Vince to come along to interview Montand for publicity for the film he had just done with Monroe. I didn't know that Montand had a PR rep in the states, but Reiss, apparently, was there to block any publicity for her client – a strange thought to me. Clashing of press agents is by now a familiar battleground, but this was the closing days of the Hollywood studios as rulers of show business. Independent press agents were just beginning to come into vogue as the studios slowly surrendered to economics and the threat posed by television.

Only this time, we came to pushing and shoving. Her formidable frame tried to herd my group away from the stairs. "Mike, I knew you when you were just learning this business, give me a break and go away. Get your story another time." I started to wonder what the hell was the matter? Was Montand drunk and going to come stumbling off the plane with some starlet, embarrassing his wife, the famous French actress, Simone Signoret? Was this the picture and story Marilyn Reiss was trying to prevent?

Just then an alert came out over the loudspeakers, "Everyone, please clear the airport. There is no need to panic. You have plenty of time. Please go slowly to the exits. Everyone, please exit the airport." A bomb scare had been called in to airport security. Everyone got a horrified look on their faces and rushed the exits in pandemonium. I looked at Reiss, who now had taken my arm and was trying to shove me toward the insane mob struggling to get through the few doors to exit the terminal. Nobody, not the formidable Marilyn Reiss, or this bomb scare was going to keep me from getting my story. Besides, I liked my job and didn't want to lose it. My boss, Charles Einfeld, 20th's Vice President, wanted this interview, and by hell or high water, I, Michael Selsman, was going to get that story.

I tried to disarticulate Ms. Reiss from my arm. She glared down at me, "Montand is not prepared for an interview. We'll send you pictures. You have got to leave," confirming all my suspicions. How bizarre, I thought - two groups of publicists, whose normal work involved obtaining publicity for paying clients, heaving and jostling each other over access to the same actor, with apparently opposite intentions. This was a new one for me. Vince, who later became the chief film reviewer for the New York Times, was enjoying this show immensely and busily scribbling notes, which seemed only to enrage Reiss more. Her assistant cowered behind her. Montand walked down the staircase, carrying his own suitcases.

Other passengers streamed out of the plane. Miss Reiss finally relinquished my arm and rushed toward Montand. Realizing defeat, she called back to me, following right in her footsteps, "All right, but no pictures, go to the V.I.P. Lounge." What a relief - one second from being pounded into the pavement by this woman, now we were trailing her and Montand to the airport lounge.

A luscious blond in tan slacks and raincoat comes rushing up to Montand and into his arms. It's Marilyn Monroe. Miss Reiss's little game was over. The flashbulbs went off. Vince and I looked at each other, knowing he had the scoop. We followed them through a door marked, "No Admittance" that led outside to a fenced-off lot and a waiting limousine. Monroe's secretary, May Reese, steps out of the limo with two glasses of champagne. Marilyn and Montand toast each other. Monroe laughs, not a care in the world, but Montand, red faced, embarrassed, looks like he'd like to hide. They climb into the limo. Marilyn Monroe is obviously having an affair with Yves Montand.

We are standing there dumbstruck. An airport cop is called to the limo and approaches Canby and me. "You're going to have to clear the area due to the bomb scare,"

Canby and I drink zombie after zombie in the airport bar, waiting to get our story. We wait for hours, drunk and bleary-eyed, to go back to the limo. Finally at 1 a.m., we see Montand's plane take off for Paris. Reiss swaggers into the bar. "I guess you boys can go home now. The bomb scare is over." Canby printed his version of these events in Variety as front-page news the next day. No such thing as bad publicity, we always said. The illicit affair got much press, but unfortunately, their movie, "Let's Make Love," bombed at the box office.

Same thing happened a few years later at the same studio, when Elizabeth Taylor and Richard Burton decided to relieve their boredom at those long waits between set-ups by becoming better friends. "*Cleopatra*" also didn't benefit by the press frenzy over two consenting adults practicing reproduction while married to other people.

Little did I know that a few years later, I myself would be representing Marilyn Monroe. The Monroe death was very strange business. My job, funnily enough, was just like Miss Reiss's that day at the airport, to keep the press at a distance and tell them as little as possible. This had the makings of a very nasty story, reaching high up into the White House, and I was told, "Tell them nothing." In fact, I had nothing much to tell.

"Mr. Selsman, what happened here last night? Is it true Bobby Kennedy was here? Is it true Peter Lawford was seen speeding him away from the house in a black limousine?" "What was an ambulance doing here?"

Bobby Kennedy was married to Ethel and they had four kids. Everyone had seen Marilyn sing for President Kennedy at his birthday party in Madison Square Garden in that famous sequined dress, but until that day only insiders knew she had been passed on to Bobby Kennedy and had become his mistress. At that time the media had an unwritten compact with high-level public figures and their representatives to keep such things suppressed.

I had been called around 4:30 a.m. by Arthur Jacobs to go to Monroe's house. "Monroe is dead. Meet me there. Pat (Newcomb) can't handle this. Take over." Pat Newcomb was Monroe's personal press agent and confidant, and reportedly had spent the night there, making her possibly the third person on the scene. The first, it is said, was her live-in housekeeper Eunice Murray. The second may have been her son-in-law, Norman Jeffries, a live-in handyman. Around 9:30 that night, August 4, 1962, Monroe would not answer Murray from behind her locked door and the nephew forced the door. Murray supposedly called Dr. Ralph Greenson, Marilyn's psychiatrist. His response was to tell her to take Monroe for a drive, "to give her some fresh air." He says he did not come until 4:45 a.m, when he told police he had to break through Monroe's window to find her dead in her bedroom, still holding the phone.

In fact, when Eunice and Norman found MM unresponsive shortly after 9:30, they called Schaefer ambulance. Somehow, Robert Kennedy and Peter Lawford beat the ambulance crew to the house. James Hall, the paramedic, tried resuscitation, but her pulse was failing. Norman Jeffries says Dr. Greenson got there a few minutes later and told the paramedic to take her off the machine. He then withdrew a "heart needle" from his bag and attempted to give MM a shot of adrenalin directly into her heart. The needle hit a rib, however, and MM died at 10:45 p.m. The police were called around 4 a.m., and were told by Murray that she had discovered the body at 3:40. The first ranking LAPD policeman to show up at 4:45 was Sergeant Jack Clemons, who suspected the apparent suicide story was false. Later, he was taken off the case and eventually fired from the force.

Natalie, Arthur Jacob's wife, told me she and Arthur were at the Hollywood Bowl that evening attending a concert with Mr. and Mrs. Mervyn LeRoy, when he received an urgent call at about 9:45 p.m. He apologized to his group for having to leave, and departed in a big hurry.

I got to Monroe's house around 6 a.m. The police yellow tape was already up. It was cordoned off like a crime scene, which, later, it became. Pat Newcomb had rushed out of the house in tears, got into a car and left. Dawn was now breaking over the Hollywood hills. The word was out. Reporters started arriving in droves. I stood at the tape barriers in front of the gated small house. The questions started flying. Arthur had told me to give out as little information as possible, but the more I said I didn't know anything, the more the conspiracy theories started to fly about the Kennedy brothers. The coroner came out, followed by the deputy D.A., John Miner. Uniformed cops and plainclothes detectives were swarming in and out of the house. This was big news, even for Hollywood. I was surrounded by reporters, who were now yelling at me for answers. It was at a time like this, heart pounding, that I wondered how I ever got into this business in the first place.

BEGINNING

The mist falling reminded me of the rainy day a few years earlier, at my father's funeral in Farmingdale, Long Island, thousands of miles and eons away from Hollywood. I was 18 years old, just graduated from high school, as I saw my father's coffin lowered into the ground. We were huddled there together, my mother, younger brother, my sister and myself. My father, only 49, had left no insurance. Suddenly it dawned on me that I was now their sole support. We had been a comfortable middle class Jewish family, my father a "song plugger," a now obsolete but romanticized occupation immortalized by Gordon MacRae, opposite Doris Day, in "Till The Clouds Roll By," the story of a gutsy band of men employed by music publishers to persuade bandleaders to add new songs to their repertoires and get them played on the radio. At the funeral, I asked my father's friends if they had any ideas for me since college was now out of the question. Carl Jampel, a successful radio show producer, for years the head guy on "The Adventures of Archie Andrews," had just slipped me the first (and last) thousand-dollar bill I have ever seen, to pay for the funeral, and said he'd see what he could do. The next day, he called to say he had gotten me a job in the mailroom at 20th Century Fox, in Manhattan. I still have the stub of my very first paycheck, for $35, a princely sum in 1955 for an 18 year-old.

THE WAY UP

I had always loved movies – I still remember crying all the way home – four long blocks in the snow, after *"Lassie Come Home."* The Movie Industry is one of most exciting and informative businesses in the world, a business where the revenue of a single feature film, such as *"Titanic,"* or *"Lord of the Rings,"* can exceed $1 billion.

The entertainment industry has always been consistently attractive as an investment vehicle for practical and emotional reasons. Through wars, depressions, and good times, entertainment has always paid dividends.

Investors from all over the globe, from Sony & Matushita to Rupert Murdoch, Coca Cola and Vivendi, traditionally stand in line to pay increasingly record sums to acquire entertainment assets, especially films. Movies, as distinct from television films, are an emotional experience that lifts the consumer above the mundane, worrisome aspects of his existence. Seated in a large, darkened room, surrounded by strangers, watching fantastical images fifteen times life-size, suspends the watcher's disbelief. Whether absorbing a wild ride through the cosmos, as in "*Star Wars*," or flying with "*Spider Man*" through the canyons of a big city, or secretly spying on a housewife's infidelity, in "*Unfaithful*," the movies offer consumers escape, titillation and, above all, temporary relief from life's insoluble problems.

Movies, always the most reliable form of propaganda, along with music, and television programs are the largest export earner of the United States, bringing in more than $100 billion from world customers.

Nations frequently use movies to propagate their lifestyles and to project desired images, whether of military might to further political goals, of paradisiacal standards of living to attract immigration of the best and brightest, to convince others that their views on religion are the truth, or to hasten a particular regime's downfall. Everyone, after all, believes their culture to be the best. The myth-making aspects of the movies, therefore, lend themselves strongly to sideband commerce including product placement, for which global manufacturers are willing to pay enormous sums, to creation of fads encompassing consumables ranging from clothes to food to cars. These additional income streams have frequently, for instance, added more cash to a film's bottom line than its theatrical distribution, a good example being the "Star Wars" franchise, which combined gross exceeds $10 billion.

An example of how important the movie business is to the economy of America is that, in 2007, box office receipts in the U.S. totaled better that $10.5 billion, with another 10.90 billion coming in from the international market and, over the last 20 years, ticket prices have gone up 46 percent.

I was excited and stayed late in the mailroom after all the others had gone home. I read everything I could get my hands on, contracts, memos, clippings, correspondence about all the actors and actresses under contract to Fox. One was Carol Lynley, a former top junior model and now actress whom I had seen month after month on the cover of Seventeen magazine and had long idealized as being the perfect future wife and mother of my children.

After several months, in the arrogance of youth, it occurred to me that I had ideas that might benefit the company. Fred Silverman, the nerdy son of the only TV repairman in my Queens neighborhood, since TV had only just debuted, whom I used to push down the stairs at P.S. 139, was already working at CBS, and Simon and Garfunkel, another mysteriously nerdy guitar-toting musical pair us "West Side Story" faux gangster wannabees in Forest Hills High School wondered at, were just beginning to make some noises in Greenwich Village. Silverman went on to become the only man who has ever been president of all three networks, and Simon & Garfunkel – well, you've heard of them. Another term for "nerdy," obviously means talented.

One evening, I wrote a memo on inter-office stationary to the chairman of the company, an elderly Greek gentleman, named Spyros Skouras. There was no response. So I wrote another, delivering it myself to Skouras' office. Curiosity got the better of him, I guess, and he wanted to find out who was sending him all these memos. I wasn't hard to locate. The head of the mailroom was furious at me when she found out, "Michael, Mr. Skouras wants to see you. "About some memos". When you're done, you better come see me." I knew I was in trouble. I went up the elevator, to the 3rd floor, and stepped off at the executive suites. I was escorted into his office, where he sat behind an acre-sized desk.

"Come in, big sot, so who are you, sending me these memos? Come in, sit down." I sat down. "I was 14 years old when I come to this country with 10 cents in my pocket, I couldn't speak English," he said. Not that his English had improved that much. I later found out 'big sot' meant big shot. "You have ambition, like I did. I expect you to sit in this chair someday. For now, you'll help my secretaries." "Yes sir, Mr. Skouras." "You will learn the business, listen in on meetings."

I don't know what I expected, but it was certainly better than being fired from the mailroom. From that day, I sat outside his office, next to his two other secretaries and I did learn about how the movie business, distribution, development, financing, from the east coast perspective, really operated. All the power at the studios in those days emanated from New York. That was where the money was, and how the Hollywood production quota and budgets were determined.

Skouras' Cadillac limo was parked in front of the building, 445 West 56th Street, whenever he was in, and I frequently accompanied him at a moment's notice to appointments he had with bankers, Greek clergy, for whom he was a generous benefactor, politicians, including the Mayor, Robert Wagner, and certain "personal" engagements. I was to take notes on everything he said, even in the steam room of the executive club on the same floor, which he visited every day for a steam and massage. He may have been naked but I was dressing in Brooks Brothers by this time, and those wool suits itched. I was among the first to purchase the revolutionary new Reynolds ballpoint pen, which was supposed to write under water. I never tried it under water, but it wasn't much good under steam.

His chauffer, Will, and I became good friends. We spent a lot of time together waiting for the "Old Man." One day we went to visit a "friend" of his, uptown. Skouras got out in front of a brick high-rise on West 89th St. and said he didn't need me any more that day, as he was going home to Rye, in Westchester County. It was in the 20's and snowing and, coatless and in thin shoes, I had to find my own way back to the office. We were many blocks from the subway and I was lucky to make it out of that neighborhood alive. I had nothing but admiration for this man, in his early 80's, and wondered if all Greeks had his stamina and virility.

An opportunity opened up in the publicity department. I asked Mr. Skouras if I could have it and he agreed. By now, I was irrevocably hooked on the film business and began to meet actors, actresses, many of them stars, producers, directors, authors from both Hollywood and from New York, and from Europe, with whom I was working, obtaining radio and television interviews for pictures they were involved in and which were scheduled shortly to be released. I thought that dreams actually could come true.

MAURICE CHEVALIER

One of my first assignments was to stage an 85th birthday party as a media event for Maurice Chevalier, the famous French actor and crooner, who was one of the stars of Fox's *"Can Can,"* which also starred Shirley MacLaine. He was in New York to promote the film. It had been rumored that he had collaborated with the Nazis after they had taken over France, but I found him to be as charming as he always portrayed himself to be. I also thought he was as gay as pink ink.

He never made a play for me, probably because at that advanced age, it most likely didn't matter anymore. A reporter asked him how he felt being 85. "Considering the alternative," he said, "fine." He passed away two years later.

CARY GRANT

I met Cary Grant when he came to New York in 1957 to do publicity for *"An Affair to Remember,"* in which he co-starred with Deborah Kerr. It was a remake, and the 75 year-old director, Oscar-winning Leo McCarey, and I had already done a bunch of interviews in which McCarey wanted to talk about how he had modernized the story, after having made it once before, in 1939, with Irene Dunne and Charles Boyer. But the really good reporters wanted to hear how he had started in silents, and what it was like to work with Laurel & Hardy after he put them together for the first time. Mack Sennett has always gotten credit for the teaming, but it was McCarey who was responsible, a point he made again and again.

Questions flew to him about whether W.C. Fields was really a drunk (he was), and were the Marx Brothers really brothers (they were), and was Mae West really a man (the jury's still out), and was Harold Lloyd the cheapest man he ever knew (he was). He said he hated to live in the past and wanted to talk about today. He was the last person I would have expected such a Zen answer from.

"*Affair*" was a fairly straightforward love story with a tragic and ironic ending, and I thought, an odd choice for the director because I found him to be hysterically funny in person. I told him so, and he reminded me he had won as Oscar for "*Going My Way,*" with Bing Crosby, which wasn't very funny. He had won his first Academy Award, in 1937, for "*The Awful Truth,*" which also had Cary Grant in the lead. He never turned down a job, McCarey told me, something he had picked up from W.C. Fields. I wonder what he would have thought of Warren Beatty's third remake of his story, which Warren changed around a lot in order to fit today's language. Warren made it in 1994, with his wife, Annette Benning. Less successfully, I thought.

The premiere of the film was held aboard a French ocean-going cruise ship, the Ille de France, docked in New York harbor. We had booked the entire ship for the party. I was assigned to Cary Grant, and I was thrilled. He had been my movie star idol since I had become a teenager and I was really looking forward to spending time with him. I picked him up at his hotel, the Warwick, in a limo several hours prior to the event, and we went to the ship. He had been given a stateroom as a dressing room, where he could change into his tux. I was shy at first, but he made me extremely comfortable by his friendliness, and lack of ego. We talked about his films and I told him one of his that first made me aware of him was "*Gunga Din,*" which was one of his favorites also. I was also a big fan of Hitchcock and I asked him about "*Notorious,*" another picture I loved because it was a thriller centered on Nazi spies made during the end of the war years, and besides, I was secretly in love with Ingrid Bergman. He laughed when I told him that and said he'd introduce me to her if I ever got to Hollywood.

Grant had brought two suitcases with him and, as he changed, called me in the bedroom. He had carefully hung up his clothes, telling me the blue suit he had been wearing was nearly 25 years old, and that, if you bought classic clothes of the best quality, and took care of them, it was always in style. Yeah, sure. If Cary Grant was wearing it. He pointed to two pairs of alligator loafers, brown and black, and asked me if I'd like to have them. He said they had been custom made for him and that he had barely worn them and had changed his mind about them. They were a little large for me but I was only too happy to accept, and wore them for years until they couldn't be repaired any longer.

Chevy Chase's career as a comedian suffered and eventually nearly expired when he characterized Cary Grant on a late night interview show as a "Nance." Grant's sexuality was long a topic of speculation in some Hollywood circles. No one really knows whether or not he was bi-sexual, and Hollywood didn't care. He was idolized by the people he worked with, and loved by others whom he allowed into his inner circle. He kept his private life very private, and that alone is enough to raise some people's suspicion. He was married multiple times, five to be exact, to Virginia Cherrill, a woman older than him, and his first acting coach, Barbara Hutton, the Woolworth heiress, actresses Betsy Drake and Dyan Cannon and to Barbara Harris, when he died. He also shared a house in the Hollywood Hills with western star Randolph Scott, for many years. So what!

ROBERT EVANS

Robert Evans, later to be known as a sophisticated chooser of film material, such as *"The Godfather,"* and *"Rosemary's Baby,"* as president of Paramount Pictures, had been a ladies pants manufacturer, along with his brother, Charles, at Evans-Picone, in New York's garment district. On vacation, at the Beverly Hills Hotel pool, the lean and handsome Evans was spotted by the legendary silent and sound screen star, Norma Shearer. Shearer was participating as a consultant in the making of a film about one of MGM's superstars of the 20's, Lon Chaney, to be entitled *"Man of a Thousand Faces,"* and the studio was looking for an actor to play Shearer's late husband, Irving Thalberg, then boyish head of production under Louis B. Mayer. Shearer recommended Evans, who until then had only toyed with the idea of acting. But faced with an enticing opportunity, he agreed to be tested – and got the part. He turned out, in a small role, to have charisma on the screen and was now, ipso facto, an actor.

Darryl Zanuck, the famous producer and one of the co-founders of 20th Century-Fox, spotted Evans in a New York nightclub later on and cast him in his production of Ernest Hemingway's *"The Sun Also Rises,"* a love story set in Spain around the time of the revolution. Evans, this time playing a toreador, was in strong company, with Errol Flynn, Ava Gardner, Eddie Albert, and bunch of other big names.

While the film was being edited back in Hollywood, Evans, now intent on movie stardom, haunted our offices, asking for interviews to be set up for him. At first, it was easy to get him space in local newspapers like the Daily Mirror, or Daily News – "Local Pants Manufacturer and Playboy Becomes Movie Star." Even a few magazines, like Ladies Home Journal, Redbook, or Look, were receptive. After all, he was rich, handsome, single, and becoming famous. He'd show up almost daily with an armload of ladies pants for our secretaries, and for our lone female publicist, Gert Brooks. It got so normal to see him that when he didn't show up, we missed him. I remember him sitting on the edge of my desk and my telling him that as the trade media publicist, there was nothing I could do for him. I loved his look of disappointment, it seemed very practiced to me and I thought it was what he used when a girl turned him down – if they ever did. Eventually, the movie was released. He looked good in tights, but John Huston's intense direction brought out Evan's weakness as an actor, and he realized he was never destined to be a movie star.

RUSSIANS IN AMERICA

A unique event occurred in my life at the office one day in 1959. The U.S. and the Soviet Union were at war – the Cold War, and I remember clearly how, just a few years earlier, in school, we were trained to hide under our desks to escape impending nuclear holocaust. The Russkis were our enemies; we heard it from everyone from President Eisenhower to Walter Cronkite. Imagine my surprise one day when Mr. Skouras told me our two countries had decided, as an attempt to lessen the building threat of war, on a cultural exchange. Russia was sending a showbiz contingent, although I doubt they would have put it that way, to America and we would dispatch a like product there. Since no one else wanted to deal with the hated foe, or had refused to, I, as a low-ranking but well-dressed corporate apparatchik was designated to greet and spend a lot of time with three Russian film people.

I went to the airport with Murray, our staff photographer and met the then-president of the Russian Film Academy, gray-haired and imperious Ivan Pyryev, their version of Marlon Brando, tall, blonde and handsome Yuri Yakovlev, and Russia's answer to Katherine Hepburn, Julia Borisova. They were attended by a large group of large men who, I was told, were "interpreters." I didn't know what an interpreter was supposed to look like, but even at my tender age, I didn't think they were that. Also, the three guests spoke no English and therefore I could communicate with them solely through one of the large men. Or, in Julia's case, a large woman.

Pyryev had directed a new film version of Dostoyevsky's acclaimed literary masterpiece, "*The Idiot*," which starred Yakovlev and Borisova, and we had decided to send them Rona Jaffe's "*The Best of Everything*," starring an assortment of young Fox contractees like Barry Coe, Hope Lange, the model of the moment, Suzy Parker, and with a cameo by Joan Crawford. Oddly enough, when I met Rona to do some PR with her, pre-release, I found out that her father, Dr. Samuel Jaffe, had been principal of P.S. 139, my public school, in Queens. She and I had been in the same classes and didn't know each other until then.

The Russians were installed at the Waldorf-Astoria and I accompanied them on a sightseeing trip around the city. The six-hour circumnavigation of Manhattan Island is to be avoided, if possible. Especially in cold weather, and if one is subject to seasickness. We did the Radio City Music Hall, the Cloisters, the usual museums, and even a jazz joint in the Village, something they especially wanted to do. We ate three meals daily together for three or four days before departing for Boston, thence to Philadelphia, where I left them as they boarded the train for Washington, D.C., where Fox's political machinery was to take over.

They were excited and wide-eyed to be in America, and I was fascinated by their clothes, their appearance, Julia's beauty, and their ability to drink copious amounts of Russian vodka without seeming to get drunk. I later found out their vodka was a mere 40 proof, compared to our 80 or even 100 proof. That was, and I guess still is, their secret.

We learned to communicate rather well through facial expressions, hand gestures, and my drawing pictures of things or pointing and naming them, with the Russians supplying their words for it. I became especially close to Yuri, the young actor and, after several days, satisfied we couldn't actually speak to each other, the interpreters left us pretty much alone. Late one night, the both of us absorbing most of a bottle of vodka, I began to suspect that perhaps his lack of English was a tiny bit overstated. In an unguarded moment, I shot Yuri a question in English – and he answered it. He was terrified and begged me not to reveal what had just happened. It would be curtains for him (my expression, not his). The interpreters were, of course, KGB, and all three of my new friends could understand and speak English, however in a limited way. They were to pick up whatever they could in the way of intelligence, not military, but opinions about themselves and their country, and to learn from our citizens what they could about our intentions.

I would like to say I was proud of my fellow Americans during the time I traveled with my Russian friends, but because we were told they didn't understand our language, some pretty crude and unflattering comments were made about them, sometimes right in front of them, that embarrassed and even shamed me, especially after I found out they understood every word. Or almost every word. Some of our slang got past them and I was grateful for that.

When we said goodbye, they plied me with presents, a half dozen bottles of vodka, several cartons of Russian cigarettes, and two exquisite lacquered boxes, which I still have. Mr. Pyryev also startled me by, after insisting we take a photo together, which I also still have, inviting me to come to Russia, where he would install me in the Russian film school and make me a director. Imagine that. That was just around the time that Van Cliburn won the Tchaikovsky competition in Moscow and made the cover of Time magazine as a symbol of a breakthrough. Had I accepted Pyryev's offer that might have been me on that cover.

He also told me something else – we had been discoursing in English by then – he predicted that in the future, not in his lifetime, but perhaps in mine, we, Russians and Americans, Caucasians both, would naturally be allies in a global war against the brown-skinned people. If that isn't what's happening now, it could well be in the future. I just saw on the news that Russia agreed to let the U.S. military transport arms across its territory to fight the war in Afghanistan.

CAROL LYNLEY

One day, an actress walked into my office. "I was told to come see you about the publicity for my film." She had just finished shooting *"Blue Denim"* for Fox. It was the girl from the cover of "Seventeen," my fantasy, Carol Lynley. I couldn't believe it. She walked over to my desk as I just stared at her.

I immediately arranged radio and television interviews for her, the first being "*Luncheon at Sardi's*," a live radio show hosted by Ray Heatherton, the father of Joey Heatherton, at the best-known theatre show biz hangout next to "21." I paid for it using a plastic card, a new invention that was designed to replace cash. I didn't think it would ever catch on. A director on the 20th Century-Fox board, Colby Chester, a former army general, was chairman of American Express, whose card I carried. The press agents of Fox were instructed to use them as often as possible. Only a couple of restaurants in New York, among them, Sardi's and Al & Dick's Steakhouse, would accept the card as money, so although I really liked Sardi's food, and I had come to know Vincent Sardi on first name basis, I yearned for something else besides Italian and steaks.

Two months and dozens of lunches and shows later, we realized we had fallen in love, or rather she realized she had fallen in love, since I had been in love with her for at least the past several years. One night, in my 1957 Plymouth, I kissed her goodnight. "Michael, you're the first boy I ever kissed, except for Jimmy Macarthur (her co-star in "*A Light in the Forest*," a film for Disney), but that was only for the movie." She was also a virgin at 18 and I was 23, with a good deal more experience. We were both loners, both living with our controlling mothers. She had been working since age five as a model and actress and was the sole support of her mother and younger brother, Danny, who lived on Central Park West. I was still living in Queens and had the same family responsibilities. Now I knew that dreams really did come true. We decided to get married.

Which wasn't easy. Carol was anxious to escape the vise-like grip her mother, Francis, had on her, and I was equally eager to get away from my mother. Carol was in Los Angeles for some screen test or other, and I flew out to join her. We set off early one morning while it was still dark, in a car belonging to our friends, Warren Berlinger and his wife, Betty Lou Keim, both young actors Carol had known in New York, who had also moved to L.A. We were about two hours ahead of Carol's mother and a car full of photographers sent by the studio. Francis was determined to stop us, and the studio was only too happy for the impending headlines. Racing across the desert as the sun came up, we reached the farm town of Newhall, which was essentially one big cattle ranch, and woke up the Justice of the Peace. No kidding. Just like Robert Taylor and Veronica Lake, or Jimmy Stewart and Linda Darnell, or what any fictional movie script couple would have done in a hundred movies we had all seen. The JP lived above his office, which was also the town jail and charged $2.00 for the license and ceremony – just like in the movies. Our wedding pictures have wanted posters in the background. We should have known. When Carol's work was finished, she joined me back in New York, and we took a one-bedroom apartment in Jamaica Estates, on Long Island – a major mistake. Carol wanted us to live in Manhattan, where she was familiar with the terrain and had all her contacts. She deferred to me, being the good little wife she was now playing, because I was overwhelmingly guilty about abandoning my mother, and younger brother and sister. I had been, and remained, their sole support, and I felt I should be geographically nearby. We signed the lease, moved in, and for a couple of months it worked out, even though we had to ride the subway 45 minutes each way just to get into Manhattan. In retrospect, allowing my young, beautiful movie-star wife to mingle with the great unwashed that populated New York's dangerous underground was truly nuts. Clearly, I wasn't thinking about her, but about my former family.

There was a great deal of guilt on both sides which, ironically, was solved by Fox ordering Carol to replace the missing Diane Varsi, original star of "*Peyton Place,*" in the sequel, "*Return to Peyton Place.*" Varsi, on the brink of stardom, simply disappeared after the success of the original film, much to Fox's consternation. Like fighter pilots, it took a lot of time and expense to develop a talent and they didn't take kindly to one of theirs rejecting the gifts they had presented. They felt the same way when another of their young hopefuls, Dolores Michaels, left the stable to become a nun. They couldn't react too violently to that one, however.

Carol thought too much of herself to replace some dingbat actress in a sequel, so she refused. It was then the days of the seven-year contract, which in practice was not very different from the arrangement Southern planters had with their African employees in the early to mid-1860s. When an actor refused to accept a direct order from their studio, it resulted in "suspend and extend," which meant the time allotted for work on a particular film was simply added to the end of their contract. Bette Davis called it "slavery," and struggled mightily to escape Jack Warner's clutches, but failed. Shirley MacLaine, however, was not intimidated, and took Warner Brothers to court, where the tenets of the contract were ruled illegal, ending the stranglehold the studios had over their actors. Some say the decline of the studios as masters of the most significant arena of show business began their decline with that court decision.

Carol was under strong pressure from Fox and her agents, MCA. When that didn't work, they turned to me. I was told by my immediate boss, Edward Sullivan (the other Ed Sullivan) that I should go home and talk to Carol and make her see the light. I told him we had had an agreement, that her career and mine were separate and that I would not try to influence her. That didn't work, so his boss, Charles Einfeld, our VP, asked me in for a friendly chat. I told him the same thing. It wasn't long before Mr. Skouras himself, asked me to tea. He explained they had already booked the film for next Christmas and that they were counting on me to make it happen. I felt I owed Mr. Skouras for every opportunity I had had, which had led in fact to this very moment, and I told him I would try. I really didn't expect Carol to fold, because although she was young, she was also tough. I mentioned it at dinner, got the response I expected and reported same to the old man.

The next day, I got a call from Jerry Wald, head of production at the studio. "Mike, my boy," he began. We had never spoken before, but in show business, it's always first names among strangers. Especially when you have something they want. "I want you to come out to the studio and learn production from me. You can be my assistant, and if you like it out here and want to stay, I'll give you a producing job." Well, what kid ever wrote a letter to Santa and got back a reply like that? I can tell you it was tempting. But I was idealistic, a factor of youth sometimes also known as stupidity. And I turned that down too. I couldn't quite believe it the next day when the old man told me how disappointed he was that I was not, after all, going to sit in his chair and that my career, which until then was on the fast track at 20th, was over – unless of course, Carol did the film.

That was the last straw. I called my friend, Harold Rand, who had just become publicity manager at Paramount Pictures, and asked him if he had an opening. He did, and it was a better job, at more money. I took it and left the shelter of Fox. I became Paramount's newspaper contact and was dealing with the top reporters and reviewers in New York City, the seat of culture in the U.S. I was happy. Except for Harold's boss, Marty Davis, whom I thought would make a terrific marine drill instructor.

Shortly thereafter, Carol did succumb, and went to Hollywood to do the hated film she had fought so hard to avoid. Well, that did it for me. If I wanted to stay married, L.A. was where I was going to have to move to. John Springer, my good friend and a revered film historian and publicist who, ironically, was also close to MM near the end of her life, had left 20th to open a New York office for Arthur Jacobs, a fabled and very eccentric Hollywood publicist, who had the best list of movie stars next to Rogers and Cowan. Springer later handled the team of Elizabeth Taylor and Richard Burton. He also wrote a book about Monroe, called "*Beyond the Legend*," in 1987.

John introduced me to Arthur, who hired me on the spot for $175 a week to work for him in L.A. That was real money. I arrived two weeks later on the last plane out of Idyllwild (before it was re-named in honor of John F. Kennedy) as they closed the airport because of snow and ice and arrived in LA five hours later where it was 84 degrees. I have not regretted that move since. Especially in winter.

Guilt is something a Jewish boy ingests in his mother's milk – and I was breast-fed. I should have seen the signs then of the coming conflict and subsequent all-out war that ensued between my mother and Carol. A fight which I tried to stay out of, but which I lost, because I lost Carol and ended up hating my mother. When Carol and I finally transferred permanently to the west coast, I foolishly decided to bring my mother, brother and sister along. We took apartments in Van Nuys, in the San Fernando Valley, directly across the street from each other, giving my mother the perfect opportunity to horn in on our marriage. And did she.

Early one Sunday morning, Carol and I were asleep, when I heard rustling about in our apartment. I was positive it was a burglar, so, cautiously, I clutched a hammer I had been using to hang pictures with, and sneaked into the kitchen – to find my mother had broken in somehow, and was making us breakfast. A charming scene, perhaps, in a Neil Simon play, but Carol was furious. In my usual placating way, saying she meant no harm, I made the situation worse. Later that day, Carol made me get new locks for all the doors.

Two years later, some nine months after our daughter, Jill, was born, Carol and I split up. We had many problems, not the least was my concern over her parenting methods. Carol was in many ways, still a child herself, and hadn't expected, or wanted a child this early either in our marriage, or her career. Looking back, I can now understand it. While she was pregnant, she lost two movie starring roles and I was the target of her resentment. She would have done the role played by Suzanne Pleshette, in "*Forty Pounds of Trouble*," opposite Tony Curtis, for Universal, and the part that Yvette Mimieux played in "*The Light in the Piazza*," at MGM. She had really wanted to work with Norman Jewison, who did the Curtis movie.

Carol took, in my view, an extremely, casual approach to being a mother. We had received many threatening letters in the mail, some forwarded by her MCA agents, and I was afraid of kidnappers. Carol would allow Jill to play outside, alone, on the lawn, while she was inside. She said she was watching her, but Carol liked to read and I could envision her rapt in a movie magazine while some thug snatched our kid. Carol was also not too adept at changing diapers (I wasn't either) and there were times I got home from work when I was positive the poor kid hadn't been changed since I left. We eventually did get a housekeeper, Petra, the requisite Mexican nanny, who at least knew how to raise a child. Jill, of course, did begin speaking in Spanish instead of English, but we eventually settled for Spanglish, the language of Los Angeles children.

She retained Ed Hookstratten, a leading show biz lawyer with big time clients. I hadn't a clue about what to do for myself. I had moved my mother (yes, again), to an apartment in Beverly Hills, where she had befriended a young attorney, Donald T. Sterling, newly admitted to the bar, living in the same complex. She asked me to come and meet him, which I did. He seemed nice, was inexpensive, and was anxious to protect my "rights."

The wisest course of action would have been for me to accept Carol's decision, agree to pay what I could for child support, and try to remain on friendly terms for the baby's sake. Sterling convinced me that my rights, especially in child custody, had to be protected. So he went on the offensive, and in no time, relations between Carol and I spun out of control. There must be a better way for people to go their separate ways in our society than the one we suffer from now. Alec Baldwin, one of my favorite contemporary actors, has been on something of a crusade the last few years trying to get equality for fathers in raising children. He has been in a war with his ex-wife, Kim Basinger, over their daughter. Suffice to say; when the lawyers got through with us, we were irrevocably parted. As is always the case, the kids suffer the most, and Jill eventually, as an adult dumped us both. I love her and I miss her. I admire her for her principles, and I can't say I wouldn't have done the same thing myself.

Don Sterling, as a result of the extensive publicity he received from the front-page divorce Carol and I eventually suffered through, not incidentally because of the ruckus he and Hookstratten stirred up, became very well known, and is today the billionaire landlord of more than 10,000 apartments in Southern California, and derided by basketball fans as the owner of the Los Angeles Clippers, perennial last-place occupiers of the Western Conference of the National Basketball Association.

THE DONALD & I

Sterling, some three years after Carol and I were divorced, got a letter from someone in New York neither he nor I had ever heard of, one Donald Trump, who was demanding several thousand dollars from me. On investigation, it was our landlord from Jamaica Estates, in Queens, who owned the apartment Carol and I moved into, and moved out of some three months later. This unknown person, (it was 1963, remember), who worked for his father, Fred Trump, threatened to attach my salary in California if I didn't come up with an additional three months rent from our abandoned lease. Donald, the son, had read about our courtroom appearances and tracked us down. Sterling advised me to pay to avoid the hassle of another legal problem, so I did. Talk about persistence and dogged pursuit. Is it any wonder that Donald Trump is so successful?

HANK, JANE & PETER

When I reported for duty at the Arthur P. Jacobs publicity agency, Arthur immediately handed me Mervyn LeRoy, the famous director of *"Wizard of Oz,"* James Stewart, Henry Fonda, his son, Peter, and his daughter, Jane, Rock Hudson, Lawrence Harvey, Marlene Dietrich, Peter Sellers, Judy Garland, Steve Allen and James Mason, among others, to represent. I was overwhelmed and not a little scared. I soon found out however, that the longer established, true movie stars were among the nicest people I had ever met, in or out of the business.

Hank Fonda was a little quirky – he grew his own vegetables in his back yard behind his mansion in Bel Air, and gave them to his friends and business acquaintances as gifts, and he liked talking about growing up as a country boy in a farm town in Nebraska. He and Jimmy Stewart were lifelong friends, much like Bing Crosby and Bob Hope. His set nickname was *"One Take Fonda,"* and directors loved him for his professionalism.

He would try to avoid talking about anything of a personal nature with the press, and with his reps. I thought he was shy, but later on in life I met other people who grew up in lonely circumstances, whether it was miles of empty prairie or distant parents, and they shared Hank's reticence. He once said to a reporter, "I hope you won't be disappointed. You see I am not a very interesting person." He had problems relating to women and married five times. His first wife, actress Margaret Sullivan, was discovered unconscious from barbiturate poisoning some years after they were divorced. Her death was ruled accidental by the county coroner.

Jane Fonda, his daughter, said once that her father was deeply in love with Lucille Ball and that the two were "very close" during the filming of "*Yours, Mine and Ours,*" in 1968.

He was a rotten parent, and admitted it near the end of his life. I remember him warning me that some people shouldn't become parents if they're too selfish or too involved in their careers. I think he was referring to Carol, who was then pregnant. He and Carol worked together on "Henry Fonda Presents the Family," for producers Yorkin & Lear.

Peter Fonda and I were close in age, and although he had been a troubled kid, he was now stable and married, with a young daughter, the now highly talented actress, Bridget Fonda. Peter was scarred, emotionally and literally, as Hank Fonda's child, and accidentally shot himself in the stomach when he was nine. He was a rebel as a teenager, as is well known, and his career as an actor providentially coincided with the rise of the independent film industry.

The 60s were very different from the years after the end of World War II, and problems between children and their parents became very visible. "Father Knows Best" was now laughable. Hollywood, always looking for trends, started hiring young filmmakers who made cheap films that highlighted dope smoking, free love and breaking of society's rules, and including hatred for the Vietnam War. "Easy Rider" epitomized counter-culture. Interestingly, it was produced by Bert Schneider, multi-millionaire, Harvard-graduate son of one of the founders of Columbia Pictures, Abe Schneider. Youth-themed films were in, especially about the hippie movement. One of the best films of that time was MGM's "The Strawberry Statement," directed by a young, very young, commercials director named Stu Hagman, whom I represented. The plot in these films always involved drugs, campus revolt, riots, police brutality, and female and male nudity. It's hard to imagine that just a few years earlier, you wouldn't have seen Doris Day in a slip in front of Rock Hudson, in "Pillow Talk." Peter Fonda and Dennis Hopper came to be the Fidel Castro and Che' Guevara of Hollywood.

Jane and I were the same age and, among all the beautiful young women I was exposed to, I counted her as the most exotic and mysterious. Her face had, to me, an

Asian quality, and although I was married to one of the most famous faces in America, I remember having erotic dreams about Jane. She was living at the time with a gay acting coach, a refugee from the Actor's Studio, Andreas Voutsinas, whose job, as far as I could see, was managing Jane's life and career.

Jane always said in interviews and in person that her dad was distant and cold to her, which Hank admitted to me. Jane dated lots of older men in Hollywood, and got a reputation for promiscuousness, which wouldn't even be mentioned in today's media. Jane left Voutsinas for Roger Vadim, the French director and discoverer of Brigitte Bardot, for whom she starred in "Barbarella," a predecessor of today's comic strip- movies like "Batman," "Spiderman," and others. She told me she was only too happy to do Vadim's nude scenes just to aggravate her father. She later married Vadim, who specialized in marrying beautiful women, and they had a daughter, Vanessa. Vadim also married Brigitte Bardot and Catherine Deneuve. Just for that, he was my hero because of how much courage I knew it took to be married to one actress.

PETER SELLERS

Peter Sellers was truly nuts or, as it would probably be called today, "Bi-Polar." Obsessive- compulsives, and he was one, are perfectionists, focused on themselves. As Peter told me, if he couldn't wear it, eat it, or fuck it, he wasn't interested. The three roles he played in "Dr. Strangelove" fit perfectly with his multiple personalities. He could have done more, and in fact asked Stanley Kubrick, the director, if he could play also the part of the American bomber pilot. Kubrick thought it more than Sellers could handle, and instead cast the cowboy actor, Slim Pickens, in the part. The image of Pickens riding the hydrogen bomb down on a Soviet missile complex, waving his 10-gallon Stetson, will always be, for me, one of the most memorable of that terrific black comedy.

We often talked about both of us having controlling mothers, which interfered with our ability to make solid connections with the women in our lives. It was hard for us to trust. Peter's hilarious antics onscreen, such as his Inspector Clouseau character, were based on childhood tantrums, which he said he had often used to get his mother's attention. That socialization worked then, so he used it on his wives to control them, as well. Eventually he was married four times. While I represented him, his wife, Anne, in London served him here with divorce papers. He flew immediately to London to get her back. She wouldn't have him, so he said he married the first woman he saw in the lobby of his hotel, a prostitute. That was Britt Ecklund. Whether she was or not, that was typical of Peter's weirdness. He said she was a hooker, but then Peter was always very mean about women in his life once they were in his past. He put her in two of his films, "After the Fox," in 1966, which was written by Neil Simon, and the awful, "The Bobo," the following year. "She's a professional girlfriend and an amateur actress," was Peter's quote about Britt. When he was in his right mind, there was no one I would rather have hung out with. He was spontaneously funny, and women flocked to him. I was only too happy to pick up his leftovers.

It was during the filming of "The Party," directed by Blake Edwards, that Peter really cracked up. He had been on drugs, like Librium and Elavil, the popular mood changing chemicals of the time, and also drinking and using cocaine, the combination of which can make anyone psychotic. I would occasionally visit the sets of films being shot with my clients to cover media interviews the studio publicists set up during lunch or breaks, but also to "show the flag," to demonstrate to our most important clients that we cared. I found myself visiting Peter nearly every day. Sometimes he was glad to see me – sometimes he wasn't. It's a good thing I didn't take his rants and insults personally. Representing stars, either of show business, or politics (more on that later), or in business can be hazardous to one's emotional health. He died in 1980, at the age of 55, an original. Although I've always liked Steve Martin, in my opinion, it's risky to emulate a real genius like Sellers in re-makes of "The Pink Panther." The comparisons can harm an entire previous body of work.

YOUNG HOLLYWOOD 1961

Carol had been good friends with young Bobby Mirisch while in Hollywood. They "dated," but it was really more companionship to see movies and go to parties at Bobby's father, Harold's home. Harold Mirisch was the head of The Mirisch Company, in those days perhaps the most powerful independent film production company. The Mirisch's were behind "Some Like it Hot," "The Apartment," "Irma LaDouce," and a gang of other hit pictures. Harold's office displayed a bunch of Oscars.

Bobby had since married, and so we hung out as couples with other young marrieds. Carol and I, Bobby and his wife, Wendy; Mickey Callen, a young Columbia contract actor, and his wife; Andy Prine, a Universal contract actor and his girlfriend, Karyn Kupcinet, would show up on weekends at Peter Fonda's Coldwater Canyon home, with tennis court, in Beverly Hills, in a small enclave called Hidden Valley, to play – and to play. We had a terrific former pro, Flo Allen, give us tennis lessons. She was tall, pretty and very strong. And she was ambitious. Rumors about Rock Hudson's masculinity were becoming gossip and, traditionally, when that occurred in Hollywood, public dating usually put them to rest. Flo dated Rock and became his personal manager. Shortly thereafter, Flo became an agent at Chasin-Park-Citron, bringing Rock with her, before joining the famed William Morris Agency, in Beverly Hills. I don't know if there was a connection.

ANOTHER UNSOLVED HOLLYWOOD MURDER MYSTERY

A moment about Karyn Kupcinet – she remains one of the unsolved mysteries that haunt Hollywood. She was found murdered in 1962, and although one of the most extensive investigations in the history of this town ensued for many years – mainly because of the power Karyn's father, the late Chicago show business columnist, Irv Kupcinet wielded, no killer was ever found. It was sad that her former boyfriend, Andy Prine, suffered career problems, probably because Irv thought he was the culprit. Those of us who know Andy, and I later became his manager, knew he had had nothing to do with it. Various aspects of the investigation turned up some bizarre theories but, like Marilyn Monroe's death, the truth will probably never be known.

On the surface, Karyn was a sweet, pretty 21 year-old Jewish girl from Chicago, who became an actress because she didn't know what else to do. Her father was able to get her a contract with Universal, and placed her under the protection of his good friend, Lew Wasserman. Universal's head of talent and contract actors was Monique James, a former agent at MCA, who quickly became ultra powerful among the soon-to-be stars. Monique didn't think much of Karyn's abilities, but did place her in guest-starring roles in a few of the 10 or so TV series the studio had running at that time.

Karyn dated around, but settled on Andy Prine, one of Monique's favorites, and a hard-working actor who mainly did westerns. Andy was a player, and had to fight off the girls. But he was also ambitious, and hanging with Karyn couldn't do him any harm, he thought, with Mr. Wasserman and Karyn's dad. After a few months, when it became clear that dating Karyn wasn't going to advance his career as much as the bigger roles he now was beginning to get, Andy tried to end the relationship. Karyn wouldn't let go, however, and became a problem. Karyn was caught peeking in Andy's bedroom one night when Andy was in bed with another girl. Karyn also left increasingly desperate messages on his answering machine, wrote him long, rambling letters to the effect of how much she loved him, and in today's climate would have been a candidate for arrest for stalking.

Her friends, including me, began to worry. Andy wasn't being nice anymore, and who could blame him. Karyn was acting strangely – not answering her phone, or her door, and being out of touch for a few days at a time. Monique wasn't putting her up for acting jobs, mainly because the producers on the lot had their choice of hundreds of more talented young women, and it wasn't improving their prospects with Lew if they hired her, either. One night, Bobby Mirisch and I, and our wives were out to dinner, and decided that he and I would go over to Karyn's apartment when we were finished, to see if she was there. We sent our wives to the Mirisch home on Elm Drive, in Beverly Hills, to wait for us. Bobby and I parked on Fountain Avenue, a little east of La Cienega, in West Hollywood, and walked up to her door. We could hear the TV on, and through the closed blinds, see blue light seeping out from the TV picture. We knocked, then pounded on the door and called out her name. No answer. It occurred to me she might be entertaining, so we left.

The next day, I was shocked to hear that Karyn was dead. Apparently her parents, in Chicago, became sufficiently worried to call another of their friends, publicist Henry Rogers, of Rogers & Cowan, who got a deputy sheriff to open the door. She was found naked, grotesquely sprawled on her couch, her head askew at an impossible angle. She had been dead, apparently, some three days. I was told the stench was awful.

The autopsy concluded from the broken bones in her neck that she had been strangled – by someone left-handed. Andy Prine was not left-handed. The Kupcinets flew out and immediately retained private investigators to aid the LAPD. A great deal of pressure was put on the police, not only by the media, but also by the film community and Lew Wasserman. Despite Andy having had an alibi, he was immediately considered the top suspect. Mainly, I think, because the Kupcinets had never liked him.

The private investigator and not the local police turned up an appalling theory for Karyn's death. Unbeknownst to us, her closest friends, and Andy, her most recent boyfriend, Karyn, evidently, was living a double life. Long before cocaine and heroin became commonplace in Hollywood, Karyn apparently, was into it, and she was hooked. In addition to her steady fifteen hundred dollars per week studio contract, Karyn also received another thousand as allowance from her folks. Seven thousand per month in 1962 was a queenly amount of money. But not enough, it seems, to support her habit. The P.I turned up dozens of potential suspects, we were told. Karyn would frequent a Santa Monica Blvd. bar & grill called the Rain Check Room, in West Hollywood, near her apartment, and would bring guys back for quickies, for the money. Also identified were service people, including a TV repairman, even a UPS deliveryman, who had been seduced by Karyn. They were all checked for alibis, and whether or not they were left-handed. The inquiry expanded until there were almost too many potential suspects to make a coherent case. Nothing conclusive was ever determined, and the Kupcinets returned to Chicago to grieve. There can be no worse punishment for a parent than to lose a child in such a horrible way.

THIS SUPERMAN WASN'T FASTER THAN A SPEEDING BULLET

I bought a house on Benedict Canyon, in Beverly Hills, in 1965. I had no idea the Colonial-style two-story house next door was the very one that Superman committed suicide in. Or at least that was the official police report. A thorough investigation was later made by a private detective well known in Hollywood, Milo Speriglio, Director of Nick Harris Detectives, an organization formed before the FBI. Speriglio claimed Superman, AKA George Reeves, the actor who played Clark Kent and his alter ego, was murdered. A movie about this was recently made, called "Hollywoodland," and starred Ben Affleck, as Reeves, and Diane Lane, as Toni Mannix.

In an article in "Movie Star News," a tabloid publication, in 1968, Speriglio, interviewed me and New York Herald Tribune Hollywood reporter, Joe Hyams, for his investigation because Joe and I had done our own research, when he and I climbed over my back yard fence and broke into the vacant house. Hyams had been following up a story on haunted houses for his newspaper, and asked me if I had anything to contribute. I told him that renters moved in and out of that house with alarming speed, sometimes overnight. I had spoken to several, who had told me they heard strange noises, and that on one occasion, while they slept upstairs, the downstairs furniture had been re-arranged. Another renter swore he saw a spirit or ghost of Reeves holding a German Luger pistol pointing at his head. Ghost busters had been called in but the apparent haunting continued, with eyewitnesses claiming doors opened and closed at will, lights would flicker on and off, and the chandelier would sway. Earthquake? Perhaps. But not next door, at that moment; at least not in my house.

Joe and I entered the house quietly, but it seemed, at times, there were groaning noises coming from the walls, almost like the sounds one hears on a sailing ship when the masts and the knots rub against each other. The house had not been lived in for some time and the real estate agent, Elaine Young, told me it was because the word had gotten out. Inside, it was dark and musty and, I have to admit, a little spooky. We didn't see any ghost, but that doesn't mean he wasn't there. Perhaps ghosts sleep during the day.

Reeves had been doing pretty well as an actor, having good roles in *"From Here to Eternity," "So Proudly We Hail," "Blood and Sand,"* and *"Sampson and Delilah,"* all major studio hit pictures. But playing Superman made him famous. 34 million people in thirty countries watched the show from 1951 to 1957. But at 1:20 a.m. on June 16, 1959, either Reeves committed suicide or someone else killed Reeves. Why criminologist Speriglio thinks it was murder is because Reeves was a ladies man with lots of conquests, some of them very prominent Hollywood married women.

During the last two months of Reeves' life, Milo told me, he had received as many as twenty death threats daily on his unlisted phone, the final one just hours before his death. He had filed police reports with both the Beverly Hills police and with the District Attorney's office, and suggested a suspect – Toni Mannix, the wife of Eddie Mannix, general manager of MGM. Mannix was a big man in Hollywood, reportedly Louis B. Mayer's "muscle." The cops said that Mrs. Mannix was also getting death threats, so they were both being terrorized. But by whom?

Reeves left all his assets, some $71,000, to Mrs. Mannix in his will, which I'm sure, took some explaining by her to her husband. Speriglio also found out that she had given Reeves a brand new Mercedes convertible for his last birthday.

Reeves' last day was spent with the woman he intended to marry, a former New York socialite named Lenore Lemmon. She had a reputation as a jealous woman who had once been thrown out of the Stork Club, in New York. That night, she made dinner for her finance' and for their friend, writer, Richard Condon. Reeves went to bed around 12:30 a.m., while Lemmon and Condon watched TV. An hour later, they heard a gunshot and ran up to the second floor, where they found Reeves naked in a pool of blood in his bed. Reportedly, he had an astonished look on his face. His gun was on the floor, next to the bed.

Nick Harris Detectives was retained by Reeve's mother, Helen Bessolo (Reeve's real name), who didn't believe the suicide story because Reeves had a lot to live for. Both his friends, actors Gig Young and Alan Ladd, said they were certain Reeves would never kill himself. He was about to start a new season of "Superman," at a large salary increase, was shortly to fight an exhibition match for charity with heavyweight champion Archie Moore, and was planning to marry Lenore the following month, with a honeymoon in Australia, where he would earn $20,000 in personal appearances.

Reasons that Speriglio is convinced Reeves was murdered include the facts, as verified in the official autopsy, that no powder burns were found on Reeves hands, meaning he could not have fired the bullet, and that no powder burns were detected on his face, so he couldn't have held the gun to his head, as the police claimed. Speriglio said that he had investigated many suicides and that the absence of gunpowder showed that the gun would have had to be fired from a foot-and-half away, clearly an impossibility. The detective also found that after the coroner turned Reeves, who was found lying on his back, over, the single shall casing for the bullet was found underneath Reeve's body. Now how could that have occurred?

More reasons for suspicions, according to Speriglio, are that the coroner found the entry and exit wounds to be "irregular," or not consistent with a usual suicide, and that the bullet was recovered from the ceiling. Reeves' head would have had to be twisted in a near-impossible manner for a self-inflicted wound. Speriglio speculated that Reeves encountered an assassin, or surprised a burglar, grabbed his own gun and had it taken away from him, which was then used to kill him.

Lastly, the autopsy report states Reeves shot himself with his right hand. In fact, shortly before he died, Reeves was in an auto accident, where his Jaguar had been totaled, and his right hand disabled seriously enough so that he had had filed a personal injury claim in Los Angeles Superior Court, asking for half-a-million dollars in damages. It seems unlikely he could have used that hand to fire a Luger.

I've pulled the trigger on a Luger many times myself at firing ranges, and I can tell you it has a nasty kick.

So, was Superman murdered? If so, it must have been because he had misplaced his Kryptonite.

WHY YOU NEVER SEE MOVIE STARS ON THE STREET

Bobby's father, Harold Mirisch, loved to entertain and, on Friday nights, had a select group of people over to watch a couple of new films, pre-release. Their living room contained Picassos, Monets and Chagalls and when it was time to begin watching, after a sumptuous dinner; at least $10 million of paintings lowered themselves automatically, revealing a projection booth and screen. I found myself, on various occasions, sitting next to Audrey Hepburn, or Bill Holden, across from Billy Wilder, sometimes Jack Lemmon, or Shirley MacLaine. The cast changed from week to week, but because Carol and I were friends of Harold's son, we were always invited.

ROCK & LARRY

Rock Hudson was a sweet and confused guy. He was represented by Henry Willson, who specialized in gay male actors, and included in his stable were Tab Hunter, Richard Chamberlain, and Troy Donohue. If he had had a Latino, he probably would have named him Tom Bien. Gay in L.A., Rock, whose real name was Roy Fitzgerald, was a better actor than anyone ever thought, since almost no one outside his tight circle knew. I found out, to my surprise, when he very gently propositioned me. I was still married to Carol and she and Rock had done a western together, "The Last Sunset," a couple of years earlier, so we had something in common after all.

He started publicly dating Flo Allen, my former tennis teacher, as I mentioned, when the rumors about him began to seep out. That happened more than the public knew, when gayness was still scandalous. The public was much more naïve than today, and believed anything we press agents and star's handlers invented.

I liked him a lot and felt very sorry for him when he had to come out as he did. How much easier and better it would have been for him these days. It took a lot of courage. A few months later, he was dead.

Laurence Harvey, another one of my clients, also was gay, or bi-sexual, as we now call it, and very open about it. I believe it was he who coined the phrase, "You suck one cock, and everyone in Hollywood thinks you're a fag." At least I heard it from him first. He was a highly skilled British actor, who had co-starred with Julie Christie in "*Darling*," and had been invited to Hollywood as the 60's version of Errol Flynn.

In his youth, in London, he married one of the first supermodels, as they came to be known, named Pauleen Stone, and they had a child, whom they called Domino. Domino grew up, as many children of famous people do, wanting a spotlight of her own. She started one of the first dance clubs in London, developed a hip clothing line, got into sex, drugs and rock n. roll, and like seemingly everyone else in the English near-show biz set, came to Hollywood. She didn't seem to fit in, having tried AMW (acting, modeling, whatever), and eventually became a bail recovery agent. What's that, you say? It's the genteel term for "*Bounty Hunter,*" usually a thug, hunting thugs who have skipped out on their bail money. Domino, being tall and almost pretty, looked good in bullet belts, holding her shotgun, which she called "*Betsy.*" A made-for-movies pose. Domino recently died of a reported heroin overdose, facing ten years in prison on other drug charges. Did I mention her life would make an interesting movie? Well it did, because Keira Knightly played her in the inevitable film version of Domino's very interesting life.

Her dad, Larry, as he liked to be called, in L.A, came under the protection of Joan Cohn, the rich and socially connected widow of Columbia Pictures founder, Harry Cohn. Joan and Larry hosted some of the best and most entertaining parties for the film community in those days. Joan was regal and powerful, and Larry was bright and funny, a killer combination. He worked all the time, starring in several hit pictures, including "*The Manchurian Candidate,*" opposite Frank Sinatra. One day, in the back seat of a limo, on our way to an industry award show at which he was to receive some fatuous honor or other we had concocted for him, he put his arm around me and his hand on my thigh and told me he loved the color of my eyes. I told him I had heard that from women all my life, and that I liked them. He sighed. A true gentleman, and you can't blame a fella' for trying.

PHIL SILVERS

I loved Phil Silvers. I thought he was sweetest, nicest guy in the world and always looked forward to working with him. When I knew him, he was in his early fifties, married to a beautiful, much younger wife, Evelyn Patrick, an actress, and had five adorable young daughters. With "*Sergeant Bilko,*" one of America's top TV hits, he was the happiest man in America, he always told me.

Evelyn missed working as an actress, and acquired her own agent at Creative Management Agency, a young man fifteen years her junior. The Silvers could afford several in help, and maids and nannies took care of the girls while Evelyn pursued her career. Phil didn't like this at all, telling me that he and Evie, as he called her, had agreed she would be his wife and a mother to their kids. But he was too afraid to say anything to her, so dearly did he love his kids. He envisioned him and Evie splitting up if he became too insistent, which terrified him. Phil was not a ladies man, and romancing women was not his strong suit.

Comics are generally shy as children and usually become comedians in order to create a persona that protects them from bullies, racists, and, strangely enough, from pursuing women. Woody Allen and Larry David have talked about their reticence to approach women when they were growing up. Indeed, Woody has made a career of casting beautiful actress, sometimes decades younger than him, in his films and having them fall madly in love with him. That is one of the benefits of power, the ability to fulfill your fantasies. And Milton Berle always said his mother was the most important woman in the world to him, and he didn't marry for the first time until she was very elderly and presumably couldn't fight back anymore.

Phil was very busy himself, co-starring in *"40 Pounds of Trouble,"* with Tony Curtis, and as one of the many comic stars in Stanley Kramer's *"It's a Mad, Mad, Mad World."* He also had begun a new TV series, *"The New Phil Silvers Show."* Between Phil's schedule, and Evelyn's ambition, they began to drift apart. Evie soon informed Phil she was leaving him and taking the girls. Oh, and she was moving in with her new agent, now her boyfriend.

That almost killed Phil. The five little girls were his late life gift, and he had truly been in love with Evie. He rallied however, and continued working up until his death of a heart attack at the age of 74, in 1985. Although he stayed close to his kids as they grew, he was never the same man.

MANIPULATING THE MEDIA

Arthur Jacobs and Warren Cowan, of Rogers & Cowan, were, hands down, the best press agents of that era, and believed in constant publicity for their top clients. If no news was available, we were told to make some up. Warren's signature idea was to create a fictitious organization and have it give a client an award. One time, Cyd Charisse was threatening to leave the agency, so Warren invented "The American Beauticians Society," or some name like that, and appointed a local hairdresser he knew; it may have been Barbara Rush's, his then-wife's, as president. There was a trophy shop down the street in Beverly Hills, where we had a huge, gold plated cup made, and staged a presentation at our office, complete with "photographers," some of which were agency employees she didn't know. We serviced those photos to all the local papers and wire services, and darned if they didn't run them. I'm quite certain Cyd never guessed.

As an aside, Barbara Rush, a beautiful actress much taller than her husband, which made for some funny pictures, was a serious actress whose film role choices made her seem less talented than she really was. Working for Warren at that time, I got to know her socially fairly well. She had none of the affectations that most of the actresses I knew did, and in her upcoming years, had to contend with minor roles in B films. But she did co-star with my later client, James Mason, in a landmark picture in 1956, called *"Bigger Than Life,"* for 20th-Fox, which was about addiction to a brand new wonder drug called cortisone.

All wars produce some beneficial results, and cortisone, an anti-inflammatory, was discovered in 1936 and used to treat wounded soldiers during the Second World War. Acclaimed as a wonder drug, cortisone was not extensively tested on humans, except on the battlefield and in veteran hospitals, before it was released generally for civilian use. It held such promise for arthritis sufferers and, later, for sports injuries, its potential dark side was not discovered until later. In the movie, Mason played a family man suffering severe pain and blackouts. Told he has a rare inflammation of the arteries, doctors say that he has only months to live, so he agrees to an experimental treatment with the new hormone. He recovers and returns home to his wife, played by Rush. He must keep taking cortisone tablets regularly to prevent a recurrence of his illness. But the "miracle" cure turns into a nightmare as he starts to overuse the drug, causing increasingly wild mood swings, endangering his life and his family. It was a cautionary tale based on real-life events, and was directed by the respected Nick Ray.

I recently encountered pain from tendonitis in my elbow, caused by typing on the computer keyboard, and was given a painful shot of cortisone by my orthopedist, Dr. Neal Ellatrache, a leading Beverly Hills doctor who treats many sports and film stars. I brought the subject of cortisone addiction up to him as a conversation piece to keep me from bolting off the table as the incredibly long needle he was inserting into my elbow pumped this burning chemical into my arm. He was surprised to hear it – said that he routinely used it usually only once on his patients, because it had a tendency to degrade surrounding tissue if used more frequently, so it wasn't an issue for him. But it might be an issue for other people whose physicians aren't as educated and talented as Dr. Ellatrache is. Cortisone addiction? Who knew?

Barbara Rush did appear in some serious films thereafter, including 1958's *"The Young Lions,"* with Marlon Brando, and *"Strangers When we Meet,"* opposite Kirk Douglas, in 1960. A friend of Frank Sinatra's, she was also in *"Come Blow Your Horn,"* with him in 1963, one of playwright Neil Simon's first Broadway hits to be filmed, and in *"Robin and the Seven Hoods,"* in 1964, with the rest of the Rat Pack. In 1967, she co-starred with Paul Newman in *"Hombre."*

Arthur's favorite scheme was to have me, on arrival at the office, put a blank sheet of paper in my typewriter, and invent ten column "items" on all my clients. I'd then send them over by messenger to Mike Connolly, the tough and suspicious gossip columnist for the Hollywood Reporter, who would run three or four the next day. Those he rejected, I'd send the following day to Harrison Carroll, the crusty, old Hollywood correspondent for the Herald-Examiner, L.A.'s other newspaper. I'd keep recycling them, adding new ones every day. After a few days, I'd be reading the trade papers while drinking my morning coffee, and be amazed at what my clients were up to – completely forgetting I had written those lies the week before.

Army Archerd, of Daily Variety, insisted on checking out everything he ran, in advance, so no lies for him.

Another gambit we press agents would stage would be phony "press conferences" for our clients. Same deal as the awards, where agency employees posed as reporters, complete with note pads. I think I brought that to Arthur Jacobs when I arrived in L.A. to work for him. At 20th Century-Fox, in New York, we frequently staged press conferences for visiting producers, directors or actors from Hollywood or Europe, who wouldn't know a reporter from an astronaut. They were impressed, and that's all that mattered.

Our publicity director at Fox in New York, Edward E. Sullivan, annoyed us mightily, because, in addition to not doing any work at all, he would come in Monday mornings, call us together, and conspiratorially tell us that, over the weekend, he had talked to "The Coast." He would let us in on the latest gossip, who was doing what to whom, what was going to be the next hit picture, and so on. We suspected he was making most of it up or getting it from his sister, who was the secretary, and mistress, we understood, to Joe Moskowitz, a shadowy executive whose office was right next to Skouras.'

The story we had heard about Moskowitz was that in the 30's, Joe Schenck, one of the founders of 20th-Fox, had gotten into some tax trouble, and that Moskowitz had taken the rap for it, spending a couple of years in the pokey. A paid lifetime vacation was his reward.

Schenck, then president of United Artists, co-founded Twentieth Century Pictures in 1933 with Darryl Zanuck, former head of production at the Warner Bros. studio. Zanuck couldn't get along with the Warners' and wanted to be an independent producer so he could make the pictures he wanted to make. Twentieth Century signed a distribution deal with United Artists and quickly became the number one supplier of films to UA. However, Zanuck became furious when UA refused to give Twentieth Century stock. Schenck resigned from United Artists in protest and joined Zanuck in starting and running Twentieth Century.

The next year, Sidney Kent at Fox Film asked Schenck and Zanuck to rescue the failing Fox studio, Twentieth Century Pictures and Fox Film merged. Kent remained president, Schenck became chairman, and Zanuck was production head of a new Hollywood major, Twentieth Century-Fox Film Corporation.

In any event, we decided we were going to smoke Sullivan out. Normally, our department issued twenty or so press releases a day, which we'd distribute no later than noon to the newspapers, wire services, radio and TV stations, and magazines. Sullivan would stay in the office until he read his set of releases, then go to lunch and that was the last we'd see of him until the next day. So, we invented a movie. The first release we wrote (which didn't get out of the office) announced the studio had acquired the film rights to a new novel, "*Street of Sorrow*," written by some name we had made up. The next week, another release was written, to the effect that a writer known to be under studio contract had been assigned to do the screenplay. The next week, a contract director signed up. We followed that up by announcing various contract actors and actresses were cast and that a start date was next. From time to time, we put press releases on Sullivan's desk about location shooting, completion of principal photography, editing, music, and the like. About six months later, Sullivan came into the office one Monday morning, assembled us in his office, and told us he had talked to "The Coast," and heard that "*Street of Sorrow*" was so bad it was unreleasable.

DARRYL ZANUCK

Darryl Zanuck, production head of 20th-Fox, although married to the same woman for fifty or so years, lived mainly in Europe, especially Paris and Monte Carlo, in those days. He loved to gamble, and it shows in many of the risky, avant-garde pictures he made, promoting the anger of the Vatican with "*Gentlemen's Agreement*," starring Gregory Peck, about discrimination against Jews in American society; "*Pinky*," starring Jeanne Crain, the first film about a black girl passing for white; "*The Grapes of Wrath*," exposing the exploitation of poor tenant farmers of the Midwest; "*The Roots of Heaven*," about preventing the extinction of African elephant;, "*Leave Her to Heaven*," the first Hollywood film about a female serial killer, and "*The Chapman Report*," based on the Kinsey Report of the 50's, the first in-depth look at American sexual habits.

Zanuck had a succession of mistresses, with whom he lived in Europe. They were actresses, naturally, usually French or Italian, and of course he found starring or co-starring roles in his films for them. He was generous to a fault. Besides, there was no reason for them to stay with him otherwise. One such actress, Bella Darvi, who was actually Polish, was more beautiful than talented. Zanuck sent her to New York to do publicity, but she hadn't been in a Fox film for several years. She had had a role in "*Hell and High Water*," and a somewhat larger part in "*The Egyptian*," so we had absolutely no luck in persuading reporters to meet with her. We would be in major trouble if we couldn't produce something, so we did an "Ed Sullivan," and had a press conference for her, in which we publicists and secretaries pretended to be the media. Murray, our reliable staff photographer, was on hand to record the event, and we produced a book full of "clippings" and photos to 'prove' how successful her trip had been.

I believe it was when Ms. Darvi was in New York that Zanuck formally christened Juliette Greco as his newest "protégé." Ms. Greco had a fairly good reputation as an actress and singer when she met Zanuck, but being known in France is not the same thing as being recognized as a Hollywood movie star, so Zanuck, clearly, was the key to bigger things. She was promptly put in "*Roots of Heaven*," and "*The Sun Also

Rises," before co-starring with Orson Welles, in "*Crack in the Mirror*." It was a lot easier to get real newspaper and TV-radio space for her. That woman had class and style. Not conventionally pretty, but arresting, she could deliver a song and an acting performance that had power. She was big hit with the press in America.

When Zanuck came to New York, he used the conference room on the executive floor as his office and Skouras would detail me to act as his aide de camp for anything he needed. I'm five foot seven, and Zanuck was shorter than me. He wore lifts in his shoes, which made us the same size. He was partial to eight-inch Cuban cigars, which he bought in Paris, and when he ran out he would send me to Dunhill for their version, which was only slightly less lengthy. What would Freud have to say about Zanuck's height and the length of his cigars, I wonder? He was brusque and at times seemed lost in thought. I would sit at the other end of the immense conference table while he puffed - and thought. I have a photo of us at that table, where I conducted a press conference for him.

WHY YOU SHOULD NEVER DRINK ON THE JOB

Zanuck's casting director of many years, Owen McLean, was known for his commitment to his Irish heritage, and his inherent right to celebrate it. McLean, like most big studio heads of casting, directed the activities of his department, but also functioned as a "finder" of young, beautiful talent for his boss. After all, that was his job, n'cest pa? As Owen aged, however, he was apparently becoming a bit out of touch. His son, Mike, also was a casting director at Fox, and a friend of mine.

One of the producers on the Fox lot at that time was Ingo Preminger, brother of the famous director, Otto. Ingo had been a leading literary agent for many years, but had decided that what he really wanted to do was produce movies. Ingo's star writer, Ring Lardner, Jr., had come up with a black comedy about the Vietnam War, called "*MASH*," based on the Mobile Army Hospital division, and was showing it to a few agents to solicit some ideas for director and actors. I thought the script was terrific, and told him so. I said I could direct it and it would be a hit, and I had no talent whatsoever. I did make some suggestions, including our client, George Roy Hill, who became famous for "*Butch Cassidy & the Sundance Kid*," and Franklin Schaffner, who also became a hot director from "*Patton*." Zanuck, however, thought the best idea was Robert Aldrich, who was one of the most accomplished directors of action/war movies, including, "*The Dirty Dozen*," and promptly told Owen McLean to make a deal for him. Here's the delicious part. As I heard it, McLean somehow transmogrified "Robert Aldrich" into "Robert Altman," a little known TV director with only a couple of obscure low-budget film credits. Owen made a firm pay -or- play deal for Altman.

Ingo, the producer, thought Zanuck knew what he was doing, although in his opinion, Aldrich would have been perfect, and besides, he wanted the picture made, so he said nothing. Zanuck, in Paris, with new mistress Juliette Greco, was fighting for control of Fox and trying to oust his own son, Richard, from the presidency, so he wasn't paying attention, and a probably very surprised Robert Altman showed up for work to direct "*MASH*." As I mentioned, the script was so good, anyone could have directed it and it would have been the smash Ingo predicted it would be. And it was. And Robert Altman was suddenly the hot new director find.

Has Robert Altman ever made a successful film in the 35 years since? Nope, despite that some self-proclaimed film mavens like the late Pauline Kael, of the New Yorker, elevated Altman to God status, based on who knows what intellectual conceit. Warren Beatty, perhaps the canniest of all modern actors, leaped at the chance to do "*McCabe & Mrs. Miller*" with Altman, which besides being a flop, was shot so darkly you couldn't see the actor's faces half the time. I know he regretted it because he never appeared in another Altman film. I always felt Altman borrowed Stan Dragoti's idea and style for "McCabe" from "*Dirty Little Billy*."

MARLENE

Marlene Dietrich, another client Arthur Jacobs assigned me to, fascinated me. She was intensely beautiful and her voice was lubricious, accent and all. I had seen almost every movie she had ever made, from "*Blue Angel*," in German, through "*Witness for the Prosecution*," opposite Tyrone Power and Charles Laughton, and Stanley Kramer's "*Judgment at Nuremberg*."

I was always a little nervous around her. Although I was 25 and married, and she was in her early sixties (she took great pains to obscure her actual age), I would have literally dived into her if she had let me. I visited her once in her dressing room backstage at the Sands hotel, in Las Vegas, prior to her nightly show and watched as she was literally sown into her silver, lame' skin tight gown.

One of my duties was to be on hand when pictures were taken of her. One such session involved the skilled Hollywood master photographer, Frank Bez. Frank and I saw quite a bit of each other because he was in great demand among the female movie stars, whom he specialized in, and Arthur Jacobs had the best list of them. Because Dietrich was no longer young, she had special requirements and, although Frank was only in his late 30s, he had studied with George Hurrell, the master picture-taker of the 1930s and 40s, who had worked with practically every MGM and other star who mattered in those days.

Frank used diffusion lenses, at times a thin coat of Vaseline, and unique lighting that Dietrich devised and supervised, to obtain the full length and portraits he took of her.

Frank also worked frequently for Playboy, and had two nude layouts in the February and March 1965 issues, the first of Kim Novak, and the second of my ex-wife, Carol Lynley.

Dietrich had a mysterious smile she would send me as though she pictured what I was thinking. I always felt my face getting hot. I learned a lot about women from her, and she knew it. God, I was in love with her.

JUDY

Judy Garland was my all-time favorite star. She led a fractious and sad life when I knew her, but unlike Marilyn Monroe, whatever demons pursued her the night before, she was kind, generous and warm to me. As much as I disliked having to work with Monroe, that was how much I looked forward to spending time with Judy.

Judy's morning was early afternoon, and one day, as I visited her in her rented house on South Rockingham Drive, in Brentwood, Liza, 14 at the time, had already become the successor to her mother, as Judy retreated into childhood and dependence. Judy descended the staircase from the second floor, wearing a robe and nursing a black eye and a couple of reddened facial bruises. She told me she had walked into a door. And then smiled. And insisted on making me tea.

We had interview dates to set up, and PR arrangements to make for her comeback (again), this time at the Hollywood Bowl, to a star-studded audience that would include all the studio heads.

Everybody loved Judy, but were unsure as to her hireability, given her drug problems, prescription and otherwise, and her fondness for champagne. A socko performance, which she was always capable of, but didn't always deliver, would put her back on top. Everyone wanted her to succeed.

Judy deferred the details to her 14-year old daughter, Liza, who took notes, supervised the household staff, looked after her younger brother and sister, and made Judy's appointments with her hairdresser, her make-up people, her agents, and lawyers, their family travel arrangements, and ran interference with her step-father, Sid Luft. I was amazed at how efficient this young girl was. She clearly adored her mother, and I could see why. Judy was a doting and loving parent, no doubt because she had missed out on just those qualities from her own mother and father. My heart went out to this small woman with the amazing talent that I had grown up watching and loving onscreen.

Vincent Minelli, Liza's father, was one of MGM's top directors, and Judy fell for him because of his maturity, gentleness and grace. He was also bi-sexual, which probably surprised Judy, naïve and childish as she was, as a protected ward of the studio.

Judy later married Sid Luft, a former bouncer, who took over Judy's management and career. She wanted someone to look out for her interests because she had outgrown MGM and was now an international star, with global travel commitments, movie, concert, recording, and stage contracts. She thought Sid was just the man she needed. It turned out that Sid had fallen into the score of his previously unsuccessful life and, tough guy that he was, intended to make the most of it. Many actresses, not to say civilians too, immediately become pregnant to prove their love to their new man, and Judy sealed the deal with two more children, Lorna, and Joey. By then it was too late to get out of the marriage and her well-known depression, aided by drinking and drugs, put her once more in the awful, but oddly comfortable victim role again.

Around this time, Judy had had a small but stunning comeback role in Stanley Kramer's "*Judgment at Nuremberg*," in which she portrayed a Jewish concentration camp survivor, cross examined by war crimes prosecutor, Maximillian Schell. She astounded audiences with the power of her acting, but in reality, it was a role she had been playing all her life, that of victim.

Once or twice, I found myself driving from Monroe's house to Judy's house on some PR function or other, and marveling at the difference in the two women. Monroe had had a hard childhood, but so did Judy. Probably a lot tougher. To me, that was part of the reason emotionally lost children became actors – to live lives more agreeable to them, to wear someone else's clothes, to be called another name, to say words written for you so you wouldn't have to defend yourself at every turn, and to enter and live in a fairy tale world, at least for a while. The disparity in the two personalities was striking to me. Monroe never lost an opportunity to show you how powerful she was, and to remind you of how many people depended on her good will. She could hire you or get you fired, and made sure you knew it.

Judy, on the other hand, was the perfect victim, and had been from the age of three, when she wandered out on stage during her parent's act and inducted herself into their vaudeville routine. She was always vulnerable because she never felt she could please anyone – three year-olds stumble, or forget their lines. Judy wanted you to like her. It wasn't hard. She knew what she was, she knew what had been done to her, and she accepted it. Because she had been betrayed by her own parents, especially her mother, her habituation to authority made it impossible for her to act decisively in her own defense – except on screen. She married badly, always hoping the next man would turn out to be her prince, or salvation. In fact, many of the songs Judy made famous contained almost those very lyrics, as in "*The Man That Got Away.*"

She mentioned to me that there were times she wished she were educated, that there was something else she could do for a living, but singing and acting was all she could do - she was trapped. I said I had always wanted to explore science or medicine, but that I had been corralled into show business myself, and didn't see how I could leave it. She said, "As long as you're breathing, you're always in showbiz. I'm the living example"

Her upcoming concert at the Hollywood Bowl was the major ticket in L.A. I was inundated with requests from the media, Hollywood studio executives, friends and friends I never knew I had. There was a genuinely positive mood, tinged with perhaps some trepidation you could feel in the community that she would somehow blow this "last chance" to make it happen once more. No one needed to be concerned. That night, Judy was at the very top of her voice and personality.

The weather report had us concerned we might have to scrap the event because of rain in the forecast. It doesn't rain a lot in Los Angeles, and not usually in September, and the Bowl is, after all, an outdoor venue. But it wasn't raining, and a huge, sold-out audience of 20,000 filled the Bowl. They came with raincoats, scarves, hats and blankets, ready to stay even if it poured.

When she walked out on a ramp over the pool, a runway deep into the audience, from which Judy could almost reach down and touch people midway through the orchestra level, the audience jumped to its feet for a long, standing ovation.

"What a nice intimate room," she greeted everyone when she first came on stage. Then, it began to rain – a drizzle at first. But no one would dream of leaving their seat. This was a night to remember, a social as well as entertainment event. And then it rained a little harder, and I began to worry. In 1961, cordless mikes had not made their way into general usage, and Judy was working with a corded mike trailing a long wire. I worried some more – that the rain would somehow work into a fray or crack in the electrical cord and that Judy would, or could be electrocuted in mid-song. At one point, her cord, when it wasn't tangled around her feet, causing her to do a little dance that elicited a roar from the audience, draped itself into the pool. I thought certainly this was it – that she'd go up in a flash of lightning. A press agent's dream.

It soon began to pour down, but Judy didn't quit, and neither did her audience. She had them pinned to their seats. From time to time, groups of young men would leap to their feet, yelling, "Bravo, Bravo!"

A good thing it was near the end of her program. She was overwhelming, and pulled shouts and euphoric applause from the hardened and cynical show business audience. We were by then pretty soaked, but Judy kept singing – encore after encore, until there was no way to continue. I've never felt such two-way love between a performer and an audience, before or since.

JIMMY

Jimmy Stewart was the nicest movie star I ever met, and also one of the most reticent. He was a determined conservative, along with his good friends, John Wayne, and director John Ford. I think when you're young and idealistic, it's easy to be a liberal, which I was, but when you get older, you realize suddenly there's a third act in your life, preceding "The End" credits, and you begin to understand the need to focus on your own and your family's needs. It's especially acute when you're an artist and conscious of the body of work you will leave behind – what it says about you, and what it might mean to future audiences, if not historians.

Stewart was a very smart businessman, which very few people not close to him knew. He owned Ambassador Oil, of Fort Worth, and made nearly a billion dollars from exploration and production - more than he ever made as an actor. He asked me to work on his oil company as he felt he didn't need personal publicity, and actually tried to avoid it, except when he was asked to promote a film. In 1961, Ambassador's net income was $1,144,515. In today's dollars it would be twenty times that, if not more.

Ambassador competed vigorously against the giants of the oil drilling and exploration business, including ARCO, Sinclair, Chevron, AMOCO, Cities Service, and others, and successfully bid against many of these for leases in Texas, Arizona, and California. Whether or not Stewart's deep pockets, from his acting career and his oil revenues, or his connections in Washington, due to his having risen through the ranks in the U.S. Air Force, helped him, was never investigated.

Stewart enlisted as an airman in the Air Force a year prior to war breaking out with Japan and Germany, and rose through the ranks to Colonel. He was awarded the Air Medal, the Distinguished Flying Cross, the Croix de Guerre and 7 battle stars As a B-24 bomber pilot he flew more than 30 missions over Germany. His last mission was over Vietnam, at his own request, following the death of his stepson, Ronald McLean, a Marine, in 1969, in combat in Vietnam. Remaining in the Air Force Reserve, he rose to the rank of Brigadier General, the highest rank ever achieved by an actor.

He loved to work, and was disappointed when Alfred Hitchcock, with whom he made some of his most memorable films, like *"Vertigo," "Rear Window,"* and *"The Man Who Knew Too Much,"* chose him as the lead for *"North By Northwest,"* but was overruled by the studio, which insisted on Cary Grant, instead.

He told me he had never taken an acting lesson, and felt that young people could learn more when actually working rather than studying the craft. Take that, acting teachers!

Stewart, Henry Fonda and Margaret Sullavan met while acting in a small theatre group in New York in the late 1920s, and stayed close friends until Sullavan's suspicious death some years after she had married and divorced Fonda. Stewart made sure that Sullavan always had a job when she needed one and they eventually did four movies together.

WHY WARREN BEATTY LIKED ME

In Hollywood, no matter your role, you can have influence, even if you don't know it. Warren Beatty, Michael J. Pollard and I arrived in Hollywood around the same time. We had known each other in New York before, with Pollard actually playing me, or a representation of me, in a TV special titled, "*Henry Fonda Presents The Family,*" a series of skits produced by Norman Lear and his then-partner, Bud Yorkin. Carol's role was, appropriately enough, a pregnant newlywed, which she was, with Pollard, as me, putting up with the culturally accepted nonsense attributed to pregnant women in 1960.

A couple of years later, after Warren became a star in "*Splendor in the Grass,*" opposite Natalie Wood, his new love, and directed by Elia Kazan, he decided to do a film called "*Bonnie & Clyde,*" and took the idea to Jack Warner, where Warren was under contract. Warner was reluctant but was talked into it by Warren, a notoriously persuasive operator.

Warren got a highly-regarded theatre director, Arthur Penn, to agree to direct it, and cast the unknown but formidable actor, Gene Hackman, Estelle Parsons, another upcoming theatre actress, and of course, Michael J. Pollard in the other roles. In a small but very effective cameo, the new-to-films Gene Wilder, filled out the cast. Every role had now been cast - with the exception of Bonnie. Natalie, Warren's girlfriend was his first choice but she didn't want to do it. Warren checked out every other actress in town, professionally, of course, and wasn't satisfied with what there was to choose from. He even tried his sister, Shirley MacLaine, but she also turned him down. The start date was coming up and Warren had a real problem. He asked everyone he knew if he had overlooked anyone.

I had just returned from a business trip to New York, where I had attended an off-Broadway performance of a new play, "*Hogan's Goat,*" and was impressed by the performances. I even signed the young male lead, whose name just happened to be Bob Hogan (coincidence) as a client.

When Warren got around to calling me, I said I had just seen this play and that the young woman in it was very talented and could very well be right for the part. I had also learned that Otto Preminger, who was casting a Columbia picture, "*Hurry Sundown,*" had been in New York, where he had made a test of this actress. I told Warren he should call Otto and ask to see the test. He did, and hired Faye Dunaway for the part. The story of the film being abandoned by Warners after it was finished, and how Warren took the print under his arm and traveled to every major city in the U.S., obtaining good to excellent reviews, thereby forcing Warners to release it, is well known. By the way, I have never met Faye Dunaway and she has no idea of the part I played in her career.

This happens more often than the average moviegoer would suspect. One of my clients in 1964 was Martin Ransohoff, the well-known Hollywood producer. He had a script called, "*The Americanization of Emily*," which was set up, also at Columbia, had Arthur Hiller to direct, and had signed the then very hot James Garner for the lead. Garner, just off the hit TV series, "*Maverick,*" was just starting his film career.

Ransohoff had in mind a certain blonde, very buxom actress for the role of "Emily." Unknown as she was, except as a very close friend of Marty's, he was getting a lot of flak from the studio. Like Warren, he had looked at what there was around town, but needed an authentic Brit for the part. I told him that Julie Andrews, star of "*My Fair Lady*," then currently the new rage of Broadway had been cast as "*Mary Poppins*," for Disney, and I suggested he look at her test, because I thought she would be perfect for his picture. And she was.

BING

I subsequently became a talent agent with Artists Agency Corporation, now ICM, participating in television packaging with the agency's client, Bing Crosby Productions. I was also involved in the early career development of James Garner, Alan Arkin, and Robert Redford.

Bing, the agency's most impressive and lucrative client, had, by then, retired to Hillsboro, near San Francisco. He had recently remarried, to Katherine Grant, a beautiful young actress some 30 years younger, his children were all adults, and he looked forward to playing golf, his favorite pastime, and fishing in the Russian River, at his camp in the Sierras. Bing, a protestant, and super rich, was denied membership in both the Los Angeles and Bel-Air country clubs, both fortresses of gentile aristocracy, because he was, gulp, in show business, and he was furious about it. He could play – they were glad to show him off, but he couldn't belong, along with Jews, blacks, and Catholics.

The Bing Crosby Invitational, was a top attraction in the Professional Golfers Association, and took place annually in Palm Springs, along with his best friend, Bob Hope's tournament, also in the desert, as well as the Dinah Shore Classic. That still didn't help him with the L.A. upper crust. Hillsboro was more welcoming, and in addition to playing all the golf he wanted, Bing, in his late 50's, began another family, having two more children with Katherine. Bing was a happy man.

Until his business manager, Basil Grillo, hit upon a sure fire way for Bing to lower his immense income tax bill. The TV business was, and is, notoriously chancy, expensive, and almost always impossible to make money in. What if, Basil reasoned, Bing was to invest in the multi-million dollar business of TV development and pilots, which would generally not be picked up, and therefore, written off? Bing agreed, and his long-time agent, George "Rosey" Rosenberg, got the OK to set up Bing Crosby Productions.

Lew Wasserman, Hollywood super agent, had just created the new practice of "packaging" by persuading his client, Jimmy Stewart to star in a Universal Pictures western, "*Winchester 76,*" at a fraction of his salary, against a gross position in the film's income. That had proven to be a jackpot for Stewart, and for his agency, MCA, headed by Wasserman. If it was good enough for MCA, it was good enough for us.

Agency client, Jim Moser, created, wrote, and produced the pilot for a realistic doctor show entitled "*Medic,*" starring an unknown actor named Richard Boone. It was breakthrough TV for its time, and the agency commissioned him to write the pilot for "*Ben Casey,*" starring Vince Edwards. It was 1961; Bing Crosby Productions paid all the bills. From episode one, the show was a runaway hit. OK, we thought, nice income for the agency – puts us on the map, but odds are it can't happen again.

The next throw, we knew, would be craps and we'd be out for at least the next couple of seasons. That would cool us off. So we let some time go by and in 1964, Bing invested in yet another pilot, financing yet another hit, this time a political drama, starring Richard Crenna, called "*Slattery's Heroes.*" It was only a modest hit, but it too, was a moneymaker. Apparently we could do no wrong.

By now, we were on a roll, much like a shooter at the craps table in Vegas. The crowd around us, in this case, the trade papers, and the local creative community, were cheering us on. One last chance for Bing to lose a lot of money – The following season, 1965, we chose a take-off on the Billy Wilder classic film, "*Stalag 17,*" and we came out with "*Hogan's Heroes.*" "Hogan's" quickly became the number one show on TV.

Bing, ensconced in delicious retirement, with only his back swing to think about, got a bad news call from his business manager. Grillo informed Bing that, due to the great rush of new money pouring into Bing Crosby Productions, Bing now owed the Internal Revenue Service millions more than he had ever paid them. Worse yet, if he didn't want to dispose of his assets in a fire sale, Bing would have to go back to work. Bing was furious, and Basil Grillo was fired.

Bing sold his five-acre Holmby Hills home in Los Angeles to Aaron Spelling, the ultra-successful TV producer, his Oldsmobile agency, which saddened us agents, since all of us drove flashy 88's and 98 Starfires, which we purchased at cost, and other of his assets. Spelling tore down Bing's mansion, and built a 50-plus-room home more resembling a grand hotel on the property. And Bing was looking for work.

Could things get worse? Yes. There didn't seem to be a way out for Bing. When were we going to fail? Bing didn't give us the chance. He sold his share of the production company, and took his losses. Which were in reality, his winnings. Is this clear?

BING'S KIDS

Gary Crosby, one of Bing's four sons by his first wife, Dixie Lee, was struggling to become either a singer or an actor, whatever would work for him. He and I were almost exactly the same age, and so I got to represent him. It was more of a favor to Bing than a real opportunity for me. Gary, a dead ringer for his old man was a moody and troubled young guy, and had a drinking problem. I got him out for a bunch of TV guest shots around town, and some minor roles in low-budget movies, a couple of which he got. He acquitted himself pretty well, but for some reason he was rarely asked back. I think it was the chip he carried on his shoulder.

Because I liked him, and he had stories to tell, which always interested me, I'd go drinking with him occasionally after work, usually at Scandia, on the Sunset Strip, the best-known gourmet restaurant in those days in a gourmet restaurant-scarce Los Angeles. Gary hated both his father and his mother. He told me that Bing had become an alcoholic early in his life, and, unlike some drunks who became happy when inebriated, Bing became mean and violent. Dixie, Gary's mom, in order to stay emotionally connected to Bing, also took up drinking, and eventually outclassed Bing in violent drunken behavior. AA people know this as "co-dependency." It seems that Bing and Dixie vied to outdo themselves in punishing their four boys – Dixie would begin during the day, and Bing would take over at night. Beatings, humiliation, embarrassment, and degradation were common for the kids of America's best-loved crooner, although the unaware public had a hero worship relationship with him.

The media then, as compared to now, would never print anything unkind about celebrities – their advertising and access to movie, radio, music and, eventually TV stars depended on keeping our heroes' dark secrets just that. Gary, however, wrote a book in 1983 about his painful life, which he called, *"Going My Own Way,"* an obvious take-off of the title of his dad's Oscar-winning performance in, *"Going My Way,"* in which Bing played a kindly priest. Gary left nothing out, since Bing had died six years earlier, and Gary didn't need to fear him any longer.

Gary related, among other things, that, as a six year-old, he had hidden his breakfast of bacon and eggs under a carpet, since he was allergic to eggs and couldn't eat them. When his mother found out, she made him eat the entire meal, which was then covered with dirt and hair. And when Bing came home, he beat Gary until he bled.

Bing eventually stopped drinking, mostly because his liver had enlarged, and his best friend, Bob Hope, worked on him to quit. Dixie, however, couldn't stop, and remained a fall-down drunk until she died. Although the names have been changed, the movie "*Smash-Up, the Story of a Woman*," made in 1947, is based on her life. She died at age 41, allegedly of ovarian cancer, but heavy alcohol use contributed to her early death.

I couldn't handle Gary after a while – he would fly into unprovoked rages, obviously aimed at his parents, but whom he could never dare confront, and would show up drunk for appointments. I asked "Rosey," my boss, who was Bing's long-time agent, if I could get off Gary's case, and to my relief, he agreed.
Gary died in1995, at age 61, predeceased by his brothers, Dennis, in 1991, from suicide, and Lindsay, also from suicide, in 1989. Philip, the last remaining Crosby sibling, died early in 2004. All four sons also suffered from long-term effects of drinking, and of the terrible lack of love their parents punished them with.

IT TAKES TALENT TO BE AN AGENT

As a movie and TV agent in those days, I had great latitude to cruise around the studios and look for opportunities for my personal clients, and those others the agency represented. Barry Diller, then a program executive for ABC-TV, invented what became known as the "Movie of the Week," a two-hour, made-for-TV film that instantly became a network and advertiser's dream. Audiences, once hooked, would presumably stay for the entire show, instead of switching channels after a half-hour, or hour. This was so successful that Diller was hired by Paramount to expand on his vision. A MOW, as it came to be known in the newly emerging world of acronyms, could be distributed outside the United States as a feature film, giving the studios additional pictures at a fraction of the production cost of regular movies. Diller eventually became chairman and CEO of the studio, before leaving to join Rupert Murdoch in creating a fourth TV network, Fox.

One such MOW producer, Ray Wagner, was sitting alone in an office on the Universal lot, wondering what his next job, if any, might be. He had a screenplay by a new and very talented writer named Barbara Turner, which had the unique and impossible title of, "*Me and the Arch Kook Petulia.*" He had sent it out to a number of agencies for casting suggestions, but wasn't getting much positive feedback. I happened in and he gave me the script to take back to my office and read, hoping he'd get a better reaction from me. I read it and thought it was terrific. I called him the next day and said I wanted a forty-eight hour exclusive to see what kind of package I could put together from within the agency client list. Ray was only too happy to agree, and I made several copies and gave them to Rosey's wife, Meta Rosenberg, the agent who personally looked after Jim Garner, and sent one to my client, Geraldine Chaplin. Geraldine was very warm in town, having come off strongly in her very first movie, "*Dr. Zhivago.*"

Both Garner and Chaplin liked the script and agreed to do it. I had a package. My first. I was overjoyed. I brought Ray in to the office to negotiate a deal for him to produce and direct. He also was overjoyed. Rosey, his wife, Meta, and their partner, Bob Coryell, older conservatives all, were concerned about the legality of representing Ray specifically for this project, as well as Garner and Chaplin, and insisted that Ray get his own legal and business advice. The powerhouse team of Mike Ovitz, Bill Haber, and Ron Meyer, who left the William Morris agency to start Creative Artists Agency, which became the leading movie packager in town, had not yet been formed and therefore, my bosses could not have gotten the message that this was the future. Ray said he wasn't interested in outside assistance and that he would be very happy to be included in the package. Bob Coryell insisted they couldn't do that.

You know how it's said that just prior to death, your entire life is said to flash before your eyes? I can testify to its truth, for I saw my package dissolving. Ray was beginning to get angry, and Coryell was too. Ray jumped up and said he wouldn't do business with us, and left. I was feeling unwell. It reminded me of Groucho Marx's line about not wanting to belong to a club that would have him as a member. Ray had been rejected, it seemed to him, when I spoke to him later that day. In reality, I tried to explain, my guys were simply trying to protect him and his interests. "From whom," Ray wanted to know? Was my agency untrustworthy? Of course not, I explained, we had one of the best reputations for honesty in the entire agency business, quite a statement in Hollywood.

Creative people are by definition, insecure, and it doesn't matter if you're a star or a studio grip. The next job is all. In making a film, a disparate group of strangers come together for a specified period of a few weeks, all with specialties of their own, and under great pressure, working 24 hours every day, make alliances for convenience or mutual support. Love happens. Affairs happen. Tragedies occur. For the director, a role similar to a British sea captain in the 1800s, a tight bond between him and his closest associates, in this case the leading actors, is vital, especially if it's your first time around. Ray thought that by not being included in the agency package, he'd forever be regarded as an outsider, and not able to count on support from the stars or their agents if he ran into emotional or professional difficulties.

Well, no good deed goes unpunished. Ray stopped talking to me and eventually lost his option on the script. Richard Lester, suddenly a hot director off the first and second Beatles films, picked up the script, quickly locked in George C. Scott and his pal, Julie Christie, had Barbara Turner do a quick rewrite, lopped a few words off the title, a good thing, and Warner Brothers put up the money for the film, now called simply, "*Petulia*." It was a wonderful film, full of pathos, and immense human drama. But of course I knew that.

FRITZ WAS A FUCKER

I represented the irrepressible and immensely talented animator and filmmaker, Ralph Bakshi, right after he completed "*Fritz, the Cat*," the breakthrough X-rated feature-length cartoon in 1972. It caused a commotion both in Hollywood and across the U.S. If you think too much was made of Janet Jackson's "boob tube" three-second shot during the Super Bowl show, you have no idea of the fuss kicked up by "Fritz" in the media. Imagine cartoon animals screwing right up there on the silver screen, fifteen feet high. And "high" is the operative word, since it became a cult favorite to see it while stoned. The film made tons of money, and a star out of Ralph. Hollywood pretends to have a moral spine, but is really just a whore interested in taking as much of the contents of your wallet as it can. All the doors were open to Bakshi. He followed "Fritz" with "*Heavy Traffic*", a violent street story based on his life growing up in a Brooklyn ghetto. His third film was "*Coonskin*," which took on the Disney classic, "*Song of the South*." The civil rights campaign was in full swing at the time, and Ralph's portrayal of black vs. white conflict caused strong protests at its first showings, forcing Paramount to shelve the picture after its first screenings.

Trying to right his rapidly-sinking career, Ralph tried science fiction, making "*Wizards*," in 1979, and actually started filming "*Lord of the Rings*," but got into trouble with the outraged Tolkien fans when they found out he was rotoscoping, not animating the film. Rotoscoping is filming live-action actor's movements and then tracing them onto animator's boards. By the way, that's now the model in making animation – Ralph was, as usual, ahead of his time. He completed the first part, but it was incoherent, using live action, animation, and still pictures, and his ending was bewildering.

The picture was shown in only a few places, but nine-year old Peter Jackson saw it in New Zealand, and fell in love with the story. He immediately went out and bought the three-book trilogy. Jackson could not have had the idea that some 20 years later he would be a filmmaker, and that he would have the opportunity to make "*Lord of the Rings*" his way. Or could he?

Bakshi gave it up for a while after that, going back to his love of painting. It wasn't until 1992 that he tried a comeback with a sexy cartoon female human character, Holly Wood, voiced by Kim Basinger, in "*Cool World*," but it too, was a miss. As usual though, Bakshi was ahead of his time, having blended animation and live-action years before Robert Zemekis made "*Who Framed Roger Rabbit*," for Steven Spielberg's Amblin' Entertainment, in 1988. Ralph is a full-time painter now.

Another observation I'd like to inject here is the unfairness shown not only to Bakshi, but to Woody Allen by Zemekis, who copped Woody's monumental achievement in making "*Zelig*," in 1983. Zemekis made "*Forrest Gump*," in 1994, using special effects to place the actor on screen with famous dead people, such as the late President Jack Kennedy. Woody did it better, and funnier ten years earlier.

FRANCIS AND ME

Having begun the acting department at our agency, I was continually scouting for new talent. I had been tipped to a young couple, Bart Patton and Mary Mitchel, graduates of USC film school and, after meeting them and seeing some of their work, I signed them up. A friend of theirs from school, a new director named Francis Ford Coppola had, like many others before him and since, got an offer to make a cheap horror picture, "*Dementia 13*," for the "King of the B's," Roger Corman. Corman was famous for giving new filmmakers their first jobs and launched the careers of Jack Nicholson, Martin Scorsese, Peter Bogdanovich, Ron Howard, Jonathan Kaplan, Joe Dante and Jonathan Demme. Others he discovered were Ellen Burstyn, Robert De Niro, Bruce Dern, Diane Ladd, Talia Shire, Peter Fonda, and Charles Bronson. He was also famous for paying cowboy wages, or just enough to eat.

Corman sent them to Ireland for the shoot. One wonders why it was cheaper for Corman to dispatch a cast and crew overseas rather than to shoot on a stage or an L.A. location. Because of the way Roger financed his films, he had blocked currency in several countries. Blocked currency is money earned in certain countries by U.S. companies or corporations that can't be exported, but can be spent there. Ireland was one of them and, besides, it would give the film a spookier look.

One of the ways Roger developed the people who worked for him, and saved money at the same time, was to give his filmmakers less money than they needed to finish their pictures. They would then have to scramble and be endlessly creative in order for Roger not to take their films away from them and finish it himself. Which he frequently did, thereby taking the percentages he had doled out to talent back for himself.

Coppola, like most beginners, surrounded himself with his friends and hired both Bart and Mary as actors and as crew. Bart and Mary got married in Dublin. As predicted, Coppola ran out of Roger's money, finished everything he could overseas and brought everyone home to attempt to complete production before Roger's drop dead date for distribution. Francis was living in a modest starter home above Hollywood and, like Orson Welles, had his editing equipment in his living room. I was anxious to see Bart and Mary, who told me to come to Francis' house to see some raw footage of the film and of them.

It was only in the editing process that it became clear that a few pieces of continuity were missing, meaning parts needed to be filmed in order for the movie to make sense. One of the film's stars, Luana Anders, played a victim of an axe murderer, and Francis had film of her sleeping unawares on a bed, the bedroom door ajar. Also existing was footage of a man's arm holding the axe. What was absent was a shot of the killer walking down a hallway to Luana's room. Bart suggested to Francis that I play that part. He agreed, picked up a hand held camera and shot me stealthily advancing toward the victim. Everyone thought I had done a masterful job of acting. I later found out I been filmed from the knees down and that I been selected because of all the people there, I was the only one wearing shoes, rather than sneakers.

Francis Coppola is a loyal guy. Both Bart and Mary worked for him for years in all sorts of jobs, Bart as an actor in "*THX 1138*", in 1971, and as one of the producers of "*The Rain People*," starring James Caan and Robert Duvall, in 1969, and Mary acting in "*Peggy Sue Got Married*," in 1986, and as script supervisor on "*Dracula*," in 1992. I read that Duvall gives all the credit for his career to Coppola.

THE REAL REASON GEN. WESTMORELAND NEVER APPEARED ON "LAUGH IN"

Just after I became an agent, a young fellow named Gary Stromberg, a publicist, whom I knew from my PR days called me. Gary was, and is extremely bright – not always an asset, since it frequently got in his own way of success. He would never do anything conventionally, but I liked him because of his oddness. He was in love with a beautiful black girl of nineteen, named Chelsea Brown. He wanted me to meet her because she had acting ambitions and needed representation. I had no one like her on my list so I went to dinner with them and was charmed by Chelsea's manner and her quick humor.

An hour variety show called "*Laugh In*" was being put together by a producer named George Schlatter, and casting was underway. They had signed the new comedy team of Dan Rowan and Dick Martin, who were being positioned to be the new Martin & Lewis, as Dean and Jerry no longer wanted to be in business together. The producer planned to surround them with a zany bunch of performers who would say and do outrageous things onscreen. And they did, which for that time was pretty daring, but which wouldn't get even a snicker today. I sent Chelsea in for an interview and they loved her – especially in a bikini. She joined Artie Johnson, Judy Carne, and a bunch of other spontaniacs, as they called them, in what became a hit show from the first episode. With a weekly paycheck coming in, Chelsea and Gary got married. It was the first, and only, Jewish-soul food affair I've ever attended. Along with cold cuts from Nate n'Al, one could have smothered pork chops with greens cooked in bacon fat. Oy.

The Hollywood community was bitterly divided over the Vietnam War at that time. The establishment, which I belonged to by virtue of working for the agency that handled Bing Crosby and James Garner, and whose owners were in their early sixties, had been through World War II, and believed in the USO. The United Service Organization, or "Hollywood Canteen," not only had centers where military personnel could relax while on leave, but was most famous for sending troupes of performers to war theatres to entertain the troops. Bob Hope is perhaps the best-known example. In WWII, everybody in the entertainment business wanted to go overseas and join in the war effort by relieving the anxieties of the front-line soldiers, marines, sailors and air force flyers. This time, however, it was different. Many of the younger people had been radicalized, including me, and were against the Vietnam action.

Naturally, being the youngest agent there, and apparently the most expendable, my bosses assigned me to be the agency's liaison to The Hollywood Overseas Committee, an association comprising all the major studios and theatrical agencies. Our job was to contact our clients and get them to sign up for a tour in Vietnam, Cambodia, Laos, or wherever the military felt they were needed. The community's response was strong – at least among the people or organizations that felt they could use the exposure and publicity. Playboy sent a group of Playmates, for instance.

Although I disagreed with the political scene, I gritted my teeth and persuaded some of our clients to participate. About a year later, a large package arrived for me at the agency bearing a Vietnam postmark and a lot of colorful Vietnamese stamps. Tearing off the wrapping, I stared at a 20 by 40 inch full color portrait of General William Westmoreland, his four-star epaulets glinting in the sun.

It was inscribed to me; "With gratitude for your assistance, on behalf of our men and women in uniform," or something along those lines, and signed. It looked like a real signature. I say that because when I worked in the 20th-Fox mailroom years before, we had a machine that we used to inscribe hundreds of photos that we sent out to fans.

I didn't know quite what to do with it. I didn't want to take it home, and there was no room for it in my office, so I stashed it in the trunk of my '65 Olds Cutlass, courtesy of Bing Crosby's auto dealership. The next time I saw Chelsea's husband, Gary, he had graduated, if that's the word, into a full-fledged hippie. He wore ripped jeans, tie-dyed tops, had long hair and beard, earrings, sandals, and a ton of homemade jewelry. He was also usually high. I showed him the general's portrait, and he offered to trade me a beaded necklace he was wearing, for it. I took his offer. After all, his wife was making the agency a lot of money.

NOW I AM A MAN

I have to say that I'm not absolutely certain of this information, but the story I heard from Chelsea, which concerned Dan Rowan, the straight-man part of Rowan & Martin, was that, at the time, while "*Laugh In*" was convulsing the nation with hilarious bits like "Here come the judge," Rowan was married to an actress and singer named Peggy King. Peggy was tiny, but had a very big voice. She looked like Judy Garland, and sang like her too. It held Peggy back from stardom, because there was only room for one Judy Garland, and Peggy acquired the not always flattering nickname of, "Pretty, Perky Peggy King," from Dan's partner, Dick Martin. For one reason or another, the Rowan's marriage wasn't going well and Dan decided to seek professional assistance from a psychiatrist. The doctor, after some time studying his client's difficulty, apparently decided the problem could be resolved if Rowan would only become circumcised.

Now circumcision is not a walk in the park, especially for a 40-something man, which Dan was. It's dangerous, and is extremely painful. This is why it's done to most males while they're infants – so they can't remember it.

One joke that made the rounds then was about two four years-olds in a hospital; one says to the other, "What's wrong with you?" "Tonsils," says the second boy. "Oh," says the first. "And why are you here," asks the second boy? "I'm getting circumcised," he replies; to which the first boy says, "Oh, that's awful, I had that done when I was a week old, and I couldn't walk for a whole year."

Rowan had the operation, I was told, but it didn't save his marriage.

MR. LINCOLN, I PRESUME?

A funny story told me by George "Rosey" Rosenberg, my agent-mentor, concerned that great American actor, the tall, gaunt, Raymond Massey. Massey was one of Hollywood's most respected performers for many years, playing everything from Abe Lincoln, to James Dean's father in "*East of Eden*." He lived alone, behind the Beverly Hills Hotel, on Lexington Drive, and in his early eighties (he lived to be 97), owned an equally elderly poodle, which was ailing.

The veterinarian, unable to produce enough of the dog's urine to test in the office, suggested that Massey try to collect some on his daily walks. Massey was well over six feet, but in his later years was no longer agile and had difficulty bending over. Late one night, around 11 p.m., in his pajamas, robe and slippers, he was out on Lexington with his dog and a paper cup. Every time the poodle lifted his leg, Massey would attempt to catch some drops, but between his and his dog's infirmities, he kept missing the stream. One time he actually captured some liquid, but in attempting to straighten up, spilled it. Pretty frustrated, he didn't notice the Beverly Hills Police cruiser that had silently stolen up behind him, with its lights out.

The ever polite BH cops asked him what he was doing with that dog. He replied he was under doctor's orders to collect urine. When asked for his identity, he replied he lived just a block over and didn't think to take his wallet. The cops suggested someone at his house might be able to say who he was, but alas, there was a daily maid, but no one else was at home at this hour. The police then thought it wise to take him to the station so that someone could be telephoned who knew him. Massey, already testy, declared that he was famous; they should know who he was just by looking at him. Why, he had received an academy award nomination for playing our 16th president, Abraham Lincoln! That cut no ice with the cops, so they loaded "Honest Abe" and his poodle into their car, and from the station house, Massey telephoned his old friend, Rosey, who picked him up and took him home.

And that's why I like living in Beverly Hills.

HOWARD HUGHES CALLING

"Rosey" was a man I looked up to. He was in his mid-sixties at the time and, as a result of having been a heavy smoker, had developed emphysema. When he walked, which was difficult for him, he trailed a small oxygen canister on wheels, to which he was connected by a plastic tube running into his nose. It was painful for me because I knew he didn't have much time left. I didn't know this until much later, but in fact, I had always sought out older men to relate to as father figures since my own had died when he was not yet fifty. I realized in therapy that as a young man, I frequently dated women whose fathers I admired, and stayed with them because of the exposure and time I was able to spend with their dads. It explains the attraction I felt toward Jack Warner later on.

Rosey and his wife, Meta, another agent and co-owner of the agency, were not getting along and had not for some time. Rosey thought she was having affairs, a possibility. Meta was some 20 years younger than her husband. In fact, Meta had had such an attraction to our client, Robert Redford, that it cost us his representation. Meta put a full-court press on the married, 25 year-old Redford, causing him embarrassment and to flee to another agency.

At least three nights a week, Rosey, not anxious to go home, and I would go to dinner at Scandia, the best restaurant in Los Angeles in those days, almost directly across the street from our offices. Scandia also doubled as the most significant show business hangout besides Dave Chasen's. Romanoff's, presided over by the fake Russian Prince Mike Romanoff, had closed and the only other places where top showbiz folks would go was the secluded Bel Air Hotel, or the Polo Lounge at the Beverly Hills Hotel, but they were mainly breakfast and drinks places.

Rosey was celebrated wherever he went and treated royally at Scandia. Each time we would be shown to his favorite table, we would pass by a lone individual, eating by himself and frequently glancing at his watch. I was introduced to Walter Kane, an elegant, white-haired man who, Rosey told me later, had been working for Howard Hughes for over twenty years. He had never actually met Hughes and, after being hired on the telephone, had never seen or heard from him again. He was on salary for $5,000 weekly in 1965, a small fortune when you could buy a fully- loaded Cadillac for less.

Hughes' instructions to King were that he would call him at some point, at 7 p.m., and to be sure to be at his phone. Precisely at 6:30, Kane would get up and hurriedly leave. He had done that, wherever he was, for more than two decades. Rosey would wink at me and smile. Hughes never called.

HOW TO GET AWAY WITH MURDER IN HOLLYWOOD

The 60's opened up society to a lot of new thought patterns - health food, runaways, marijuana, sexually-transmitted diseases and foreign culture; the Brits, of course, because of their music, and Indians. Not the peace-pipe kind, although there was some of that too, but Indian-Indians, from India. Most everyone remembers the Maharishi, the cute little guru to the Beatles. Once he opened that door, in came the Bhagwan, Baba this and Baba that, even a few masquerading Americans, of which the best known was Tim Leary's LSD-pal, Richard Alpert, who called himself Baba Ram Dass.

L.A. was then the biggest little town in the lower 48 states. Even during rush hour, there wasn't much traffic on the freeways. You could hardly find a restaurant open after 10 p.m. The air was a lot purer than it is now. The streets were safe, you could walk anywhere. The ocean was clean and the beaches were empty. You could even sleep on the beach and find your shoes right where you left them when you woke up. It was paradise. The population swelled. Among them was a tall, handsome East coaster, and Harvard business school grad named Jim Baker. Jim came west to find his fortune, and to get away from the cold. He looked around, saw what was happening, and started The Aware Inn, a health food restaurant on the Sunset Strip. The TV series of the same name was just starting to advertise the good life out here, so it seemed like a natural tie-in.

Coupled with the still-bizarre but growing health food movement, Jim figured he'd ride the wave. Just across the street from his place, two struggling young actors named Harry and Marilyn Lewis had opened a hamburger joint called the Hamburger Hamlet to pay their bills while they waited for their big break. Jim Baker met Judy, a young and beautiful struggling actress, and married her. They fixed up the attic above the restaurant and lived there while building the mainly showbiz clientele into a very respectable business. Carol and I went there often, and so did our friends. L.A.'s population soared, the city boomed, the national media caught on to the weirdness here, and the Aware Inn was a hit.

Among the cultural anomalies abounding, besides free sex, cheap drugs and street corner rock n' roll, was the healthy alternative; body-worshipping, vegetarianism, yoga and karate. Arnold Schwarzenegger was around then. Jim Baker, 6' 4 and strong, a former college athlete, captain of his wrestling team and varsity tennis player, got into karate. Meantime, Judy was working her tail off, waitressing, hostessing, supervising, ordering, and cleaning-up. It's hard work running a restaurant, and Jim and Judy drifted apart. One day, Jim came home unexpectedly and found Judy upstairs in a prone position with a young stud from her acting class. One thing led to another, and the stud wasn't breathing anymore. Hard to do when your Adam's apple's been liquefied. Jim got off, since it was, apparently, self-defense. But as he and Judy didn't have a lot in common anymore, they divorced. As so often happens, she got the house - in this case the restaurant.

Jim moved to Northridge, in the San Fernando Valley, as far away from LA as he could go and still be around. Today it's a suburb, then, it was orange groves, where 5 acres and a house would cost you maybe $40 thou, with 5% down. Jim led a pretty solitary life for awhile, even getting himself a German shepherd to keep him company while he opened a new restaurant, also called Aware Inn, in Tarzana, right where the Ventura Freeway ended. Though Jim's place was expansive, his dog felt the need to check out the territory and spent a lot of time pursuing the neighbor's bitch. The neighbor wasn't happy, so informing Jim, but despite Jim's best efforts they had a problem. One night, the neighbor showed up at Jim's door, mad as hell. Maybe he had heard about Jim's past, maybe not, but the gun he was toting didn't do him any good. Killed him, in fact.

Well, the cops tried, but the law is, if someone pulls a gun on you, on your territory, you've got a right...and so forth. Jim got off again; same old self-defense. Two people dead and he's still looking for the meaning of life.

Valley people in those days were more or less unsophisticated by LA standards, and the Aware Inn, with sunflower seeds on their salads, didn't make it. Jim found a buyer, sold out, and was once again looking for something to do. By now, 1968 or so, the country was going to hell in a hurry. Gone were the peace and love days. Now in were tense demonstrations against the war, cops beating on innocent political protestors, and civil rights marchers, bad drugs and acid rock. Dark and dangerous streets replaced the all-night love-ins. The sunset strip, now a magnet for runaway teenagers, teemed with drug dealers, rock bands and the hawks that preyed on them, from mobsters to agents to gurus. Many of these kids came from solid, middle-class homes in small towns all over America. They had family and religious values, but they were bored. The media glamorization of the new freedom plus the liberating effects of now-prevalent drugs and audacious lyrics drew them to LA like moths to a flame. They were out of their depth, and easy pickings. When their money ran out they lived in crash pads, in the streets, hand to mouth. They stole, sold their bodies, anything to avoid going home with their tails between their legs...back to their small, boring towns.

Jim Baker, like almost everyone else, continued to search for meaning in his life, experimenting with Buddhism, psychotherapy, meditation, LSD, chiropractic, acupuncture, EST and Primal Therapy. Finally, he had a vision. Not surprising, since he probably had a lot of recreational drug residue roaming around in his brain. In any case, he was re-born as Baba Jim. He was convinced he was the very latest reincarnation of God. He still had quite a few bucks left, to which he added the proceeds of the sale of his Northridge acreage for a shopping mall, and set out to change the world.

Now dressed totally in white, complete with turban, as befitted a personage of his station, he traded his Cadillac for a Volkswagen van and joined the throng on the strip. Sensing his mission was to save these poor unfortunate boys and girls, he collected a few, one at a time, putting them up at low-rent motels along Sunset Blvd. At first, they were grateful for the food and a place to stay. Jim was kind and generous, they could come and go, and keep on smoking dope, but sooner or later, if they wanted to stay dry and keep their tummies full, they had to hear his message. Which, by the way, he was still working out as he went along.

Pretty soon, the ones that didn't leave became his pupils, his acolytes, his subjects. He dressed them all, boys and girls, in white, with turbans, just like himself. His reputation grew along the strip. His believers, in keeping with the times, gaily decorated his van in day-glo, so he could be seen blocks away. Jim had become hip, acceptable, in demand, and the kids were flocking to him. He was giving them not only a home, but a religious overlay that reminded them dimly of their upbringing, even if it was as far from Christianity as one could imagine. Nothing like having your own cult for ego gratification. I understand. Who doesn't want followers?

Jim's little band increased and it was chaotic, filling several motels, blocks apart. One day, Jim bought a run-down thirty-room mansion in what was once a fashionable Pasadena neighborhood, and moved them all in. He had almost sixty kids living there, from 15 to 25, and now he needed organization. Having worked out the basics of his new religion, he decided that boys and girls would be segregated. Those little love affairs that had either been in progress or begun under his roof would end. His new rule was that they would all be celibate; except for him, of course. He immediately married all of the girls. Occasionally, he would assign others to marry and live together, but only platonically. Sex existed only to procreate with the Godhead...himself! What a deal. Only by now, he was running out of money. It cost a bundle to feed, clothe and house this bunch. They would have to start working. Jim was a pretty tough guy, used to giving orders and getting results. Besides, how could you say no to God?

He organized a janitorial service and laundry, buying a few used trucks and vans, painting them white, of course, and some cleaning supplies. Pretty soon, his army of scrubbed and polite little drones was out scouring offices and stores, picking up and delivering laundry for restaurants and small hotels, and the money was rolling in. His little cult, now numbering over a hundred, kind of got lost amongst all the craziness happening up and down the coast; what with Ken Kesey's Merry Pranksters on their tie-dyed bus, the turn-on tune-out antics of Leary and his Hollywood Hipsters, and the studio pitch meetings that began with the ceremonial "taste." All of this was duly recorded by the international media, especially Hunter Thompson and Rolling Stone, which bore down in a feeding frenzy, establishing LA around the world forever as the Capital of Strange. But Baba Jim might not have been as good an influence on his young tribe as they once thought. True to the design of any worthwhile cult, disagreement, much less disobedience to the leader is punishable.

Every now and then, one or two got it into their heads to leave. Some did, not returning from their jobs, which is how the stories finally got out. Most were too afraid to try. Still, the kids continued to believe in God. Baba Jim, that is. Well, hard work and no play, etc., and Baba decided to take a vacation. Selecting a representative group of worshippers, including a few strong young men to schlep, and a bunch of nubile young beauties to sooth his fevered, heroic, God-like brow, they set off for Hawaii. Arriving on Maui, they took over a motel and went native. I'm told there was a lot of flesh visible, but they kept their turbans on. The new sport of parasailing had just emerged; you start out water-skiing behind a speedboat, gradually unfurling a parachute behind you, which, as it fills with air lifts you high above the water.

Baba Jim, probably the very first God-athlete, had to try it. His little turban-clad band gathered on the beach to watch. At first, all went well. There he was, some two hundred feet over the Pacific, sailing along, dripping holy water from his skis, smiling benedictions down on his subjects - when the rope broke! Unfortunately, as the air pressure equalized and he dropped to earth, the prevailing trade winds blew him over the beach, so when he landed, it was with a mighty thud! He was hurt. Anyone could see that. Something to do with the compound fractures of both his legs that caused his tibia bones to peek out from his skin. The blood seeping from under his turban wasn't a good sign either.

The beach crowd and staff from the parasail outfit were there in minutes. Someone called for an ambulance and the cops, which for a small, relatively undiscovered island arrived quickly. But by then, Jim's mighty band of believers had formed an arms-linked cordon around him, refusing to allow anyone near. "Don't touch him, he's Holy", one yelled. "He's God", screamed another, "he'll heal himself". Someone who was there later told me he could see in Jim's eyes that he knew what was going on and couldn't resist an ironic smile.

By the time the cops could pry the fanatic human Maginot Line apart to try to administer some aid, Big Jim was gone - passed on to that great Jim Jonesville in the sky.

I always like to think, regardless of what Einstein said, that God does have a sense of humor.

WHY LEW WASSERMAN HATED ME

In my wanderings around Universal Studios just after Lew Wasserman took it over, I met a young former MCA agent, Ned Tanen, who had started at the agency as Lew's driver. Wasserman had had to choose between keeping MCA, the super agency he and Dr. Jules Stein built, which the Justice Department decided had become a monopoly. Lew had taken Ned with him to the studio but as yet, Ned had no assignment. I had known one of MCA's top agents, Jay Kanter rather well, as he was one of Marilyn Monroe's agents and also was Marlon Brando's representative, and he suggested to me that Ned and I cook something up together. I had an idea.

Bart Patton wanted to strike out on his own as a producer, away from Coppola, and I was looking for a way to get him started. Sam Arkoff and Jim Nicholson had one of the most successful low budget studios in town, American International Pictures, and specialized in teenage comedies and horror films. In fact, Roger Corman distributed many of his films through them. They had the lock on cheap B pix. But Bart, having had the Roger Corman-Francis Coppola experience, also knew how to make those kinds of films. I suggested to Ned that Universal start a production division that would compete with AIP's, and he leaped at the idea. Bart was not a director, and we needed one to make up the unit.

I had been to a comedy club a few weeks earlier on the recommendation of a friend, and watched a rotund and loud comedian named Lennie Weinrib perform. I wasn't interested in representing him as an actor, but I remembered that he said his big ambition was to direct. I put him and Bart together and they hit it off. I took them to meet Ned and we decided on a clone of AIP's *"Beach Blanket Bingo,"* and called it *"Beach Ball."*

We had to come to a business arrangement, so I proposed to Ned a seven year deal, two pictures a year, with mutual approvals of script, cast and budget. Bart and Lennie would co-own the profits with Universal, their films would not be cross-collateralized, and their fees would graduate accordingly. Ned took the deal to the business affairs department and to my delight, contracts were signed. Ned had a mission. The key to making these cheap films was to keep them off the lot, and to remain below the radar, as they'd be targets of the various craft unions, and be socked with overhead charges that could add fifty percent to their budgets.

The film was made and it wasn't terrible. It wasn't terrific either, but it was serviceable. It did the same kind of business that AIP's films did, and a sequel was immediately planned, this time, called *"Wild, Wild Winter,"* same shenanigans, only in the snow.

While that picture was being completed, against my specific orders, fat, loud Lennie Weinrib decided to have lunch in the Universal commissary. He wore a red sweater. During lunch, he marched up and down the aisles, glad-handing and backslapping, and making a fool of himself. Seated against the wall, as usual every day, was black-suited, icily cold-steel Lew Wasserman, and his cohort. Who was that idiot, Wasserman wanted to know? When he found out that it was his employee, and that this loudmouth was making pictures for him with a deal that nobody had, not even Hitchcock, Lennie and Bart's deal was rescinded, their contracts cancelled, and they were kicked off the lot. I nearly was, also. Lennie recently died in Chile. (He'd probably make a joke about that, too).

Ned, however, was able to show Lew that he could make films at a price the studio mechanism couldn't touch, so his division was allowed to continue, and he went on to make a few more, until he got the chance to head feature production. Ned, too, died recently. He was a terrific guy who had two obsessions; women and cars. One of his wives tried to poison him. Among his collection was a 1930's Mercedes that once belonged to Adolph Hitler.

SONDRA

Sondra Locke was recommended to us by Alan Arkin, who was a client of the agency and whose representation I shared. He had just completed the Warners film, *"The Heart is a Lonely Hunter,"* by the famous Southern novelist, Carson McCullers. Sondra, at age 21 played a 16 year-old deaf-mute, and won rapturous notices from the critics, including an Oscar nomination for Best Supporting Actress, 1968.

Sondra was born in Shelbyville, Tennessee, and was married to a young man named Gordon Anderson when she moved to L.A. to pursue her career. She became my client. I immediately designed a public relations plan for her to impact the community. Another of my clients, a hot new director named Noel Black, whose first film, *"Pretty Poison,"* had been a hit, had made a deal with Fox. I immediately secured a co-starring role for her in Noel's next film called, *"Run, Shadow, Run,"* subsequently released as *"Cover Me, Babe."* I also managed to place two of my other clients, Robert Fields, and Suzanne Benton, in the other leads.

Sondra was waif-like, soft-spoken, with a southern accent, naturally, but possessed of a steel will for stardom. Although I was used to ego and had worked with many actors, including major stars, there was something about this young girl that frightened me just a little. Sondra and Gordon were their own special unit growing up, they told me. They didn't play with other kids from about age ten on, but hung together, going to the movies and dreaming about Hollywood. She and Gordon put on their own little plays, making the costumes, the sets, with Gordon doing Sondra's and his make-up and hair.

When I would schedule an appointment for Sondra to "go-see" a casting director, a director or producer, Gordon would do Sondra's hair and makeup, including individually gluing on each of Sondra's false eyelashes. And he would accompany her on her rounds, to the dismay of certain casting people and directors, who complained about Gordon's lurking about when he couldn't actually go in the office with her. It was becoming a problem and Sondra and I clashed about it more than once. She was intensely loyal to Gordon, saying he was her husband and manager. I couldn't quite grasp the husband part.

One day during the filming of "*Cover Me, Babe*," at 20th-Fox, I received an emergency call from Joe Scully, the casting director on the film, who asked me to come over to the studio immediately – There was a problem. He asked me to meet him outside Women's Wardrobe.

I had known Charles LeMaire, the head of Women's Costumes at Fox when I had worked for Arthur Jacobs as a press agent. LeMaire had been one of our clients and I had arranged media publicity for him. Joe and Charles were waiting for me at the wardrobe door. Women's Wardrobe, a cavernous building half the size of a sound stage, contained thousands of items of clothing dating back more than fifty years, some of which had won Academy costume Awards. The problem was that Gordon, Sondra's husband, was inside and refused to come out. He had been "researching" some ideas for his wife and, apparently, had been trying some garments on. When asked to cease and desist, he had refused. That's where we were, and I was asked to go in and talk him out. I felt I needed more firepower, so I walked over to the stage where the picture was shooting, and waited until Noel had finished a scene and was waiting for the grips to complete a new set up. I whispered my situation to him, and he excused himself for a few minutes while we walked back to wardrobe. Noel's authority as Sondra's director convinced Gordon to emerge. I was told he had had on Linda Darnell's dress from "*The Mark of Zorro*."

SWIFTY

I worked for Irving "Swifty" Lazar for several years before he died. Linda, my then wife, his aide-de-camp for a quarter of a century, told him that he was losing a lot of business because he traveled so extensively. Irving was out of town or the country for at least six months every year. He had worldwide contacts and friends and would visit them at their exotic homes in France, Dominican Republic, Switzerland, England, even Africa.

I was, at the time, a personal manager, with a list of anywhere between 10 and 15 clients, mostly actors, writers and directors, and worked from my home office in our house on Linda Flora Drive, in Bel Air. Linda suggested to Irving that I occupy his small office while he was away to manage his inflow of literary material for sale by publishers, answer his voluminous correspondence, summarize expressions of interest from studios for transmittal to him, wherever he was, and generally make sure that nothing slipped away. He was meticulous in his personal life, and strove to be the same in business. Linda was the best personal assistant in Hollywood or she wouldn't have lasted one day with him. He was tough to deal with, petty, touchy about his short stature and downright ugliness, and extremely penurious for a man so wealthy. She was in great demand and could have earned a lot more money working for various other producers or movie stars, but she and Irving had this love-hate, angry father-submissive daughter relationship that fascinated me and seemed to work for them. After Irving's death, Linda became the great songstress and composer, Peggy Lee's assistant and, later, looked after affairs for Armand Deutsch, a wealthy industrialist and member of Ronald Regan's "kitchen cabinet".

Irving had remained a bachelor for 55 years until, like the lyrics in the Eagles song, "*Desperado,*" he decided to "let someone love him before it's too late." He met a former airline hostess and model, Mary Van Nuys, who had previously been married three times, and married her, instantaneously making her one of Hollywood's premiere hostesses in a highly social town.

Mary flourished, making their art-adorned home in Trousdale, high above Beverly Hills a favorite gathering place for Irving's friends and clients, including the Billy Wilders, the Jack Lemmons, the Harold Mirisches, the Alan Jay Lerners, Roald Dahl, and his wife, Patricia Neal, the Irwin Shaws, the Henry Kissingers, even the Richard Nixons. Lazar was heavily criticized in Hollywood when he took on the representation of Nixon and the sale of the former president's memoirs. Nixon was considered persona non grata among the overwhelmingly liberal crowd of Lazar's friends, but Irving, who was known for his voracious appetite for money, as evidenced by the enormous sums he obtained for his clients, retorted by allegedly saying he'd represent Hitler if there was ten per cent in it for him.

I met Michelline Lerner through a mutual friend, who asked me if I'd represent her, as she had a writing-producing job in the works with a local production company. Michelline had been one of many wives of Alan Jay Lerner, co-creator, with Fritz Lowe, of "*My Fair Lady*, "*Camelot,*" and a gang of other hit Broadway musicals and films. Lerner was a compulsive marrier, Michelline said, eventually compiling seven wives, I believe, because he was unable to function unless he had a woman with him to "take care of things." I'm never surprised about how many creative men need the same. If you go into their past, inevitably you'll find distant, absent, or compulsively attentive mothers at the core of their lack of ability to exist alone.

Michelline told me a funny story about Lazar, which only proved what everyone knew – that he never read anything he sold. When the first draft of *"My Fair Lady"* was complete and ready to be given to Lazar for his opinion and suggestions prior to it being sent to Jack Warner for production, Michelline yanked a couple of hairs from her shoulder length coif, and inserted them in the middle of the script, which would have fallen out had Irving ever opened it. Several days later, when Alan and Michelline were at Irving's home for a dinner party, he raved about Alan and Fritz' accomplishment and gave the Lerners the script back. Later, at home, they opened it and there was Michelline's hair, undisturbed. Irving Lazar, the super salesman, could have sold smoke to a fire.

In fact, his reputation was so powerful that when I sent out material in his absence to the studios for potential sale, I didn't get back the usual letters, saying "Thanks, but no thanks," I got telephone calls from the studio heads, almost apologizing for not buying it, and saying they hoped that wouldn't preclude our sending them material again in future. That was unique for me.

Lazar always told me that everyone in Hollywood, and he meant everyone, had two agents – their own, and him. If he heard of or saw an opportunity, he'd leap in and make a deal for whomever the buyer wanted. And then he would call the talent and say he had gotten them a job – without specifically identifying the exact facts. Insecurity is everyone's co-pilot in show business and no-one ever turned down Lazar's deal, because it was always better than the one their agents could have negotiated – if they had known about it to begin with.

Swifty got his nickname from Humphrey Bogart, who challenged Lazar to get him a job during the lunch they were having at Romanoff's. Bogart was represented at the time by an agent named Phil Gersh, and Lazar was trying to steal him. In the next two hours, Lazar got him three deals. Another pricelessly original story about Lazar involves Frank Sinatra. Lazar, barely five feet tall, and the word ugly, when applied to him would seem a compliment, could only attract highly-priced prostitutes. Even though Henry Kissinger famously said that power was the world's most potent aphrodisiac, it didn't seem to have much of an effect on Lazar. He paraded them around at the best restaurants and parties in Hollywood, London, Paris, Rome, and wherever he happened to be in his ceaseless traveling, eventually convincing himself, if not his friends and hosts, that they were "actresses" who just happened to be in love with him.

Lazar loved to take these women up to his apartment to show them his custom-made wardrobe, which he had installed behind mechanized automated sliding doors. One night, as the story goes, when he and his date of the evening were at the Brown Derby, Frank Sinatra and one of Lazar's clients, George Axelrod, who wrote *"The Manchurian Candidate,"* which starred Sinatra, and had also written the screenplay for *"Breakfast at Tiffany's,* not coincidentally, because Lazar's other client, Truman Capote, was the original author, stole up to Irving's lair. They were met by a construction crew from one of the studios. Several hours later, Lazar and his "love" arrived and, proudly pressing the buttons on his remote control, Irving was horrified to find – a brick wall. It wasn't funny to Swifty for several reasons – not only couldn't he perform sexually – there was some strange connection between his libido and his clothes, but because everything he wore had to be custom-made, including his shoes, he literally had nothing to wear until he could bring workmen in to tear down the wall.

Irving was near 80 when I worked for him. His physical energy was phenomenal, but his memory was beginning to go and, as it ebbed, he became even more short-tempered and difficult to get along with. I was able to move on, but poor Linda was stuck. She stayed until the bitter end, when his health finally failed and, after a couple of operations to improve the flow of blood through his veins didn't help, he refused further medical assistance, and resigned himself to death.

There is a horrific scene in the famous, academy award-winning film "*Zorba the Greek,*" starring Anthony Quinn, when the old woman character being played by Lilia Scala, appears to have died in her hovel. Neighbors rush in and begin stripping the home bare of its furnishings and even the old lady's clothes, when she wakes up, weakly protesting. That doesn't stop the looters however. The same thing happened to Lazar.

Mary, his wife of over 30 years, predeceased him by five years, suddenly coming down with advanced cancer that was undiagnosed. Like Alan Jay Lerner, Irving had become "accustomed to her face," and life without Mary no doubt hastened his end. He was left in the care of Philippine housekeepers, his doctors, and Linda. The walls of Irving's home were festooned with original paintings he had acquired in the 1940s by young and upcoming artists like Matisse, Marc Chagall, Joan Miro, Salvador Dali, and Pablo Picasso, whom he eventually represented. Owning multi-million dollar artwork and displaying it on your walls at home was the height of fashion, and Lazar's friends, Billy Wilder, Ahmet Ertegun, founder of Atlantic Records, and Harold Mirisch copied him. Wilder eventually built a world-class collection, which he sold at auction just before his death. For Lazar, however, it meant less and served mainly to demonstrate how perspicacious and rich he was. He told me he had paid a couple of hundred dollars for most of them and they were now worth some thirty million dollars.

As Irving lay dying, he was visited by his "friends," who took to selecting certain items of Lazar's property as they left, to "remember him by." Among them, I was told, several of the Picassos, Miros' and Chagalls were taken for "safekeeping" by the Erteguns, Ahmet and his wife, Mica. Other mementos, including Irving and Mary's jewelry, also disappeared. The housekeepers, who spoke little English, were in no position to object.

Somehow, it all fits. Irving Lazar, a legend in Hollywood, who compiled great wealth because of his boldness in robbing the robber barons, in the end, had it stolen from him.

RATMAN

Bruce Cohn Curtis and I became friends around that same time. Bruce is the grandson of Jack Cohn, brother of Harry Cohn, founder of Columbia Pictures, one of the original major studios, and I found him, like Ray Wagner, sitting alone in an out of the way office at the studio. Bruce desperately wanted to be a producer and had started in the business as a minor executive in Columbia's London office. He had actually been instrumental in getting a film called "Otley," off the ground there, and had a producing credit. "*Otley*" starred Malcolm McDowell, soon to become a star in Stanley Kubrick's shocker, "*A Clockwork Orange*." But making a small film in England at that time didn't mean much in Hollywood circles and, despite his pedigree, he was having problems gaining traction. I promised to find him a shootable property, and proposed we partner on it, as I was ready to make the jump from agent to producer. He agreed and I started looking. It took some time, during which Bruce, unable to function here, returned to London.

Our agency had a reciprocal deal, as did some of the other agencies, with literary agencies in New York, London, Paris and Rome. One of our London contacts sent me a newly published short novel entitled, "*Ratman's Notebooks*." It scared me, and I don't scare easily. I called Bruce, commented on how it was published in England, and sent it to him. A week later he called me back to say he had hated the book, didn't see a movie in it, and what was wrong with me? Who would go see a movie about rats?

We sold the book to ourselves essentially, to Bing Crosby Productions, who else, and it was produced under the title "*Willard*," in 1971. It starred Bruce Davison, and my client, Sondra Locke, and grossed over $100 million. It also spun off a sequel, called "*Ben*," in 1972, which made, as sequels usually do, about half of the original's take. It was remade in 2003 and fared poorly. Bruce would have been even richer than his trust fund from his grandfather, and I would have been a producer much earlier.

THE UNFRIENDLY SIX

Hollywood has always been liberal, if not exactly Left. Our chief literary agent at the agency was George Willner, an avuncular and soft-spoken man in his late 60s, who had been one of the premiere literary agents of the 1950s. He and his wife, Tiba, had been members of the communist party, in Los Angeles, along with many of his famous writer clients.

Marvin Josephson, a former CBS lawyer, struck out on his own as a manager of on-air personalities, and had under his wing, when I met him, such broadcast luminaries as Edward R. Murrow, Eric Sevaride, Marvin Kalb, and the most trusted of national newscasters, Walter Cronkite, among others. Josephson was an ambitious and brilliant business strategist, who wanted to quickly own a major show business entity.

With backing from his brother, a founder of Bear Stearns, a leading Wall Street brokerage, he acquired several New York and Los Angeles theatrical agencies, gaining their stellar client lists, as well. One of the agencies he bought in California was Rosenberg-Coryell, where I was employed. Melding it with several others, including Ashley-Famous, headed by Ted Ashley, who subsequently became Chairman of Warner Brothers, he changed the name to Artists Agency Corporation. Josephson eventually built his holdings into what is today the third largest theatrical agency in America, International Creative Management, or ICM.

I've always admired Marvin for hiring George Willner. George looked after the careers of at least six of the famous "Unfriendly Ten," or those who would not name names in front of congress. When the purge hit Hollywood, George, along with his clients, lost his job, his savings, and was relegated to obscurity. At one time, just to buy food, George was reduced to selling notions in the 42nd Street subway station, in New York. George's client list, prior to his being named as a communist, was stunning. He represented, among others, Dalton Trumbo, whom Kirk Douglas rescued as an act of defiance against the House Un-American Activities Committee and Senator Joseph McCarthy, who had ruined so many lives, by hiring Trumbo to do the screenplay for "Spartacus," under his own name. Trumbo had been writing under assumed names and had won an Oscar, in 1957, for the screenplay of *"The Brave One,"* which he had done under a pseudonym, Robert Rich. He was unable to retrieve it.

The Ten consisted of Alvah Bessie, Herbert Biberman, Lester Cole, Edward Dmytryk, Ring Lardner, Jr., John Howard Lawson, Albert Maltz, Sam Ornitz, and Robert Adrian Scott, as well as Trumbo. They had written or directed many of the best-known Hollywood films of the war era. Most of the Ten's best films included *"Hotel Berlin," "The Master Race," " Crossfire," "Sahara," "Pride of the Marines," "Destination Tokyo,"* and *"Thirty Seconds Over Tokyo,"* all dealing with antifascist themes. One would have thought these pictures alone would have cleared the Ten of any suspicions that they ever had the replacement of the American political system in mind.

Other scriptwriters who were also named as communists were Abe Polonsky, Walter Bernstein, and Arnold Manoff who wrote most of the *"You Are There"* segments, a CBS television series about cultural victims such as Socrates, Jesus, Joan of Arc, and the Salem witches. Ring Lardner, Jr., and Ian McLellan Hunter wrote *"The Adventures of Robin Hood"* series.

Woody Allen starred as a beard, or a stand-in, for blacklisted writers in a 1976 movie called, "*The Front*," which was directed by Marty Ritt, a blacklisted director, and which also had in the cast, former communists Zero Mostel and Herschel Bernardi, among other lesser-known names. Walter Bernstein, another former communist, wrote the script.

Other writers couldn't stand the constant pressure from the government and the contempt of many of their friends and colleagues, who were anti-communist, including Ronald Reagan, then president of the Screen Actor's Guild, and Charlton Heston, and left town, or in some cases, went along with the government and "confessed" to save their careers. Hugo Butler wrote scripts for Luis Bunuel in Mexico City, and Jules Dassin, who settled in France, had major box-office hits with "*Rififi*" in 1954 and "*Never on Sunday*," in 1960, which he made in Greece. Dassin, who was married to Greek actress and later, member of the Greek parliament, Melina Mercouri, star of "Sunday," outlived his wife by a number of years, and passed away recently, in his nineties.

A few writers besides Trumbo, like Alvah Bessie, worked under the radar in Hollywood and insiders knew that Nathan E. Douglas, the Academy Award writer of "*The Defiant Ones*," in 1958, really was blacklisted Ned Young. In 1960, Otto Preminger broke the blacklist by giving Trumbo credit for scripting "*Exodus.*" Michael Wilson, who had written "*The Bridge on River Kwai*" and "*Lawrence of Arabia,*" revealed his participation in those films.

Every reaction has an equal and opposite reaction, say physicists, one of the basic laws of the universe, and it wasn't long after the disgraceful blacklist, that the Left in Hollywood began to fight back. The 1960s, a radical period in U.S. if there ever was one, the studios started making films with radical themes. Ring Lardner, Jr., wrote the anti-war movie, "*M*A*S*H*" in 1970, a Korean War satire that became one of the all time most popular television series. "*The Molly Maguires*," directed by Marty Ritt, and written by Walter Bernstein, tackled unfair labor themes, as did "*Norma Rae,*" another Ritt project, this time written by Irving Ravetch and Harriet Frank, Jr., also former communists. "*Silkwood*" and "*Matewan*" also pushed for fairer treatment for workers. "*Daniel,*" in 1983, dealt with the execution of Ethel and Julius Rosenberg, and Warren Beatty starred as John Reed, an American reporter during the Leninist takeover of Russia in 1917, in "*Reds,*" in which Beatty filmed interviews with still-living radicals, including Scott Nearing. "*The China Syndrome*," made in 1979, made us wonder if nuclear power was in our best interests, and "*Go Tell the Spartans*," and "*Coming Home*," both in 1978, "*Apocalypse Now*," the following year, and Kubrick's "*Full Metal Jacket*," in 1987, criticized the Vietnam War. "*Wall Street*" predicted the current greed of our economic system, and "*Missing*," in 1982, examined our dubious influence in Latin America. Robert Redford, who until then, had soft-pedaled his left wing views, used the blacklist as a plot point in "*The Way*

We Were," in which Barbra Streisand, a committed Communist, was married to a liberal screenwriter, played by Redford.

Vietnam veterans threatened Jane Fonda, and the media savaged her for her opposition to the Vietnam War, and Ed Asner, president of the Screen Actors Guild, had his *"Lou Grant"* television show canceled after a strong protest campaign by right-wing groups. Vanessa Redgrave, who criticized Israel, had several contracts cancelled after demonstrations by Zionist groups. Redford, Jack Lemmon, and Gregory Peck were criticized for attending Cuban film festivals.

Lillian Hellmann, a former communist, wrote *"Scoundrel Time,"* and Dalton Trumbo produced *"The Time of the Toad"* to highlight this awful time in Hollywood. Elia Kazan, in his autobiography, *"A Life,"* in 1988, wrote that he was justified in being a friendly witness even though he regretted turning on his friends. He was one of the best American directors ever to make movies, including *"Streetcar Named Desire," "Viva Zapata," "On the Waterfront," "The Glass Menagerie," "Gentleman's Agreement," "Pinky,"* and many other classics. Just before he died in 1993, he got a special academy award. During the ceremony, many current stars, directors and writers pointedly did not applaud. He died at age 92, still hated by many of his former friends and co-workers.

JACK L.

Speaking of virulent anti-communists, a few years later, I had the opportunity to work with Jack Warner. Stan Dragoti, a leading advertising copywriter at Wells Rich Greene, in New York, wanted desperately to be a film director. He and his partner, Charlie Moss, had written a screenplay about Billy the Kid, entitled, *"Dirty Little Billy,"* and Stan was willing to give up his job for his dream. He was married at the time to Cheryl Tiegs, perhaps the top model in the country and figured her income would tide them over until he got started in movies. I was, by then, a personal manager and represented Michael J. Pollard, whom Stan simply had to have to play Billy. I met Stan at the Polo Lounge, read the script, agreed with him that no one else should play the part, and committed Pollard to the film. Financing was the next obstacle. Stan went to Mary Welles, who was the majority owner of his ad agency and because she didn't want to lose him, said she would put up fifty percent of the budget, $750,000. She didn't think he'd be able to find the rest.

Cheryl, however, had a lawyer, Arnold Grant, who was married to the former Miss America, Bess Myerson, later to become a New York City commissioner, whose major client was – Jack L. Warner. Warner had recently sold his studio for $47 million to a company called Seven Arts, headed by a New York financier named Elliot Hyman. Warner, age 80, suddenly, after 70 years, was unemployed. He had taken a luxurious suite of offices in the new Century City, a huge development by the Alcoa Corporation, on the site of what once the 20th Century-Fox lot, in Beverly

Hills, a fire-sale result of the cost overruns on *"Cleopatra,"* and was wondering what to do with the rest of his life. Every morning, he had a haircut, a manicure, and a massage. Then it was time for lunch.

Grant called Warner and told him of this opportunity to co-finance this film for a fraction of what films normally cost in those days, and he agreed to listen to what Stan and Charlie had to say. They flew out from New York and literally acted out every role in the film in front of Jack's desk. He bought it and the film had a start date. Two of my other clients, Lee Purcell and Richard Evans, filled out the rest of the major casting and I became an integral, if uncredited part of the production. Stan and Cheryl took a house in Beverly Hills and off we went to Tucson, Arizona, to shoot at the Old West set outside of town.

Warner, whose name had been on more than 1500 films, as Executive Producer, in his fifty years at the studio, had actually never produced anything. Stan was off shooting, Charlie had returned to New York, where he was more at home, and Jack and I got to spend a significant amount of time together. It was exciting for me because Warner was one of the actual pioneers of a business that in a short period of time had become the major cultural influence of not only America, but of the world. I had begun with another pioneer, Skouras, at Fox, and by now was becoming something of a historian of the movie business.

Jack L, as he liked to be called, told me wonderful and fascinating stories about his early years, how he and his father and mother and his three brothers traveled the wilds of Canada with a projector and a sheet, and showed silents for a nickel admission. Jack also was a boy tenor and performed during reel changes. I heard about his knockdowns with Bette Davis, Jimmy Cagney, Errol Flynn, Bogie, Eddie Robinson and a hundred other famous names. And he also told me that when Warren finished *"Bonnie & Clyde,"* he had hated it and refused to distribute it, saying he had made the same film a dozen times in the 30s with Cagney and Bogart. And he had.

Warren came to him and begged, literally begged, he said, getting down on his knees. Warner was known as a crusty, difficult and extremely vain man, but I found him to be a warm, generous person. Perhaps he had mellowed over the years and his age allowed him to relax a bit. Or perhaps he was now a general without an army. Or maybe I was still seeking a strong father image and it flattered older, successful men to have eager young men to teach.

He said he was embarrassed by Warren's pleading so he allowed him to take the film out himself. He readily admitted he had made a mistake and that Warren had "saved his ass."

Warner enjoyed knowing from me more about the actual details of making an independent film, since he had been so isolated at the top of his studio for so many years. I had recently spent several years making low budget independent films in right-to-work states such as Montana, Florida and Texas where, as the producer, I also hauled lighting gear, drove the day's shooting negative to the airport late at night, chose each day's menu from various local restaurants serving as caterers, and even appeared as the third Indian on the right, in a scene from a film called *"Grey Eagle,"* where Ben Johnson and Lana Wood were menaced by a renegade band. Also appearing with me was one of our truck drivers, and a costumer. We were high on a ridge, on horseback, in silhouette, so, covered in a blanket, complete with feathers, we passed.

Jack L. had also bought the film rights to a moderately successful Broadway musical, *"1776,"* a very patriotic reminder of our roots. He was a leader during World War II in producing films that celebrated American heritage and was recognized for his efforts by our government. The film version, alas, was only moderately successful, as well. It might have done better in these troubled times.

BRIGITTE, CLAUDIA & THE MAESTRO

Michael J. Pollard, the odd, snub-nosed little character actor, and his wife, Annie, were Best Man and Matron of Honor at my marriage to Linda Jones, daughter of the late comic bandleader, Spike Jones, in New York, in 1968. As a wedding present, the Pollards gave me a visit to the famous, or infamous, "Dr. Feelgood," Dr. Max Jacobson. He was renowned in showbiz circles for his "vitamin" injections that gave recipients sustained vigor for a week. I waited in his anteroom with at least a dozen members of the current hit Broadway musical, *"Hair,"* until it was my turn. It was rumored that Jack Kennedy and his wife, Jacqueline, were also frequent visitors. I got my shot, and that night, our daughter, Alexandra was conceived, and born exactly nine months later. Linda and I had lived together for five years and although no birth control was used, we never even had a scare. When the Manhattan D.A. busted Dr. Jacobson, it was revealed his "vitamin" shots contained, besides some B vitamins, a goodly amount of Methedrine, or "speed." I know it works.

Pollard and I went to Burgos, Spain, shortly after that, where he was to star in a western, *"The Legend of Frenchy King."* Frenchy King was to be played by Brigitte Bardot, in black leather, while the good guy, or in this case, the good girl, was Claudia Cardinale, in white leather. Pollard was the comic relief – in case the comedy inherent between Bardot and Cardinale wasn't enough.

Claudia was a doll – gorgeous and sweet, and I tried to have breakfast with her on the patio of our hotel whenever she wasn't on call. Bardot was another case. She moved at the center of a pod, consisting of her hairdresser, makeup person, secretary, bodyguard, and whoever else was in her employ. She and her group kept their distance and lived on their own planet. I did, however, near the end of shooting, get to meet and talk with her when, on the ancient train which served as another character in the film, she was waiting for the crew to set up. She was out of costume and wore very tight hip-hugger jeans, as they were known in those days. She also was wearing what can only be described as a pornographic belt. A very large buckle depicting an exotic sex act and, of course, made in Paris for her. I admired it, if that's the word. She said in her limited English, "You like...?" And took it off and wrapped it around my waist – still warm. I can still feel it.

I didn't know if I needed to smuggle it back to the U.S., but I did hide it securely in my luggage. I still have it of course, but very few occasions arise where I can wear it. I liked Brigitte, with all her eccentricities. I've always thought she was shy and that's what made her keep people at a distance.

I got a call from Rome while Pollard was finishing "*Frenchy*," from Federico Fellini. The Maestro was planning a film called "*Satyricon*," and famous as he was for casting "faces," he wanted to meet Pollard, whose face was about as funny as faces ever get.

We flew to Rome on a hot August morning, when all the Romans had fled to the seaside and only American tourists were on the street. Fellini had sent a car for us and we were driven to a restaurant, whose name escapes me now, that appeared to be closed. In fact, it was closed. Our driver knocked, whispered a few words to a slightly opened door, and we were quickly ushered in to a darkened dining room and seated at a large round table. I was introduced by the owner to a perfectly awful-tasting drink called Fernet Branca which, he told me was a collection of 12 beneficial herbs, in an alcoholic base. It was good for whatever ailed you, and would prevent future discomforts of the digestive tract. I remembered reading as a child, stories about the explorer, Sir Richard Burton (not that Richard Burton), in the mid 1860s, who, in order to curry favor with his Arab hosts while crossing the Sahara, pretended to adore eating the eyeballs of a sheep. I winced, but it went down better with alternate sips of very strong espresso. I always have a bottle of it on hand in my home as a nifty after dinner digestivo. Scares the hell out of my guests when they first taste it.

Suddenly, and I mean suddenly, the door to the restaurant flew open and there was an apparition. A huge figure, dressed all in black, including hat and voluminous cape advanced toward us. It was Fellini himself. The man just loved to make an entrance. He had with him his delightful wife, Guilietta Massina, who starred with Anthony Quinn, in Fellini's masterpiece, "*La Strada*." Guilietta didn't speak much English so we communicated mainly through gestures, hand symbols, and smiles. The Maestro, however, did have a strong command of our language, and was charming, funny, and just what you'd expect in an Italian uncle. We had a delicious three-hour lunch while Fellini studied Pollard's face, which made Michael pretty nervous. He didn't get the part though – the Maestro thought he looked too modern.

KISS MY NANNY

I sent Pollard home to L.A. and flew to London to see a couple of my agency clients. Juliette Mills, daughter of the great English actor, Sir John Mills, and sister to Hayley, Disney's newest star, and I were attached in business, but we hardly knew each other. Juliette's primary agent, Fred Specktor, had left the agency to join a start-up called Creative Artists Agency, and I was assigned several of Fred's clients. An agency producer-writer client, A.J. Carrothers, had created and sold to the ABC-TV network, a funny TV pilot script called, "*Kiss My Nanny*," which was, as you can imagine, about the adventures of an English nanny in Hollywood – kind of a real-life Mary Poppins.

Very few British actresses were living in L.A. at the time, and Lynn Redgrave had already committed to an MGM comedy feature called, "*Every Crook and Nanny*," so Juliette Mills, the right age and available, got the part. Another example of agency "packaging." Juliette and I hit it off immediately. Part of our mutual attraction may have been that she and her then-husband had recently split up, leaving Juliette with custody of their three year-old son. She was feeling lonely and rejected. I was sympathetic because virtually the same thing had happened to me when I was married to, and then divorced from Carol. We understood each other.

RITA HAYWORTH

I boarded a TWA 707 in London to return to L.A. via New York, and settled into my aisle seat next to an apparently older woman, who seemed to be mumbling to herself. I said hello but she didn't acknowledge me. Just as well, I thought, a six-hour flight and I had brought some magazines. As the drinks cart came around, I ordered a couple of bloody mary's and offered to help the lady on my right. She was fairly incomprehensible. She didn't even seem to want to eat, so I kept to myself.

When we arrived in New York, the flight attendant asked me if I would help the lady get to her change of planes, as we were both booked on the same flight to Los Angeles. A wheelchair and attendant had been provided, and I agreed. We made our way down the terminal to the departure gate and I saw her to her seat. I had arranged to have the seat next to her, as I was feeling protective of her at this point.

Arriving in L.A. some six hours later, I helped her off the plane, where some people met her. The flight attendant then told me I been sitting next to one of the great movie stars of my time, Rita Hayworth. Alzheimer's disease had not yet been discovered or identified as a condition at that time, and Hayworth was an early victim. She began to show symptoms as early as age 42, and she was 44 when I met her. She had been in Europe for a job and had begun filming her part when, according to what I later learned, she became too ill to continue.

It's only because it was confirmed that it was she, that I believed it. There was no comparison to the gorgeous international movie star, once the bride of the wealthiest man in the world, the Aly Khan, to the woman I had just spent eleven hours sitting next to. I wish I had known then, because I would have reminded her of the great parts she had played in so many American classic films, like "*Gilda,*" "*Pal Joey,*" "*Cover Girl,*" and, co-starring in Orson Welles' "*The Lady from Shanghai,*" while also his wife, and what she meant to world audiences.

TRUHEART

Linda Jones, then my wife, had had a highly dysfunctional relationship with her boss, Irving "Swifty" Lazar, perhaps the best-known literary agent of all time, which eventually lasted 25 years. Spike Jones, her father, was distant and she gravitated toward strong, older men to fill that paternal need. Irving and his wife, Mary became godparents to Linda's and my daughter, Alexandra. Linda established close personal working relationships with a number of Lazar's famous writer clients, such as Truman Capote, Roald Dahl, and Irwin Shaw. Lazar always referred to Capote as "Truheart," but then he was unafraid to call Cary Grant "Archie," Grant's real name.

Capote, especially, became dependent on her and she kept his personal books. Truman had a small house in Palm Springs, with a pool, and insisted that Linda and I take advantage of it when he wasn't using it, and we did. One weekend, we found a brand-new yellow convertible Jaguar XK-150 in the garage and a note from Truman saying he'd sell it to us for $5,000. It seems he had fallen for a 19-year old garage mechanic and had bought the car for him for $8,500, a large amount of money for a car in the early 60s. The romance lasted one week and Capote had taken the car back. I took it out for a spin. It was a two-seater sitting atop an immense engine that took you to 60 mph in second gear. If it had been pink, from a distance it would have looked just like a penis. It was much too much car for me, especially as I was co-raising my year-old daughter by Carol, so I had to pass. If you can even find a comparable version today, you'd have to pay better than $150,000 for it.

THE CHAPLINS

I met Geraldine Chaplin around that time. She had become a client of the theatrical agency I was now working at, and was assigned to me. She had just finished her first film, "*Dr. Zhivago,*" and was in Hollywood to meet other producers and look for a follow-up picture to take advantage of the heat being generated by the David Lean film.

She brought with her boyfriend at the time, a young Spanish director named Carlos Saura. He was getting to be well known in his native country but didn't speak English and was therefore unable to work here. I've always liked to cook so I made dinner for them to welcome them to Hollywood, and invited a few producers and directors who might have future work for her. Both Geraldine and Carlos were crazed about American westerns and as a gift, I rummaged around in my file drawers and found a captain's badge from the school safety patrol, which I had worn as a ninth grader at Junior High School 157, in Queens, and gave it to Carlos. I proclaimed him sheriff of Beverly Hills. He loved it. So did Geraldine.

I later visited Geraldine at her father's home, in Vevey, Switzerland, and got to meet 86 year-old Charlie Chaplin, a thrill for me. He was pretty sprightly for his age and very sexy with his much younger wife, Oona, the daughter of the famous Irish playwright, the late Eugene O' Neill.

I had gone to Vevey to see James Mason, the brilliant British actor, who had just become a client of mine. Mason's house was just down the road from Chaplin's. James was married at the time to his latest and last wife, a beautiful Japanese woman. Luckily for me it was in the spring, because I hate the cold.

Marty Ingels, the flap-mouthed redheaded comic who's been married to and separated from Shirley Jones so many times for so many years, was my lieutenant on the school safety patrol. Only he was known as Marty Ingelman then. His badge was red, while mine was blue. Blue was better. I was his boss and never let him forget it. Marty had an original device to call attention to him when he hit Hollywood and was looking to get established. He would call all the commissaries at the film studios during lunch hour and ask to speak to himself. The loudspeaker would boom above the din, "Phone call for Marty Ingels." He did this for years until he got the co-lead in the TV show, "*He's Dickens, "I'm Fenster,*" with the late John Astin.

MARILYN & CAROL

The next time I met Marilyn Monroe was one cold, rainy, November night as Carol and I pulled up to Marilyn Monroe's apartment at 882 N. Doheny Drive in Hollywood, several months later. Carol and I had a cozy little place on Coldwater Canyon, part of a three-house compound owned by Marjorie Lord and her then-husband, Randy Hale. She had previously been married to another actor, John Archer, with whom she had a daughter. Marjorie was playing Danny Thomas' wife on the "*Danny Thomas Show*," and Randy was operating a little theatre group in the Valley. Their 14 year-old daughter, Anne, who was a young beauty even then, and Marjorie's parents made up the rest of the cluster. Anne Archer went on in her mother's footsteps and became a successful actress, slaying Glenn Close, in "*Fatal Attraction.*"

Carol was nine months pregnant, due any moment. I couldn't and didn't want to leave her at home by herself, so I took her along to Monroe's apartment. MM was to look at negatives from a photo shoot she had just done with the hot new photographer, 21 year-old, Doug Kirkland, for Look magazine. I knocked on her door, as Carol stood shivering beside me. MM opened the door and looked at Carol, whom she knew, since they had adjacent dressing rooms at the studio, and said, "You come in," motioning to me, "but she can wait in your car." This was unexpected and I was momentarily stunned. Carol and I exchanged glances, and I assured her I'd be out in 15 minutes. I was frankly scared. Monroe was one of our biggest clients and I did not want to confront her, or lose my job. After all, how would I support my wife and new baby, completely rejecting the reality that every Friday there was a check in our mailbox, addressed to Carol, from 20th for 20 times my salary.

Every other actor I worked with would use a red grease pencil to put an X through the negatives they didn't like, but not Monroe. She took a scissors and cut out every one she did not like, then cut those into tiny splinters and threw them in the wastebasket. This laborious process took three hours, during which I repeatedly got up to leave. MM kept ordering me to sit down. To be young is to be stupid, someone said, and if I were ever in a situation like that again, I might be out of a job, but I might have still had a wife. It was my first evidentiary of Marilyn Monroe's capacity for cruelty. Kirkland himself, in a recent photo book he published, entitled, "*An Evening With Marilyn Monroe*," remembered how terrified he was of her that night, as she meticulously destroyed negative after negative. He relates he told her that they were his property – that he could be trusted to keep them locked up if that was her wish. That didn't deter her, of course.

Finally she was done and I went out to the car. Carol, young as she was, looked at me with what I swear was pity. Then she got mad. "What the fuck happened in there," she wanted to know. "Did she try to screw you?" I tried explaining, but I was so wrong, I had no defense. "I'm younger than her, I'm prettier." At last an opening. I rushed right in and told her she was the most beautiful girl on the planet, because I really thought so. "And I'm a better actress." I quickly agreed. "And she's jealous because I'm pregnant, and she's not."

Looking back, this may have been the beginning of the end for us. Older than she, more worldly, and certainly more sophisticated, as I imagined myself to be, I probably sold myself that way to her. It's clear to me now that being put out on the street to work at age 5, as she was, and learning all about rejection, double-dealing and broken promises in years doing the Sears catalog with her contemporaries, Sandra Dee and Tuesday Weld, Broadway, in "*The Potting Shed*," with Dame Sybil Thorndike, and the 'sincere' world of Hollywood, made her a hell of a lot more sophisticated than I had ever hoped I was.

The next day, around 10 a.m. at my office desk, I got a call from Carol. She was in the labor room at Cedars of Lebanon hospital, on Fountain Avenue, the predecessor to the now famous Cedars Sinai, near Beverly Hills. Independent, as always, and not wanting to take me away from my job, she had called a taxi. She'd be delivering any minute and said not to bother showing up until I checked with Dr. Garber later. It was well before the days when fathers were mandatory in the delivery room, or even welcomed past the nurse's station. I arrived around four that afternoon and Carol, looking no worse for wear, presented our daughter, Jill.

One of the first films I had ever worked on at Fox was "*Carousel*," starring Gordon MacRae and Shirley Jones, and the words from the soliloquy rambled at that moment through my mind, "A sweet and petite little tintype of her mother, what a pair." Unfortunately, we were children having a child. The marriage failed and we were divorced in 1963.

DATING IN HOLLYWOOD

Among the young ladies I dated while I was getting over Carol, was Alana Ladd, daughter of Alan Ladd. Lannie was 21, beautiful, slim, with movie star looks. Acting wasn't for her, though, she wanted a home and family of her own. Which she got by marrying the other Michael Jackson, the urbane long-time L.A. radio talk show host. She lived with her family in a mansion on Mapleton Drive, in Holmby Hills, where a lot of big name actors, producers and directors lived. For example, the Playboy Mansion is nearby.

Alan Ladd, who was ill and near the end of his life, was living permanently in their Palm Springs home, and Lannie's mother, Sue Carol, spent much of her time there. When I arrived at the house for our first date, Lannie showed me around the lavishly furnished home. In Alan Ladd's den was a set of beautifully leather-bound scripts from all the films he had done. And they almost filled a bookcase. Nothing new there, I had seen the same in many movie star's homes. Then Lannie asked me if I would like to see the bomb shelter. Bomb shelters were very big in the early 60s among the movie and TV crowd. The Mirisches had one.

In the kitchen, the door to the pantry also contained a staircase to what I assumed was the wine cellar. However, underneath the house, extending under the expansive lawn was a fully equipped three-bedroom abode, complete with stored food, water, and everything necessary to survive a nuclear attack on L.A. It even had a replica of Alan Ladd's den. Complete with a duplicate set of beautifully leather-bound scripts. I immediately thought about what future archeologists might make of this. I was distressed to learn recently that Lannie, who has been married to Jackson for more than 40 years, had a stroke, at age 63, and is physically handicapped.

Another young lady I liked being with a lot was Denise Alexander, also 21, again a child actress from New York, who had spent a number of years on "*Days of Our Lives*," a popular soap. She, like I, had only been in L.A. a short time and we decided we just had to go to Mexico – the popular thing among young people in showbiz. We drove to Tijuana and bought a few tourist items, a couple of bottles of tequila, and ended up at the Plaza De Toros for the Sunday afternoon bullfights. We were excited, along with the crowd, by the pageant, the colorful matadors, toreadors, the blindfolded horses of the picadors, and the familiar music. Denise was doing fine until the first bull was killed, spilling a large amount of blood on the ground. She said, "Excuse me," and left her seat for, I thought, the bathroom. When she didn't return after a half hour, I went to find her – and did – on the street, throwing up against the outside wall. First and last time either of us went to a bullfight.

Denise recognized the appeal California had for east coasters like us, especially when it got cold, and figured refugees, especially in the entertainment business, would need places to live. She socked every cent she made into buying small houses she rehabbed and rented and, last I had heard, was exceedingly wealthy. Wish she had told me her plans.

One of my clients as an agent was Deborah Walley, the second "*Gidget*" after Sandra Dee. She was married to a young actor named John Ashley, and had a little blonde son of two. Redheaded and cute, she had been a professional ice-skater with the Capades and was now heading toward stardom. One Saturday morning I visited her at her home in the Hollywood Hills, facing the San Fernando Valley. It was very hot and she suggested a swim. I didn't have a suit so she offered me one of John's. He was away in the Philippines, shooting a movie. We were in the pool when her phone rang. John was calling. She took it inside and after a long while, Deb came out of the house, crying. John told her he wasn't coming back – that he had signed to do another film there, and that he had fallen in love with a local girl. I stayed for most of the day, made dinner for us – she was still breast-feeding, and did what many agents, personal managers, even press agents do – assume roles as confidants, amateur psychologists and even as temporary best friends, until the crisis passes. Of course, "best friends" has multiple meanings. Sometimes it crosses over to lovers, which it did for us eventually. Others take advantage of the situation and attempt to control the careers of the emotionally distraught. It usually ends in disaster for all. Debbie went on to do a few more films and some TV, but it didn't work out for her in Hollywood and she eventually moved to Colorado. I was very surprised and pained to read of her death from esophageal cancer, at the age of 51, in Denver. Such a sweet girl.

I liked Diana Hyland perhaps best, among my actress clients. A regal and sophisticated blonde, she was down to earth while projecting a queenly presence. I got her a continuing role in the TV series, "*Peyton Place*," based on the hit movie. Diana also had a featured role in "*The Chase*," starring Marlon Brando, Robert Redford and Jane Fonda, in 1996. I was stunned when she began an affair with a very young John Travolta, 17 years her junior, who was just coming becoming known in "*Welcome Back, Kotter*," a TV series hit. It didn't last long, however, and I thought I had a chance with her. But she thought business and pleasure was a bad mix, and fell for a handsome dude named Joe Goodson, a nephew of one of the owners of "21," the showbiz hangout on 52nd St., in New York. They bought a house off Doheny

Road, in the Hollywood Hills, with a view to forever and thought they were in love. I couldn't believe it when Diana called me to her house one day, and cried to me about Joe having cheated on her, and that she had thrown him out. That rat! I never would have cheated on that woman. What a score she was. I was crushed when she died unexpectedly, within three months after she was diagnosed with breast cancer, in 1977. Today's advanced treatment and drugs, unknown then, might have kept her with us longer.

Kathleen Nolan was lots of fun. She was the female lead in the raucous 1964 Universal TV series hit, "*Broadside*," along with Sheila Kuhl, formerly of the "*Dobie Gillis*" TV series, and a former state senator in California, and Dick Sargent, later to become Elizabeth Montgomery's husband in "*Bewitched*." Kathy was the first woman ever elected as President of the Screen Actor's Guild, in 1975. Like many actresses I knew, Kathy was entirely unsuccessful in picking mates, and had just kicked out her husband, whose name was Dick, which I thought completely appropriate, for cheating on her. It seemed to be an epidemic.

Kathy and I both had 3 year-olds, her son by Dick, and my daughter, Jill, from Carol. We would take our kids on Sundays to the pony park, on the corner of La Cienega and Beverly Blvd., where we could spend a couple of hours relaxing while our infants were occupied pulling the ponies' hair. I called Sundays at the pony park, "father's day," since I would see many of my contemporaries with visitation, anxiously, sometimes, desperately, trying to use up their allotted six or eight hours, before gratefully returning their hyperactive and needy children to their nannies.

Nina Blanchard owned the Nina Blanchard Agency, in Los Angeles, during the 1980s, well known as the top modeling agency on the West Coast. Nina "discovered" Cheryl Tiegs, a local girl who swiftly became the first "Supermodel." I met Cheryl when she married Stan Dragoti, who happened to become my client, and whom I mentored in the ways of Hollywood when they moved here so Stan could direct "*Dirty Little Billy*," for Columbia Pictures. And of course, through the Dragoti's, I met Nina.

Nina vectored Cheryl's success into representing the cream of the beautiful young women in the 1970s thru most of the 1980s, when she sold her name and agency to one of her competitors. But before she did, she found and built the careers of Vanna White, of the long-running "*Wheel of Fortune*," Lindsay Wagner, who signed with Nina at age 13, Christie Brinkley, Christina Ferrare, and Rene Russo, who later became a movie star in such films as "*Lethal Weapon*," with Mel Gibson. Nina also wrote a best-selling book, "*How to Break into Motion Pictures, Television, Commercials & Modeling*."

Nina gave regular parties at her home in the Hollywood Hills to show off her "talent" to the usual suspects among producers, directors and studio executives. Occasionally, one of her clients would actually get a role in a movie or TV show. Mostly, the producers, directors, and studio executives got laid. Naturally, Nina invited me. However, instead of being attracted to the cohort of near 6-foot tall, stunning females competing to look the sexiest, Nina fascinated me more. I've always liked smart, ambitious, and good-looking, of course, women. My mother was like that. Nina couldn't believe I really wanted her, an "old lady" of 45. Married unsuccessfully once, and since utterly devoted to her business, Nina had just about forgotten about men. In fact, most of them were too entranced by her "protégés" to even notice her. After I convinced her I was serious, we had a short but very satisfying relationship. I broke it off because she smoked heavily, and I tear up and wheeze around cigarette smoke. I'm not one to tell someone else how to live their life and, sure enough, a few years later, Nina died.

THE MEXICAN CONNECTION

In 1986, while a producer at MGM studios in a first-look deal, I met a young woman named Joan Beck, through a mutual friend, a Mexican jet-setter, named Alfonso Lopez-Negrete, whose aunt had been the beautiful and fiery Hollywood star, Dolores Del Rio. Joan, an American, and a native of La Jolla, California was in her early 30s and had the facial features of Bette Davis at the same age. She dressed beautifully and had a great figure.

Alfonso was known to his friends by his nickname, "Poncho;" he loved having a good time, and was my host in his Acapulco cliffside home, his Mexico City townhouse, and his vacation home in Cuernavaca. He had been a friend of Joan's former boyfriend, Carlos, another wealthy playboy. Joan and I hit it off and started seeing a great deal of each other. I was curious about her Mexican connections, since she seemed to have spent a lot of time there, but she was vague about dates and places, and the whereabouts of Carlos. Which only made me more curious.

Several months into our relationship and after Joan was prodded by Poncho, I was stunned to learn about Joan's real life. I was open-mouthed by her story, which she proved to me by showing me yellowing newspaper clippings, and by my confirming it all with Poncho. I immediately thought, "Screenplay."

Joan was an abused child of wealthy, alcoholic parents, who grew up without love. One evening, at a party in San Diego, when she was nineteen, she met a handsome, charismatic, affluent Mexican businessman twenty years her senior. He was kind, attentive and sophisticated. Before long they were in love. Carlos Kiriakides owned several businesses, including the Mercedes agency in Tijuana, two restaurants and a laundry. She said they lived a fairy tale existence and were happy together for six years. They skied in Biarritz, gambled in Monte Carlo, and had homes in New York City, Beverly Hills, Paris and Mexico City.

One night, with Joan driving them in her Rolls Corniche, a gift from Carlos, on their way to a party for then-President Echeverria at the Palace in Mexico City, their car was ambushed at a red light. Vanloads of machine-gun toting masked men surrounded them, hauling them out, beating Carlos brutally, slapping Joan, blindfolding and handcuffing her. She was thrown onto the floor of a van and taken to the "Black Palace," Leucumberri Prison, where she was thrown into the "hole." She told me she had no idea what happened to Carlos, or to her. For eight days, in the dark, an inch of oily, fetid water on the floor, her only companions' cat-sized rats and millions of cockroaches, her bathroom a bucket, she said all she did was cry in terror.

Finally, she was dragged out into the light, brutalized, screamed at punched, and horribly tortured, and still had no idea what had happened to her, or why? Two of the cops, she said, were blond and blue-eyed and spoke very bad Spanish with an American accent. It came out that Carlos, without her knowledge, had become one of the western world's leading drug and arms smugglers. They told her he had had the presidents of Mexico, Bolivia and Colombia on his payroll. She refused to believe them because Carlos was rich when she met him. He wouldn't have gotten himself into that, what did he need with more money? Joan told them she didn't speak Spanish, they were rarely in Mexico and Carlos kept his business dealings secret.

The awful truth, she found out, was that three years into their relationship, Carlos had been approached to finance a drug operation that brought him so much money so fast, he was unable to stop. With all his income, he spent lavishly and still owed millions from his gambling. With his eventual political connections he was contacted by the CIA to act as a conduit: he could continue his drug operations unmolested as long as he paid the left-wing guerillas and the farmers they protected with weapons left over from Vietnam, supplied to him on unmarked ships, which would be used to destabilize local governments in Columbia, Bolivia, and elsewhere.

With the republicans now in office, Nixon was pressing the "war on drugs", both to embarrass the Democrats and to ensure his re-election. And it didn't matter if a few innocent Americans got in his way. Mexico isn't America. No one has the right to a lawyer or a hearing, much less a trial. With Joan knowing nothing of all this, and unable to speak in her own defense, she was sentenced to 30 years in the Black Palace.

Her parents, frantic with worry, got no help from the U.S. Embassy, who told them Joan was dead. Now doing their best to be sober, they sold everything they could to finance a search throughout Mexico for their daughter. She was marked for death, learning to protect herself from the Mexican Mafia and from female criminals jealous of her former life and connections. Passing the children's play area one day, she noticed a baby, head stuck between the bars of a playpen, choking to death. Joan saved the child's life, giving it CPR, only later finding out it was the daughter of the main Mexican gang leader. The woman's gratitude was endless, and then on Joan had a measure of protection. There were nearly a hundred other American women, from all over the country, being brutalized behind the bars of the Black Palace.

Some were guilty of minor infractions, others, like Joan, innocent. Such as the 65 year-old grandmother from San Diego who, while backpacking through South America was asked by her grandson to pick up a schoolbook for him in Mexico City. The book held a small vial of hash oil, and she too, was sentenced to 30 years. With her new protected status, Joan organized the prisoners, becoming the spokesperson for the Americans, and of the helpless Mexican women. Her cell became the center of political and social action as she began a letter writing campaign, ingeniously smuggled out in the underwear of the Amnesty International women who visited them, to President Carter and every congressman and senator they could remember, telling them of the hell American women were being forced to endure.

Occasionally, when one of the women went over the edge, tried to end it all and failed, they inevitably ended up in Joan's cell, where she would sew up their wounds or pump out their stomachs with an ancient hand-cranked pump, and give them the courage to continue. Nearly every day for three years, Joan's father stood on the steps of the American Embassy to ask, then beg, and finally demand the ambassador find and protect his child. And he was ignored.

Carlos meanwhile, had been taken to another prison, where he had been tortured in a particularly gruesome fashion dating back to the Aztecs. His whereabouts had been kept secret from Joan, but with her growing notoriety, as human rights groups picketed the border at San Diego and petitioned congress, causing the media to play the story on the front pages, she was able to force the authorities to recognize her "conjugal rights." In Mexico, all prisoners are entitled to see their wives, husbands or lovers weekly. One night, awakened at 2 a.m., Joan was blindfolded, handcuffed and taken for a long, bumpy ride in the back of a sealed van. She thought they were finally going to kill her for all the trouble she had caused them.

Hours later, they arrived at a mental institution, Teppepen, miles from civilization. The floor was a vast ward of beds, dimly lit by a single bare bulb. She went from bed to bed, and finally located Carlos by the veins on his hands. He had been beaten so badly the right half of his face had been pushed back half-an-inch, and he was in coma. Joan demanded her rights, and every Sunday thereafter for three hours, they were allowed a private room at the prison. Over the next two years, Joan slowly brought Carlos back to life.

There were a few light moments; like the time she was first arrested, desperate for any information as to why her world suddenly fell in on her. She begged an unseen guard for something to read, a newspaper, anything. His response the next day was to slip under her door a dirty, ripped copy of Ram Dass' "Be Here Now."

Or the Christmas, when with dollars smuggled in to her by her parents, she broke out of her cell and into the Directora's office. Using the phone, she ordered 350 Kentucky Fried Chicken dinners delivered to the prison by taxi as her gift to the other inmates and the staff.

Finally, partly as a result of Joan's efforts, the political pressure on congress and the glare of the media's attention, the United States and Mexico signed a prisoner-exchange treaty. In fact, in Congress, it was titled the Joan Beck Amendment. The doors to the Black Palace swung open and a hundred bedraggled and hurt American women swarmed out into the arms of their loved ones. All except Joan. She said that the U.S. attorney in San Diego, angered and embarrassed by her political action and his failure to break her, illegally kept her from release. After threats from the Justice Department, he was forced to capitulate. Put on a plane for the U.S., and under the impression she was bound for San Diego, where the media, as well as her family and friends were gathered, the plane landed in Los Angeles, where the FBI re-arrested her.

Taken to Sybil Brand Institute, an unprecedented Sunday board meeting was held to determine what to do with this political hot potato. However, this time it was America; due process, civil rights, and Melvin Belli. The famed criminal lawyer was retained with the last few dollars the Beck's could scrape together, and shortly thereafter, Joan was found innocent of all charges, except for a minor one of transporting more than $10,000 across a border without registering it, and was released to pick up the pieces of her life.

Several weeks alter, Joan was handed an itemized bill by her parents for the money they had spent on trips to Mexico, lawyer fees, bribes, food, lodging, etc. They settled for her Rolls convertible. Joan had no money, since her parents had taken the only possession she had, and because of her felony record, which Belli had to accept as a condition of her discharge, had trouble finding work, so she agreed to my suggestion. We spent the next six months researching, taping her recollections, flying to San Francisco to see Melvin Belli, and talking to other women who had been in that same prison with her. I finally produced a very hard-hitting movie script that took on the Nixon administration, the DEA, the Mexican government, and unloving parents. It was immediately optioned by MGM, and promptly got caught up in development hell, as it's known.

It was my first screenplay and, although it had been bought on the spot, the studio insisted on hiring better known writers. Two years later, Joan and I got the script back. We had been paid for MGM's options, but had lost a lot of valuable time while the administration of the studio changed twice. The script was optioned twice more, once for television, but still has not been produced.

I asked Poncho, if Carlos had this great love for Joan, why he didn't get her out of the way when it got hot. He could easily have deposited her in La Jolla while he worked things out, if he could. Poncho said that no matter how rich a Mexican is he always feels like a wetback in the U.S. An American girlfriend is a very prestigious possession and Carlos was too selfishly conscious of his status in his world.

Joan and I continued as boy and girlfriend for another year and a half, and I thought things were going well, when I bumped into her on the street, and she introduced me to her husband, a Brazilian man named Humberto, whom she had married on the spur of the moment the previous week. Again, I was stunned, a regular occurrence with this girl. Joan loved to salsa dance, I knew, and had a weakness for Latin men, and at a club, she and Humberto were so good together, she simply had to have him.

That was a long time ago. Joan and I are still good friends, and Humberto is long gone.

MARILYN (ONE MORE TIME)

So here I was standing outside Monroe's house. In spite of how she treated me, I felt sad she was dead. After all, there really was no Marilyn Monroe; it was only an invention, a fictional character. So then, who, really, was dead?

Marilyn Monroe was an empty suit, that whoever was playing her took off when she came home. Like Superman, who was really Clark Kent – or was it the other way around - the scared girl-woman, home alone at night, only became powerful when she climbed into the Marilyn Monroe costume. Thus, mightily dressed, she could influence the world. She could make huge studios tremble; she could bring dominant, academy-award-winning directors like Billy Wilder to tears. She could keep the most powerful man in the world, the president of the United States, infatuated and distracted from his job of taking care of the rest of us. She could terrorize stupid kids like me. Talk about living a double life. How could she, she probably wondered, be so weak and so strong at the same time? I would have been confused too. I suppose similar thoughts occur to actual schizophrenics.

No doubt she hoped all that clout might bring some security, some confidence to the little girl playing dress-up movie star. What she really needed was a director she could trust – not a movie director, but some commanding, authoritative, male figure to give her the cover to venture into her emotional past, so she could discover, once and for all, the origin of her pain.

She tried many men – Jim Dougherty, her first husband, who recently died at the age of 84, Johnny Hyde, her first agent, Lee Strasberg, her first acting coach, Arthur Miller, her first intellectual, Joe DiMaggio, her first sports hero, Sinatra, even mafia man Giancana – all the way to the top – JFK. Like all of us, she wanted control over her emotions because they were hurting her. But she didn't look in the right place, where it always was – inside herself. It was fear, most likely, that kept her from going there. Abused children lock the doors on horrible memories, and she struggled to repress them, presumably until the moment her heart stopped beating. It's difficult to believe anyone could have helped her. Or saved her.

She had just been fired by Fox from "*Something's got to Give*," which would never be finished, and told that Jayne Mansfield, a top-heavy blonde actress Fox had recently signed, specifically, I remember, as a back-up to MM in case she crashed, would replace her.

Finally, I told the reporters I would meet them the next day at my office, at 449 South Beverly drive, and I'd have more for them then. They weren't happy, but they finally dispersed and I was able to leave.

The rumors continued to build. *That night, according to several sources, including Joe Hyams, then the intimately-connected Hollywood reporter for the New York Herald Tribune, the Secret Service went to the Santa Monica offices of Pacific Bell and confiscated the punched paper tapes of all the calls from MM's telephone the night before. *Her last call was to Peter Lawford. *Or it was to Joe DiMaggio. *No, it was to Joe DiMaggio, Jr. Only the Secret Service, or perhaps the FBI, since J. Edgar Hoover took such a proprietary interest in the Kennedys, knows. *Pat Newcomb, her personal press agent and best friend, left immediately that morning for Hyannisport, supposedly hired as a press agent for the Kennedys. *A Beverly Hills cop, Lynn Franklin, reported seeing a black limo speeding down Olympic Boulevard at 12 a.m. the night before. He stopped the car and was surprised to find Peter Lawford at the wheel and Bobby Kennedy in the back seat.   *A Marine Corp helicopter from El Toro was reported to have landed on the beach in front of Lawford's house that night in Santa Monica and taken Robert Kennedy to San Francisco, where he gave a hurriedly-arranged speech the next day. *Monroe had had an abortion, or a miscarriage several months prior to her death, at Cedars of Lebanon, and she wasn't sure whether it was Jack's or Bobby's.

And my personal favorite; *People who work at morgues are low-paid and are attracted by certain benefits. Among them, the opportunity to have sex with beautiful, famous women (and men?). When such a dead person shows up, preferably unmarked, as in the case of Natalie Wood and MM, the call goes out to the various nearby county morgues and the ghouls line up. And that occurred that same night, before Dr. Thomas Noguchi's autopsy the next day (courtesy, again, of reporter Joe Hyams.)

The FBI was watching MM at this time. On their website, information can be found that in February of 1962, Marilyn Monroe went to Legat, Mexico, supposedly to buy Mexican furnishings for the first house she ever bought for herself. "The reason I never bought a house before was because it was like being married, but being alone." Someone who accompanied her, a close confident, reported on this trip to Mexico to the FBI.

And this was not the first time this person reported to the FBI. The source reported that Monroe was associated with the ACGM, the American Communist Group in Mexico. Monroe was also against nuclear testing and let this be known to President Kennedy. Monroe was accompanied on that trip by three people, Pat Newcomb, her hairdresser and Eunice Churchill, an interior decorator and also assistant to Dr. Wexley, Monroe's then-analyst. Monroe was very disturbed by Arthur Miller's remarriage on Feb. 20, 1962 and felt like a "negated sex symbol." Frank Sinatra had dumped her. She called Frank to come down to Mexico to comfort her. He refused. At 5 P.M. on February 21, 1962, a man visited Monroe in her suite #1110 at the Hotel Continental Hilton for about an hour.

Two days later, they went to Toluca, Mexico together for the entire day. That night, they were again alone in Monroe's hotel suite. The confidant reported this man as being "completely infatuated with Monroe." His name was blacked out on the FBI report. Who was this man? Could his initials have been RFK? The FBI considered MM a security risk, giving her a code file of 105, which translated means foreign intelligence, which in this case meant communist. She was also getting a series of mysterious, threatening phone calls that scared her.

Robert Kennedy had became deeply involved with Monroe and, at some point, hinted he might divorce his wife to marry her; preposterous, considering the Catholicism of the family, and his multiple children. Monroe returned to L.A. to film *Something's Got to Give*, with Dean Martin, but once again was having emotional problems and was always late to the set. The director, George Cukor, did not get along with her and found her "difficult." Fox was in financial trouble at the time with *Cleopatra*, starring Elizabeth Taylor. Monroe was fired from the film. She was replaced with Lee Remick. Dean Martin, however, walked from the picture, saying his contract was to do the picture with Marilyn, not Remick. The picture was never completed. Monroe's contract with Fox was canceled.

The FBI files also say that Monroe telephoned Robert Kennedy person-to-person at the Department of Justice from her home in Brentwood, to see if he could help with the canceled contract at Fox. He told her not to worry; he would take care of it. When he didn't call back, she called him again, only this time they had an argument. He told her not to keep calling him there and that it was getting too risky for his career, and that he had to stop seeing her. She threatened to make their affair public if he did not come see her in person.

On the day she died, Robert Kennedy was in town. His coterie denied it, but Darryl Gates, L.A.'s police chief, said so. That afternoon, according to Eunice Murray, Robert Kennedy visited Monroe at her house, to break it off in person, as she demanded. Reports say they had sex, which turned into a violent argument during which, according to the FBI, who had apparently bugged the home, MM said she "felt like a piece of meat being passed around and then dropped, just like at the parties when she was a starlet, just like the abuse when she was still a kid. Nothing had changed since she became famous." Then Bobby said he had to get back to Northern California, where his wife and children were staying at a friend's ranch, and left with two aides.

Monroe was distraught, apparently. Her contract with Fox had been canceled, and now her hopes of marrying Kennedy were over. She was left all alone, age 36, with only her housekeeper.

Norman Jeffries says Robert Kennedy and Peter Lawford returned to her house at 9 p.m. and told Jeffries to leave. He came back an hour later. Kennedy and Lawford were gone. On the FBI tape there are sounds like a search being conducted – like hangers in a closet being pushed together –and crashing noises that sound like books being dumped on the floor. A bugging device was being sought. Not only the FBI, but also the Kennedys themselves had bugged her house. This confirms the feud raging between FBI director, Hoover, and the Kennedy brothers. Both men left the house shortly thereafter. Billy Woodfield, a friend of most of the people involved, says Lawford told him that he had sent a driver to pick up Robert Kennedy at 10:30 that night at his house on the beach and take him to the airport to catch a United Airlines flight to San Francisco.

Robert Kennedy flew to San Francisco and checked into the St. Francis Hotel. Dr. Ralph Greenson, the psychiatrist treating Monroe, was trying to get her off barbiturates. But on this occasion, he prescribed 40 seconal, an unusually large quantity, given the frequency of her appointments with him, and her past history of real or staged suicide attempts.

Even her husbands had failed her, maybe even used her. First Arthur Miller, then Joe DiMaggio. She had even broken with Sinatra and Lawford. Sinatra had allegedly set her up with Sam Giancana, the Chicago-based "Godfather of Godfathers," for a weekend at Cal-Neva Lodge, in Lake Tahoe, a former mob hideaway Sinatra now owned and used for those "special" times. Other Rat Packers also used the hotel when they wanted to be away from prying eyes.

Billy Woodfield, one of MM's favorite photographers, who also happened to be a trusted friend of Sinatra's, was called by Frank and asked to personally and secretly develop a roll of film taken that weekend. There were nine frames showing Giancana behind Monroe, in what Woodfield said on camera, was a position on the floor where he was either "riding her, or something else." Giancana grew up in Sicily, where the oppressive Catholic upbringing of young people made virginity mandatory for women. Young people customarily relieved their yearnings utilizing other available bodily openings. That socialization, apparently, carried over to Giancana's adulthood to the extent he preferred such sexual intercourse. Woodfield says he showed those nine frames to Sinatra and asked what Frank wanted him to do with them. "Burn them," he said. It's not difficult to believe that may have been a personal nadir for Monroe.

The rumors of murder were started by an article in Photoplay Magazine, "Marilyn Monroe's Killer Still at Large!" that sensationalized her death at the time and sold many, many copies. But I believe they were just that, rumors, and that after taking all those pills, trying to sleep to escape all her troubles, she depressed her nervous system, causing her heart to stop beating.

However, the curious thing is that everyone intimately connected to Marilyn in her last moments died violently. Sam Giancana, the Chicago mafia head, was introduced to her by Frank Sinatra. Giancana was supposedly connected to the Bay of Pigs Cuban invasion under JFK in 1961, which turned into a disaster as JFK pulled back his support at the last minute. Giancana, prior to Fidel Castro, ran the casino business in Havana. After that, Robert Kennedy launched a major investigation of Giancana by the F.B.I., and was heard saying on a taped conversation, "I want that Dago Sam Giancana put away for life." Giancana felt betrayed, since he claimed he delivered Chicago, and, hence, Illinois to JFK, helping him win the presidency. It also was documented that Giancana was recruited to help assassinate Fidel Castro. It was known he visited MM at her last home in Brentwood and had placed bugs there. He was known to have tape recordings of Bobby Kennedy's visits with MM. He claims to have been the last one to "sleep" with MM at her house in Brentwood. I doubt he ever "slept" with her. Why don't people call it what is is? Could Giancana have had anything to do with MM's death, which would and did cause a huge embarrassment to Robert Kennedy, Giancana's enemy?

Many coincidences: Bay of Pigs disaster in 1961, MM dies August 4, 1962. JFK assassinated November 22, 1963. Did this have anything to do with the failed Bay of Pigs, and Giancana's failure to regain control of his casinos in Havana? RFK was assassinated on January 5, 1968. Any connection with Giancana fleeing to Mexico because of RFK's investigation into him for racketeering? The F.B.I. report on Sirhan Sirhan, supposedly the only gunman, has always been questionable. One report said he was tackled to the floor of the pantry at the Ambassador Hotel by the maitre'd after firing only two shots from his .22 caliber revolver, and then the gun was pushed away. However RFK was shot three times and five others were wounded. The killing bullet was fired from behind RFK's right ear, from an angle not possible to be fired by Sirhan Sirhan, who was front and sideways. RFK died 24 hours later at Good Samaritan Hospital. Two separate eyewitnesses at the scene later testified that they saw a blond man in a gray suit standing behind RFK put a gun in a holster, and a tall dark haired man in a black suit fire two shots and run out of the pantry. Of the eight bullets fired, one was never recovered, having "been lost in the space of the ceiling tiles." Some reports said not all the bullets recovered matched the barrel marks from Sirhan Sirhan's gun.

The bullet that entered RFK's brain exploded. The police report was not released until 1988, after 2400 photos had been destroyed as duplicates, the ceiling tiles and door frame from the pantry with the bullet holes were destroyed because, "they wouldn't fit into the file cabinets." Of the 3,470 interviews, only 301 were released.

Giancana was brought back from Mexico to testify before the Senate subcommittee on the plot to assassinate Fidel Castro, and placed under the witness protection program of the FBI. Shortly before the hearings, Giancana was shot in the back of the head with a silencer in his home in Oak park, Illinois, on June 19, 1975.

On the other hand, MM was herself a user. She used her first husband, Jimmy Dougherty, to avoid going back to the orphanage. She used Johnny Hyde, a top William Morris agent, to introduce her to producers and directors. Hyde left his wife and small children, one of whom, Jimmy, I knew as a young William Morris agent, to be with her, and she eventually dumped him. He never got over it, his son Jimmy told me. She always ended up alone. And now it seemed her career was over, too.

Many reports that MM was being threatened were making the rounds. Jack and Bobby Kennedy were said to be warning her to dummy up about what she knew; from advance knowledge of the Cuban Bay of Pigs invasion, to a CIA document that Mike Rothmiller, an investigator for the LAPD says he read, that speculated she may been told of a secret plan to send an anonymous bomber to take out China's nuclear sites; to a story that on August 3, 1962, another CIA document, written only a day before her death, revealed that some high government officials were in a state of extreme anxiety over the fact that the Kennedy brothers had been imparting sensitive information to Marilyn, and that she was writing it down in her little red "diary of secrets." And I love this one: The CIA document apparently referred to one of the secrets everyone was afraid of; that Marilyn might have written down "the visit by the President at a secret air base for the purpose of inspecting things from outer space," i.e., JFK had told Marilyn about the Roswell UFO crash and the retrieval, in 1947, of debris and alien bodies.

Fox was saying she'd never work in Hollywood again, and even the Mafia, especially Giancana, was worried about her unstableness and the rumor she was planning a press conference shortly to blow all this up for the world to see.

Oddly enough, Giancana and JFK shared a girlfriend, a young actress named Judy Campbell, whom I also knew as part of young Hollywood. I was aware she was one of JFK's close personal associates, but didn't know about the Chicago connection until years later, when several investigative reporters revealed it.

When you consider that Jack Kennedy's father, Joe, was a bootlegger in the 20s, and associated with crime figures then, the connection between the White House and Chicago becomes less of a fantasy. And then there were those rumors that Illinois was delivered to the Kennedy camp in the general election.

Marilyn drank the whole bottle of Dom Perignon 1953 that she had opened for Bobby. On the night of August 4, 1962, Eunice Murray, the live-in housekeeper, put the bottle of 40 seconal tablets on Monroe's nightstand. Eleven other medications were also initially found on the nightstand. Later, only eight were in evidence. Previously Monroe had attempted suicide, but had been rescued with her stomach being pumped, and the previous attempts were seen as only a cry for sympathy. This time no one intervened. Dr. Greenson made arrangements with the coroner for a psychiatric board of inquiry to be appointed by the coroner, a most unusual procedure. This was done so she could be found emotionally unbalanced at the time of her death, thereby relieving any physician from responsibility for the multiple prescriptions she had from him, Dr. Hyman Engelberg, and others. Later, Engelberg was quoted as saying that he and Greenson had gotten their signals crossed and that they were each prescribing contraindicated medicines for her, resulting in a "horrible medical mistake." Billy Woodfield says he asked Greenson years later why he had prescribed chloral hydrate, a strong depressant, to an already depressed MM, knowing she was a prodigious drinker. The two, together, could kill her. Greenson agreed. Greenson, her psychiatrist, even though called while she was alive, did not come to her home until after she was dead. Pat Newcomb was flown to Hyannis port 48 hours after the body was discovered. She was given a permanent job in Washington, D.C. with the Motion Picture Division of the United States Information Service. Eunice Murray, Monroe's housekeeper and her nephew, the handyman, disappeared from sight for the next twenty years. The investigation ground to a halt.

The coroner, Theodore Kurfy, who took an amazing 13 days, ruled the death a "probable suicide." Or perhaps, as other pathologists, Dr. Robert Garnier, of hospital Fernand Widal, in Paris, and Drs. Ken Shorrok, a forensic pathologist, in London, along with Dr. Cyril Wecht, a London coroner, and Dr. Robert Forrest, a forensic toxicologist, have said on the record, after studying the autopsy reports, there's no evidence of a fatal enema, or dissolved capsules, or any needle marks on Monroe's body. It's clear she took nembutals steadily throughout the late afternoon and evening, with alcohol, which, because she was habituated to them didn't put her to sleep as usual. She then took a dose of chloral hydrate, a potent hallucinatory, which slowed her respiration until it stopped her heart. She didn't mean for it to happen that way. It just did. She probably would have been diagnosed today as manic-depressive, says Dr. Engelberg. Too bad Prozac hadn't been invented then. It might have saved her life.

Her funeral was a big event, even by Hollywood standards. Arthur Jacobs and I were in charge of giving out tickets for seating to the media. The rest of the tickets were under the control of Joe DiMaggio. DiMaggio gave Frank Sinatra ten tickets and the studio, 20th Century Fox, twenty tickets. Sinatra wanted control of the funeral, but he backed down when Joe insisted he was going to handle it. Tickets were scarce since Westwood Village Mortuary is very small. Reporters came from all over the world. There were more photographers there than I had ever seen in my life.

A gray Cadillac hearse, led by several police on motorcycles, slowly pulled up in front of the mortuary. Fox security guards waited on both sides of the driveway, until the hearse gradually came to a stop. The four security guards picked up the coffin and carried it inside. The mourners, the top celebrity names at the time, including Frank Sinatra, Dean Martin, Sammy Davis, Jr., of the famous "Rat Pack," of the original movie "*Ocean's Eleven*," slowly filtered in, following the coffin. Fox's Movietone News filmed everything, and then released it at theaters and on T.V. Jerry Geisler, the Hollywood divorce lawyer that represented MM in her split from Joe DiMaggio, was there, as well as all the tabloid columnists of the time. After the ceremony, her coffin was carried out to the hearse, and slowly driven to her final resting place, one crypt in a large wall of vaults, with a vase for flowers on it. She was interred into that crypt on the back wall, away from all the traffic on Wilshire Boulevard. Joe DiMaggio, in tears, walked up and placed the first of what would be weekly bouquets of red roses into the vase. He did this every week, while he was alive. Now permanent pink plastic roses have replaced them.

Conspiracy? Yes. No. Maybe. Conspiracy, perhaps, not to help her, as had been done before, and as she probably expected. This time it was a conspiracy to let her die. Sometimes people get too difficult to be around. Friend "fatigue" happens.

She's a much bigger star today, almost fifty years after her death, than she ever was alive. Lots of people are still making lots of money off her. The public always loves tragic stories, from Jesus to Judy Garland, to Michael Jackson, and Farrah Fawcett. It also helps to die young – we'll always remember JFK, Elvis, Mozart, Judy Garland, Michael Jackson, Farrah, and Marilyn, as they were, young and beautiful. After all, what commercial value would 83 year-old Marilyn Monroe have today? She might have emulated my other client, Marlene Dietrich who, in her 70's had the good sense, like the beauteous Greta Garbo before her, to retire from public view. And that's how we remember them.

Maybe MM's death really was just an "accident." I still don't know to this day and neither does anyone else. But I know why MM still lives– We won't let her die.

ORSON

In 1972, I represented as an agent a UCLA professor, Donald Freed, who was also an author. Well-known as a leftist in politics, he had written the first draft of a screenplay based on his book, "*Executive Action*," which purported several conspiracies in the assassination of JFK. That screenplay was bought by Burt Lancaster's production company and turned into a film starring him. Lancaster was also deeply sympathetic to left-leaning causes.

Freed followed that up with another conspiracy theory bundled into a screenplay, this time connected to the slaying of Robert F. Kennedy, the former Attorney General and then candidate for the Democratic nomination for president for the 1968 election. This screenplay was entitled, "*RFK Must Die*," and accused the CIA as the main force behind RFK's assassination. In his script, Freed included the so-called "woman in a polka dot dress," some people on the scene in the kitchen of Los Angeles' Ambassador Hotel claimed to have seen. Freed also imagined a CIA agent who "ran" Sirhan Sirhan, the alleged and later convicted murderer. I was charged with selling the script to a production company or major studio. I was unable to secure any interest in it.

Freed knew a wealthy woman, Sally Bernard, who wanted to be in the movie business. Her husband owned many downtown Los Angeles parking lots.

The Bernard's lived on Alpine Drive, in Beverly Hills. In her mid-forties, Sally was a tall, handsome woman, who had a teenage child from her former marriage. Jim was a widower, a good twenty years older than Sally, but gladly took her and her offspring, including Vicki, 18, into his life. Sally didn't have much to do of a practical nature, her children fending for themselves and the household help doing the rest. All was well with the Bernards.

Freed had remarried, this time to an interesting intellectual, Patty, a teacher who could also cook and who had a sizable monthly income comprised of alimony and child support for her two small children by her former husband. The Freeds entertained extensively, the guests ranging from certain members of the Black Panther party, Jane Fonda, Donald Sutherland and, not at the same time, his ex-wife Shirley, the daughter of the former Canadian Prime Minister, Tommy Douglas, himself known as a leader of Canada's political left. Others usually in attendance were the cream of the political left wing of Hollywood – writers, directors, producers, among them Edward Lewis, Lancaster's production partner, Burt himself, Norman Lear, and, occasionally, me.

I hung out a little with Shirley Douglas, for which she had to find a baby sitter for her young son, Kiefer. Shirley was a committed political child of the left and we argued and twisted each other's philosophies, which didn't leave us much time to get into a relationship.

The discussions were lively and centered around what the left always suspected – that the government was operating in secret, that conspiracy was the order of the day, and that our civil liberties were in mortal danger. The political climate was beginning to swing to the right, which was inimical to the establishment funding yet another "The CIA murders anyone who poses a threat to the established order" movie.

At dinner at the Freeds one night, Sally volunteered to arrange the money needed to make the RFK film. She would contact her investment advisors both in L.A. and in New York, and entice sympathetic investors to join her. I was designated the producer, since I had the knowledge to manufacture the film, plus the industry contacts, with Sally assuming the normal Executive Producer role designated for backers.

A budget of million-and-a-half dollars was drawn up, of which Sally promised $300,000 of her own and Jim's, leaving a million two to be raised.

The first call I made was to "Swifty," whom I immediately consulted with regard to the director opening, and ideas for some key casting. He told me Orson Welles was in town, and offered to set up a meeting for me, which he would agent on behalf of Welles for the role of the CIA man behind Sirhan. He didn't actually represent Welles, but was proud to say that everyone in Hollywood had two agents – their own – and him. In other words, he would blithely get someone a job, and then inform him or her that he expected a commission. Should that talent accept the opportunity Swifty had arranged, and they usually did, they would also owe their contracted agent another 10 percent. And were happy to pay it. Of course, other agents resented the hell out of Lazar, not only because they looked bad to their clients, not having known about the opportunity, but because their self-respect was damaged for the same reason.

Lazar called me to say Orson would meet me the next morning at his rented home in the flats of Beverly Hills, at 6 a.m. I was a little taken aback because business usually began in Hollywood around 10 ten, occasionally preceded by an 8 a.m. breakfast date at the Polo Lounge, or Beverly Wilshire hotels, or at Nate n' Al's deli.

Nevertheless, thrilled to be meeting the legendary creator of *"Citizen Kane,"* my favorite film, also regarded by most critics as the best American movie of all time, I was a little nervous as I parked in front of his house, at 703 Maple Drive. The house was set back some 50 feet from the street, as were all the houses on that block. There was a flagstone path leading to the front door and, as I walked to the door, I noticed perhaps some twenty small brown piles scattered around the lawn. I mused to myself that Orson must have several very large dogs and that, as a renter, he hadn't engaged gardeners to clean up the yard.

I took a deep breath and rang the bell. A few moments passed and the door opened, to reveal a mountain in a blue caftan. It was Orson Welles himself. He looked to be about six foot four inches, and, I guessed, at least 350 pounds – maybe more. He was smoking a foot-long Churchill cigar – at 6 a.m. He opened the door wider and threw his cigar out onto the lawn. At that moment, the sprinklers came on, and the question I had had about his large dogs was answered.

He invited me to the kitchen, where he said he would make us some tea. I was in historical and cultural heaven as I followed him. I noticed his lower calves, which is all I could see under his caftan. They were thick, of course, as a man of his size would be, but also heavily striated with bulging, blue veins. He walked, I thought, with difficulty, as though it was painful. I waited with him, exchanging pleasantries while the water boiled, answering his questions about how the project came into being, who Donald Freed was, where we intended to make the film, who I had in mind for the director, and other proper thoughts.

Orson and I, I later found out, shared the same dentist,"Painless" Phil Rubin. Dr. Phil, as his patients call him, has and had many celebrity patients. I once settled into the same impression, left warm by Clint Eastwood, and occasionally followed the late, sometimes lewd comedian, Buddy Hackett. Dr. Phil always relayed the latest Hackett jokes. Made the drilling that much easier to take. Orson was so huge that Dr. Phil had to lift both arms of his chair to accommodate Orson's bulk. Orson was also very afraid of pain, so before he would allow Dr. Phil to work on him, he always insisted on doing some magic tricks for the staff. As always, he was baffling, but would never reveal his secrets. Dr. Phil, to get him to relax, offered him oxygen, which Orson gratefully accepted. The "oxygen," however, was nitrous oxide, which I always insist on, even for a cleaning. Orson too, from then on, always specified "oxygen."

We went into the library and he told me how much he thought of the screenplay, to be sure to tell Donald Freed how much he liked it, and looked forward to playing the part. He mentioned, demurely, I thought, that due to his size, would I mind if he played the part sitting down, perhaps at a desk. Not at all, I said, almost giddy. Orson was always accompanied by his tiny dog, Kiki, a Maltese, which he would pick up and hold to his face, demanding a kiss, which Kiki tried valiantly to avoid. Orson's head was bigger than the dog, and I swear the dog was repelled by Orson's cigar breath.

Welles had not actually finished a film of his own since "*Kane*," and I had a theory about why. He had begun "*The Magnificent Ambersons*," for Warners, while still hot from the controversial "*Kane*" release, but the film had been taken away from him due to cost overruns and released in a much-truncated version. He had begun half-a-dozen pictures over the next decade or two, but had taken so long in production that some of his actors had died waiting; thereby guaranteeing the films couldn't be completed.

Welles had created "*Kane*" at the prodigy age of 26, an age when one can easily believe that one is a genius, especially when told over and over by critics, friends, and sycophants, that one is. It can warp you for life – especially if you have an underlying disbelief in your own ability, a result of a disjointed childhood, as Welles is said to have had.

I had read somewhere, years earlier, that Abe Lincoln, upon getting a stony silence following the Gettysburg Address from the back of a railroad coach, thought he had bombed, and that it wasn't until several days later, down the tracks, when the newspapers caught up to him, that he learned his speech had been so powerful that his audience had been shocked into stillness. He allegedly then said, Imagine if I had burped.

My theory is that Orson was terrified of burping – that he couldn't bear having any films of his compared to "*Kane*," for masterpieces are awfully difficult to replicate. Not impossible, as Francis Coppola proved with the sequel to "*The Godfather*," but not easy, either.

I left Orson's house promising to compile a list of potential directors and actors, and to negotiate a deal with Lazar for his services. Irving said Welles would do the one-week role for $50,000, and approval of the director, which I conditionally agreed to, subject to confirmation from Sally and from Donald Freed. They were both excited and backed me up, and a letter contract followed. Lazar suggested his friend, Tony Curtis, for some part in the film, but outside of Sirhan, there was no role for him.

Lazar told me that Orson preferred meeting my director suggestions at the same time he met with me – 6 a.m. This was going to be a problem, I thought. What accomplished director would audition for Orson Welles in the first place, and at that impossible hour, as well. I called agent friends of mine for director possibilities, and got half-a-dozen good ideas in no time. I sent scripts to the agencies and, within two days, had arranged all six interviews – at 6 a.m., on successive days. I was stunned. Welles clearly was an idol to filmmakers, and the opportunity to work with him was worth apparently anything.

Also going on at this time were daily conversations with Donald Freed and Orson, with Orson ever so gently making suggestions to Donald about how his role could be improved by dialogue that sounded more like what he would actually say, and so on. Freed was positively childlike in his dealings with Orson, madly scribbling ideas down and faxing them over to Orson for his comments. Orson's role eventually grew from a shadowy figure rarely but significantly seen, to what was becoming the major starring role in the piece. I got a call from Lazar. Orson would have to work a good deal longer due to his expanded role, so we added another week – and another $50,000, to the great man's schedule.

Each director meeting went well, just as my initial one had. The door opened promptly at 6, the cigar was thrown onto the lawn, tea was made by the great man, and a pleasant, usually an hour, conversation took place. Orson ruled out one or two of these candidates immediately, because he said he hadn't gotten a good feeling about the man's ability, or because he thought they wouldn't get along. The others, none of whom he had said he had ever heard of, because he lived overseas and didn't keep up with Hollywood films, were possibilities, but he wanted to see some film they had made. I asked their agents for samples and got them delivered to Orson's house, where we would look at them on his living room Kem editor.

Orson was always making films – not finishing them – but always in production. He took acting jobs to support his habit and, wherever he was domiciled, in Madrid, or Rome, or Paris, or on location in Russia, or another God-forsaken place, he somehow attracted disciples, usually film students, to fetch and carry and to promote loose ends of unexposed film, the loan of a hand-held camera, an editing machine, and down time at an obscure lab for film development.

Such was the case on Maple Drive. Orson had a film studio in his living room and a set in the garage. A new secretary, Lyn Lewin, and a host of young film acolytes from the UCLA and USC film schools also came and went. Orson eventually didn't care for any of the director candidates, and I won't mention them here because it wouldn't be nice, and we were basically at an impasse. Orson's attachment to the film had become one of the chief fund-raising attractions for Sally and her bankers, and he knew it.

Finally, he offered – and I should have seen this coming, to direct the film himself. I couldn't believe it – I might be, considering Orson's health problems, the last, perhaps the only producer to complete an Orson Welles-directed film since Albert Zugsmith, the listed producer on "*Touch of Evil*," some twenty years earlier. Orson had an expression from those days. He and Zugsmith hadn't gotten along, and a coded threat between Orson and his crew when something went wrong was, "I'll Zugsmith you."

We were pretty far along into pre-production, having made a deal with Sal Mineo to play Sirhan - he looked a lot like him, and I had been interviewing actresses for the "polka dot" woman, when I got another call from Lazar. Yes, Orson was now starring in our film. Yes, he had largely, with Freed, re-written the script. Yes, he was now going to direct. Orson wanted half-a-million dollars, and twenty-five percent of the film. I gulped and went to Sally and Donald. Sally went to her bankers. As Marlon Brando said to Karl Malden, the sheriff, in "*One-Eyed Jacks*," after having shot villain Tim Carey, "He didn't leave me no selection." Orson had us.

Orson had a unique way of communicating, besides his voluminous memos and lengthy phone calls in the middle of the night. He called it "MP, TP" and "YP." It took me a while to figure out what he meant. Orson loved being a step ahead of you. Gary Graver, his cameraman, finally told me it meant, "My problem, "Their problem," and "Your problem." Graver said "YP" was the usual answer.

He also coined a neat phrase, which of course I misunderstood for some time, until Lynn, his secretary clued me in. Each morning, Orson assembled his troops and distributed his "Turds." You can imagine my being mystified, especially when no one blinked, but went about their jobs. "Turds," it turned out, didn't refer to either the putative large canines on the lawn, nor indeed, to Orson's own personal production, which, based on his size, would have been truly heroic, but to "Tasks, Urgent Responsibilities, and Decisions."

The budget was now north of two million dollars; a goodly sum in 1972 for an independent movie, considering *"Easy Rider"* was made for a fourth of that. Sally was getting frantic because she had been unable to that point of raising any additional funds other than the money she and her husband had pledged, and Jim wasn't going any further, including a second mortgage on their home. Her bankers suggested she come to New York to meet personally with some institutions, and she asked me to come along as she hadn't the foggiest notion of how a film was made, or distributed, or how, and if it ever made its money back.

My office was in Sally's house and Vicki, fascinated by what I was doing, hung out. She liked to tell me of her dating adventures, which sounded pretty risky to me, and I said so. She seemed to draw closer each day and she was getting difficult to ignore. She was not only young, but also beautiful, with a killer body. I was being seduced, and I knew it. She cornered me one day when we were alone, and one thing led to another. I was terrified this would create a giant problem with her mother, but she assured me Sally knew of her feelings, and approved, since she liked me so much. I was 20 years older than Vicki, but she was eighteen, after all. Sidney Beckerman, a well-known Hollywood producer, who was based at Paramount at the time, once told me "You're only as old as the girl you feel."

Orson and I had lunch every day at his house – he didn't go out much, understandable when you considered how tough it must have been for him to heave that bulk around. He would shoot film every night in his garage set, so as not to tip off the neighbors – and the Beverly Hills police – ending at daylight. Hence the 6 a.m. meetings. Orson's cook was a petite, middle-aged French woman, who prepared six exquisite, tiny courses daily for the two of us, or sometimes including his cameraman, Gary Graver, and Lyn Lewin. Delicious. Lyn told me that as soon as I left, Orson would send one of his acolytes down to Nate n'Al's for four corned beef sandwiches and a couple pounds of potato salad, which he would scarf down. It took a lot of effort to put on as much weight as Orson carried. I guess though, he didn't want me to see it in progress.

Orson, whom I eventually took to calling, "Awesome," gave me the same runaround on casting that he had put me through with the directors, and rejected all the photos and film I had shown him for the "polka dot" woman. Finally, one day, around 9 a.m., he said, "I have an idea." I began immediately to worry.

"Let me show you some film I have been working on," he said, and instructed Graver to load up the Kem. He and I sat in front of the tiny screen while I watched a willowy, dark-haired, very pretty naked woman run across a field from right to left.

The woman then ran across the screen left to right. Then the woman ran straight at the camera. It was pretty grainy, but I had to admit she had style. "What do you think?" Orson said. "Uh," I said. "She's perfect for the role," he said. "She is my co-star in the film I'm making now. I know we can afford her, and she's used to my style. Since we can't agree on anyone better, I suggest you meet her and, if you like her, I'll personally make a deal with her." I agreed of course to meet her. I already knew a lot about her.

Orson lumbered from his chair and made it to the bottom of the circular staircase leading up to the second floor, and called out, "Oh, Oya, please come down, there's someone here I'd like you to meet".

A few seconds later, after I had joined Orson at the bottom of the stairs, the lady from the Kem machine appeared at the top of the stairs and, like Loretta Young, floated down towards us, this time elegantly gowned and made up. At nine a.m. Had she perhaps had a clue?

"Oya, I'd like you to meet our producer, Michael Selsman. Michael, this is Miss Oya Kodar, the actress I've been telling you about."

The film Orson had been making had been in process for almost ten years. It was called "*The Other Side of the Wind*," and I have no idea what it was about. Perhaps Orson knew, but since it, like all his films, was unfinished, we'll never know.

Oya was indeed beautiful, and looked even better in person. Perhaps not as interesting clothed, but a sight nonetheless. She spoke English with a soft accent I later learned was Czech. I subsequently found out (from Lyn Lewin) that Oya was, and had been Orson's mistress for the past ten years, or from the time he began "*Wind*."

Orson had us again. I sighed. Dealing with Orson was like being an alligator wrangler in those pit stop amusement parks along I-95 in Florida – Perhaps you only intended to put your fist into the alligator's mouth, but somehow you looked down and your entire arm seemed to disappear into the darkness. I have a serious amount of correspondence from Orson, who loved dictating long memos, like David O. Selznick, and sending them by acolyte to me. It began with "Dear Mr. Selsman," and when he liked me, it was "Dear Michael," sometimes, "Dear Mike," and when I resisted his demands, it was "Dear Mr. Selsman," again. He's one of my best memories.

Time was now critical. We had a full cast, start dates, pay or play contracts, film on order from Kodak, a sound stage located. We had spent most of Sally's stake in the film, and I had had another call from Lazar. The package of Orson and Oya now cost us a full 50 percent of the film, and $700,000 of our $2.1 million budget. And we didn't have the rest of the money we needed.

HOW (SOME) FILMS ARE FINANCED

Sally and I departed for New York. Vicki, now my girlfriend, and Jim, Sally's husband accompanied us to the airport and saw us off with hugs, tears (from Vicki) and cheers for a profitable trip. We arrived in New York in mid-winter. It was cold, and it was snowing. I recalled immediately why when I left New York a dozen years earlier; I had vowed never to return in winter.

Sally's financial people set us up for breakfast, lunch, and dinner meetings with interested parties – institutional types, other bankers, broker-dealers, and a private investor or two. Nothing doing. The film business was a risk, there was no guarantee of a return, we had no distribution, and so on. And they were right. Things looked bleak, and we made plans to return to L.A. and make a graceful exit from the project. It had been fun while it lasted, I had gotten to spend time with one of the largest legends in the biz, and I had a sexy, young, rich and beautiful girlfriend. Things had been worse in my life.

Sally got a call the next morning as we were preparing to go to the airport for our flight home from her banker, asking us to make a triangle stop (at no more fare) in Miami for a lunch meeting he thought would solve all our problems. A lady named Irene Miller, heiress to the Swanson Frozen Foods fortune, was interested. Sally and I looked at each other, shrugged, and agreed. What was one more drop of water to a drowning man?

We left bitter cold New York, and arrived in 89-degree humidity several hours later. It was so hot, it took your breath away. We lugged our suitcases to a taxi and gave the driver the address of a motel (!) in Fort Lauderdale, where we were to meet our prospective benefactor. I don't do well in extremes of weather, which is why I live in Los Angeles, so I was already grumpy on the long drive. Sally, trouper that she was, kept smiling.

We arrived at a motel that seemed, in addition to being somewhat seedy, to be closed. Even the driver said he'd be happy to wait in case we had gotten the address wrong. We left our bags in the cab and went inside. No one about. I rang the bell on the desk. Silence. I turned to Sally, as if to say, let's get the hell out of here, when a thump behind me made me jump.

A tall, balding, hawk-nosed man was behind the desk. Two hooks where his forearms and hands would usually be, rested on the wood. He only looked sinister.

Yes, he said, we were expected, and to go to the other side of the pool, where there was a clubhouse – lunch was in progress. In progress, I thought. Wasn't it just between Irene and us? Sally suggested I wait a few moments while she went in alone to meet Irene and get to know her, girl to girl, as it were. A meeting of rich equals. Then I could come in to talk movies. Sounded good to me. Irene had arranged for us to have a room to freshen up in for the meeting and Mr. Sinister indicated I could take the bags up myself – his having hooks and such. I did, and was glad of it. I did a quick wash up, changed shirts, and came down, expecting to see Sally and Irene at a table, with a third chair waiting for me.

What I saw was a table of ten, almost finished with their lunch. And what a group. Irene Miller reminded me of Jabba, the Hut, from the sequel to "*Star Wars*." She was five by five and not pleasant either to look at or to talk to. And she seemed to resent my being there. Apparently, she had been told Sally was coming alone. I was confused, and not a little pissed off.

Sally was seated to Irene's right. Irene grudgingly introduced me around. To Irene's left was Alice, a bleached blonde, obviously drunk, woman Irene's age. Next to Alice were Wallace Atkins, and his wife. Atkins, tall, bald, with glasses, was an inventor, whose resume' included those little yellow reflectors encased in rubber that guide you down a dark road at night. Irene said he earned a quarter-of-a-cent for each one.

Next to Sally were a handsome blonde man, named Sven something, who was president of Norwegian-American Lines, and his chief financial officer, another Scandinavian. Next to the Atkins' was a young, clearly Italian man, overweight, sweating, and bulging out of his black wool Cardin suit. He scowled a lot. His companion, also a young guy, introduced himself with a Jewish name, and said he was the Italian's accountant. Irene's doctor rounded up the group. He looked disreputable at the least, with his stained tie and wrinkled seersucker suit. I pulled a chair over and began to feel sorry for myself.

It turned out that Irene was a financial backer to Atkins, and had made a pile of dough on the reflectors. Atkins had come up with a new idea, which fit right into the political situation happening in the world at that moment. The Arabs had formed a consortium, and had limited oil supplies to the west, particularly to the United States. If you're old enough to remember the gasoline shortage in 1972, you know what I'm saying.

Atkins' device was a machine you fed garbage into at one end, and at the other end, it spit out a "dense log," as he called it. This dense log could be burned cleanly for energy – a solution, so it seemed for the oil shortage. The Norwegians wanted in so they could run their ships; the Italian guy, I found out, was from a large "family" in New Jersey, who were in the waste removal business, who now, instead of dumping it somewhere, could sell it to the operators of this miraculous machine. Both groups were potential investors, along with Irene, in Atkins' latest brainstorm.

Hey, perhaps Irene was the real thing. I was beginning to feel a little better. The group broke up a few minutes later, leaving Irene, Sally, Alice, the doctor and me at the table. Irene and Alice seemed to have a few nasty words, following which Irene dismissed Alice, her girlfriend, I later found out, into the care of the doctor, and they left.

Irene said she couldn't really focus on our situation at the moment, and said she would be clear the entire next day, and why didn't we stay overnight, have dinner with her, see a few sights, get a good night's sleep, and work all day tomorrow. Made sense, so we checked in. Two rooms, as usual.

I asked Irene why the motel seemed to be closed. Because it was, she said. She owned it and used it as her operating center and office. When people came in from out of town, they stayed there. It was easier than traveling around town, and she could call in a chef and staff whenever she needed to. In fact, that was exactly what was in store. Irene suggested we rest up and meet her in the bar at 5 p.m.

Sally and I went down together, dressed more casually this time, and met up with Irene and Alice. The bar had miraculously been transformed from closed to lit up and happening. Not only a bartender and waitress, but also a Cuban band, going full tilt. A pitcher of margueritas appeared. I knew Sally didn't drink – a more proper lady hardly existed, but I suppose in the spirit of friendliness, and the plain fact that Irene seemed to be our last hope, she had a glass.

We talked movies, financing, and distribution until Irene got bored, and, ignoring me, concentrated on Sally. Another pitcher of margueritas showed up, and then another. Alice kept getting drunker and was by now talking to herself, since Irene was otherwise occupied with Sally. I was feeling no pain either and was content to leave negotiations to Sally and Irene.

Irene, annoyed by Alice, and probably me, suggested I dance with Alice. I came to with a start and, not knowing what else to do, stood up and took Alice's arm and led her to the floor. We were both pretty ripped but not enough so that I didn't get an earful from Alice about what Irene was all about. Irene and Alice had been "together" for six years, and "that bitch" (Alice's words) always cheated on her. And that's what she was doing right now with Sally. Hmmm, I thought to myself, this could get interesting. Of course, Sally had no idea she was being stalked, and I wasn't going to tell her either. After all, Sally was a big girl, we had a picture to make, and sometimes, you just have to take one for the team.

The only person not drinking was Irene. She ordered dinner for all of us, and I was glad we were not going anywhere. I was pretty sure Sally couldn't drive either. A little while later, Alice spilled her glass of wine on Irene. Irene slapped her, and Alice fled. We heard the shriek of tires as Alice pulled away. God help the other motorists.

Sally was now slurring her words and I had decided this was just a big circle jerk and that nothing was going to come of it. I regretted being there and couldn't wait to get back to my little honey, Sally's daughter. I didn't know what else to do and I didn't want to leave Sally helpless in Irene's clutches, so I stayed at the table while Irene spun her web.

About nine, Irene suggested we go up to my room and smoke a joint. By now, I was fully cognizant of Irene's intentions, but I was going to attempt a Hail Mary to save the day. I thought I'd try to extract a promise from her to get involved in the funding of our picture in exchange for my getting out of her way vis a vis Sally, if that's what Sally wanted. I didn't know exactly what Sally wanted, but she couldn't have been that drunk.

The three of us sat on the floor of my room and we passed a joint around. Sally said, and it was obvious, she had never had pot before, but that she knew her daughter smoked it, and she didn't disapprove – it was the early 70's, remember. I had the feeling Sally was bursting out of her protestant shell that night, and far be it from me to blow against the wind. She was essentially my boss, remember.

Things got a little rowdy after that. We were all pretty high. Irene was closing in on Sally, and was impatient to be alone with her. I told Irene I'd leave if she promised to fund the movie herself, otherwise, she could get the hell out. It was all I could do. Of course Irene agreed. I even had her write it out on the notepad in the room. I took Sally's room key, went next door and crashed.

A bell went off in my head and a red light was flashing somewhere! I had had some hangovers in my time, but this was an original. It slowly dawned on me that it was the phone. I picked it up and I heard Vicki say, "What are you doing in my mother's room at 6 a.m.?" I don't recall exactly what I said, but it couldn't have been the right answer because she was yelling louder, cursing too. She later told me I had said Sally was in the shower, which only made it worse. I said, "Just a minute, I'll get her," and dashed next door. I pounded on the door for what seemed like five minutes, until a bleary Sally poked her head around. She wasn't entirely dressed. I explained in a kind of urgent way that her daughter was on the phone, and the rest of the situation. "Oh my God," Sally said, or words to that effect, slammed the door, and reappeared in her room a few minutes later, more decently.

She and Vicki had an exceptional conversation – something to the effect that we had switched rooms for some reason or another, and that my remark about her being in the shower was a mistake. I got back on the phone with Vicki and could tell she wasn't buying it. I told her we would be back on L.A. later that day and she said she'd be waiting. I didn't like the sound of that.

Irene and Sally were now dressed, Irene looking like the cat that swallowed the canary, and Sally looking like a shy schoolgirl. Irene said she'd be by at noon to take us to the airport, and went home. Sally and I said nothing special to each other at breakfast and then waited under the portico for Irene's Caddy to appear.

Which it did, promptly at noon. As I was loading our bags into the Caddy's trunk, Alice's car came hurtling at us, stopping inches away with another shriek of tires. She waved what looked suspiciously like a gun. "Oh, God," said Irene, "Get in," she said to me. I did and we pulled away, Alice in hot pursuit. Irene knew some shortcuts, but so did Alice and it was like a Keystone Kops chase, only potentially more deadly. I kept looking behind us from the back seat and suddenly saw another car join the chase. Irene did too, and said, "Thank God." It was the doctor, who cut Alice off, and we were alone at last. We got to the airport, a tearful goodbye was said, kisses were exchanged (by Irene and Sally), not me, and we boarded.

Six hours later, we landed in L.A. I expected to see Vicki there, but I hadn't counted on Jim as well. It was obvious they thought Sally and I were, and had been secret lovers, and the money-hunting trip we had taken was just an excuse for us to be alone. As though my apartment or local hotels weren't available.

That was the end of Vicki and me. The picture was called off. Orson never got to finish another movie, and I wasn't the producer of the last Orson Welles film. Orson and I spent a year together preparing a movie about the assassination of Robert Kennedy. He sunk it like he sunk all his films from "*Citizen Kane*" on because he was afraid anything he finished would be unfairly compared and he would be remembered as a flop.

A few weeks later, I got a call from Vicki. It seemed Irene had arrived in L.A. a week earlier and had been staying with them. Jim had moved out and filed for divorce. What did this all mean, Vicki asked me? I hadn't the heart, or the nerve, to tell her.

SOUND & FURY, SIGNIFYING NOTHING

Donald Freed, of the conspiracy theory, is never short for material. In 1976, the Chilean Ambassador to the U.S., Orlando Letelier, was blown up in his car on the streets of Washington, D.C. This energized the entire left wing of Hollywood, with known liberals jumping all over this opportunity to blame the U.S. administration. Mark Rosenberg, former student radical and now, in 1980, head of production at Warner Bothers studios, and his wife, Paula Weinstein, former student radical and daughter of another well-known left wing radical, optioned a book, "*The Letelier Affair*," written by Eugene Propper, the former U.S. prosecutor, with the help of Taylor Branch, who had co-written "*Blind Ambition*," the John Dean story of his participation in the Nixon White House. Propper, with the aid of the FBI, tried, convicted and jailed three Cubans for the murder. The book attracted Sydney Pollack as the director, who brought in David Rayfiel to write the screenplay. Rayfiel had written "*Three Days of the Condor*," another spy story directed by Pollack, starring

Robert Redford. Redford was immediately cast if and when the picture got a go-ahead.

Freed, however, had other plans. He immediately wrote his own novelized version of the story, called it "*Death in Washington*," and hurriedly published it, using a sympathetic left wing east coast publisher. He then wrote the screenplay, and entitled it, "*The Quartered Man*," based on the four major parts left of Letelier's body after the explosion. I was brought in to package the now-competing film. Freed, naturally, inferred that the CIA had been behind the assassination, just as he had claimed they were the culprits in the Jack Kennedy and Bobby Kennedy killings, thereby setting up the Warner pictures story as fiction. There were now two movies about the very same subject racing to get made – one, the Warners film using documented facts posing as entertainment, and the other, Freed's using entertainment as a cover for the "real" facts.

Propper, a neophyte to Hollywood, insisted his version was the truth and that the truth would win out. Yeah, sure, when pigs fly. He insisted Freed's suppositions were scandalous, if not libelous, and would never be filmed. Freed said in an interview that "Propper's version is the government's story. It has Propper and the FBI as heroes who cracked the case. In other words, Mr. Propper is Robert Redford. Cuban exiles were blamed and convicted, but who recruited them, and who paid them?"

Of some 200 movies usually in development at any studio, only between 8 and 10 actually get made, but Warners had the money, the distribution, and the promotion and advertising dollars, and the political ambition to make a statement We (Freed and I) were able to attach Mark Lester, a friend of mine, as the director. Mark had only done a few young audience films, but he was talented, wanted to graduate to serious films, and besides he had access to some funding. We all scrambled about for a year or so, Warners unable to get a screenplay that satisfied Redford, Pollack, and the budgeteers, and we unable to raise all the money we needed to go into production. Of course Freed blamed government pressure on the left wing potential financiers we approached. In the end, neither movie got made, and the murder of the first ambassador of a communist government of Chile to the United States remains unsolved. The story's available to you would-be producers out there.

HOW SOME OTHER FILMS ARE FINANCED

One of the legendary film producers of our time is 85 year-old Dino DeLaurentis, who got his start right after World War II, in Italy. He partnered with producer Carlo Ponti, and made several films with director Federico Fellini. When their partnership dissolved, De Laurentiis built his own studio, which eventually failed. Dino had to get out of Italy, and turned to Hollywood, but needed a base and a distributor from which to operate. He found both in the then-president of Paramount Pictures. While

Robert Evans ran the production side, making *"The Godfather* I & 2," *"Love Story," "Chinatown", "Paper Moon,"* and *"The Great Gatsby,"* The Paramount president brought Dino in, partially to offset the great personal publicity Evans was getting. He was heavily disliked in the business because he was brash, tough, and thought he knew it all. He even wrote screenplays, which made him think he knew more than the writers that Paramount hired.

Dino had mixed results at Paramount, starting with *"Serpico,"* with Al Pacino, in 1973, *"3 Days of the Condor,"* starring Robert Redford, in 1975, *"King Kong,"* in '76, and finishing with *"Ragtime,"* with Dustin Hoffman, in 1981.

Paramount was owned then by Gulf & Western, the model of what came to be known in American business as a conglomerate. Charles Bluhdorn, its owner, an overbearing Viennese immigrant, built his company by nerve, canny judgment, and luck – riding an upsurge in the U.S. economy. Something made him suspicious of the relationship between his Paramount studio chief, and Dino and investigated. The story I heard started with an alleged anonymous letter, which led to a safe deposit box maintained by the studio head containing a serious amount of dollars traced to Dino. He was out. Both have had their ups and downs since. Dino introduced Arnold Schwarzenegger to the world as an actor in *"Conan, the Barbarian,"* and celebrated American vigilantism with the *"Death Wish"* series, starring Charles Bronson. He also made a litter of flops such as *"Hurricane,"* the disastrous *"King Kong"* remake, and *"Dune."* Michael Medved, the film critic, wrote a book in 1980 with his brother, titled *"The Golden Turkey Awards*," and in it referred to Dino as "Dino Di Horrendous." The moral here is to be nice to everyone on the way up – because you'll see them again on the way down.

CATCH 22½

Orson's and my path's crossed again when I was representing a sexy, 21 year-old actress named Suzanne Benton, whom I put in three movies, as a co-star, in the two years I represented her. I sold her to my client, director, Noel Black, who was doing *"Run, Shadow, Run,"* for 20th-Fox, along with Sondra Locke, and Robert Fields, from *"The Sporting Club,"* directed by Larry Peerce, who first attracted attention with a thriller set on the New York City subways, *"The Incident."* I also obtained a co-starring role for Suzanne in Robert Altman's thriller, *"That Cold Day in the Park,"* and as Orson Welles' girlfriend in *"Catch 22,"* directed by Mike Nichols, in 1970.

Suzanne had a burning desire to be a movie star and was perfectly positioned to become one. Her husband, Jay, was a Los Angeles Police Department motorcycle officer, and she had total control of him. So besotted was he by her that she periodically left him to pursue her dream, whatever it took. I found out later that, like many actresses, including Marilyn Monroe, Suzanne used relationships with men to achieve traction in a very competitive business and her husband knew it. When her need for that particular man ended, she returned to Jay for protection. Suzanne let me know she was counting on me to make it happen for her.

My wife, Linda, and I were having problems and I moved out to my own apartment in Beverly Hills for a trial separation. Suzanne moved out on her husband, Jay, into a one bedroom at the beach, in Malibu. She and I collaborated very closely on her career, occasionally working so hard we spent the night in one or the other's place.

When the role in "*Catch 22*" came up, casting was beginning in New York City before moving to L.A. I decided to go there with Suzanne to beat the competition in Hollywood. New York had a great selection of actresses, but the obvious sex symbols tended to congregate on the west coast. On arrival, I called the casting office and got an appointment for Suzanne. She wowed them with her sensuality and her sexiness, but they wanted to see other actresses as well. I put a call into Orson, who was living at that moment in the city and asked him if he would see her. He said it wasn't necessary, that if I thought she was right for the role, he'd put in a word with Mike Nichols. Orson loved to have you indebted to him.

I later found out that just as I was spending quality time with Suzanne, so was John Calley, a highly placed executive at United Artists, which was financing the film.

One afternoon, while I was at Suzanne's Malibu apartment, Jay Benton's LAPD motorcycle rumbled up. LAPD cops are a cross between Hitler's SS and George Lucas' "*Star Wars*" Storm Troopers, dressed in black, sunglassed, and bristling with armaments. He dismounted, and, with his hand on his holstered gun, told me he thought it would be best if I immediately left and it was his wish that he never saw me again. And he didn't.

Jay didn't last long after that as he made the greatest error an actress' husband could make – he asked her to give up her career to be his wife.

SOUTHERN COMFORT

In 1974, a notorious agent, Gene Marshall, introduced me to a southern director, Charlie Pierce, who had recently completed a small-budget scare picture called, "*The Legend of Boggy Creek.*" Pierce was a product of a farm-raised childhood outside Texarkana, Arkansas, but that didn't stop him from fulfilling his long time dream of moviemaking.

Charlie was a husband and father of three small kids, eking out a living selling advertising, when he approached a local chicken manure kingpin and convinced him to put up $25,000 for this film in return for executive producer credit and a chance to play in the movies. Charlie rounded up his brother-in-law, Steve Lyons, all three of his kids, his wife, some local film students, rented a camera and a pick-up truck and headed for the bayous. He put Steve in a gorilla suit, shot him clumping around at a distance, added some scared faces of his family and a few other locals, and had a film.

I say notorious in connection with Marshall because he was a "swinger," and hosted swing parties at his double condo, on a golf course, in Palm Desert, California. He had bought condos next to each other and had the common wall removed, installing a large indoor hot tub that "seated" eight. Those early 1970 years pre-dated the first case of AIDS-HIV in the U.S. by at least eight years, so swinging was relatively safe. I say relatively, because the usual STD's like gonorrhea and chlamydia were easily curable with penicillin, and the participants took great care to avoid being even temporarily out of commission. They would voluntarily stay home rather than be banished forever.

Charlie and I were invited one weekend, and enjoyed ourselves greatly. I became a regular myself, and made some good friends. Later, on trips to Europe and Mexico, I attended what could only be characterized as orgies, as "swinging" was strictly an American custom, usually involving husbands and wives. The gatherings overseas typically involved very wealthy, well-connected, jet setters and beautiful women of all races and colors, complete with gourmet food and fine wines. How I miss those days.

After spending his last few dollars on editing, Charlie found an elderly distributor, a man named Joy Houck, that's right, almost like the *"Boy Named Sue,"* song made famous by *"The Man in Black,"* Johnny Cash, in Metairie, Louisiana, who affected bow ties and slicked-back hair. Houck was a real old-timer who had gotten his start distributing silents. His company, Howco Distributors was well known in a three-state area, primarily Arkansas, Louisiana, and Texas, for films such as *"Lost, Lonely and Vicious,"* *"Teenage Monster,"* *"The Undertaker and His Pals,"* and *"My World Dies Screaming."* He had made millions over the years, lived extravagantly and even had his own twin-engine plane. Charlie was awed. Houck viewed the picture and agreed to take it on, but he wanted the entire U.S territory. A more experienced producer would have objected, even rejected such an offer, but Charlie was out of money and Houck wanted some action on his investment, so a deal was struck. Howco spent some money on advertising and opened the film on a four-wall basis in the area surrounding Dallas. Four-walling, now long out of practice, was done by local distributors who would "buy out" a theater, or theatres, paying their overhead and a reasonable profit, for a specified amount of time, and collect all the proceeds each night from the box office. This was something of a risk if your film didn't do business, but on the other hand, if you had a hit, you could do very well. *"Boggy Creek"* opened strong, and Charlie made the rounds of the various theatre box offices at 11 p.m. every night to collect the cash in a brown paper sack. He was hooked.

Eventually, "*Boggy Creek*" expanded, still on a four-wall basis, around the country, studiously avoiding the big cities, where Howco knew it wouldn't play well and where it was very expensive to promote. Over the next year, "*Boggy Creek*" had raked in over $37 million; more than $300 million in today's dollars, and Charlie was very rich.

A Baptist, and teetotaler before becoming a filmmaker, Charlie had graduated to avoiding church, drinking, and looking around for other women. Some say this is a natural consequence of show business, but I think it's also true of big and unexpected success in any business. Dennis Kozlowski, of Tyco, comes to mind.

The next film Charlie made was "*Bootleggers*," for about $200,000, in Hot Springs, Arkansas. He had graduated to some real actors, like Slim Pickens, and discovered a new young actress named Jaclyn Smith, who became famous in the original "*Charlie's Angels*," and shot the film in wide-screen Todd-AO, an even larger negative than Panavision. He kept his original crew, however, since they were mainly high school kids over whom he had control. "*Bootleggers*" also did well, and Charlie sunk it into a 10-acre spread on a lake eleven miles outside of Shreveport, Louisiana, building himself a Xanadu of a home, the living room of which contained an editing facility MGM would have been proud to own. He also bought a custom-made bus, which slept eight, his own private plane, a twin engine prop-jet Mitsubishi MU-2, a jet boat, a white Cadillac limousine, twin Cadillac sedans for himself and his new girlfriend, Cindy Butler, who was younger than Charlie by about 20 years, and all sorts of expensive toys for his three children. And of course, a maroon Coupe DeVille for me.

We lived on that bus, which was plusher than many people's homes, driving it from location to location, from Montana to Texas, from Texas to Wyoming, from Wyoming to Florida. I collected comely associates along the way, who would accompany us to our next film site, and Charlie's plane would fly them home.

Charlie worshipped the great director, John Ford, and decided he had to make movies just like the ones Ford had made. He had an outline written for a mountain man-Indian picture, circa 1780, similar to the time scale in "*Jeremiah Johnson*," a mountain man picture that starred Robert Redford, directed by Sidney Pollack. Charlie, like many European directors, didn't necessarily need a full screenplay, as he shot visually. He had an artist's eye and his films always looked like paintings.

"*Winterhawk*," as he called it, was the first film I worked on with Charlie. Because it was his biggest budget yet, just over one million dollars, he now needed the assistance of Hollywood. I had the cachet, the connections, and the knowledge, so he and I made a deal, and I co-produced the film with him, in Kalispell, Montana. He offered me associate producer credit, but I declined.

"*Winterhawk*" turned out to be a John Ford-like film, with beautiful vistas and characters, which I cast very much in the Ford tradition. Michael Ansara played the title role, supported by a great cast of elderly character actors, some of whom, Jack Elam, the one-eyed villain, Arthur Hunnicut, Dub Taylor, Woody Strode, L.Q. Jones, and Elisha Cook, Jr., the quirky heavy in "*The Maltese Falcon*," had actually worked for Ford. Leif Erickson, Buck Taylor, and Dawn Welles, just out of "*Gilligan's Island*," the TV hit show, joined them. Charlie's son, Chuck, Jr., played the 12 year-old boy lead.

FLYING SO HIGH WITH PLAYBOY MODELS IN THE SKY

The film called for a dance hall crowded with at least six easy women of the time. I had a brilliant idea, and called my friend, Marilyn "Mo" Grabowski, who headed the photography department at Playboy. Playboy, at the time, had a modeling agency, another income stream for Hefner, and Marilyn suggested I interview a dozen or so of the girls, and make my selection. The first pictures I had seen of them were nudes, and seeing them dressed threw me somewhat off. I chose six girls, made the financial arrangements with Playboy, and booked Charlie's plane from LAX to Kalispell for the next week.

We all met up at 6 a.m., at Van Nuys airport, in the San Fernando Valley, settled in on the plane, which sat eight, including the jump seat, which covered up the on-board toilet, and took off for Salt Lake City, as far as the Mitsubishi MU-2 would go without fueling up again. Charlie had employed a new pilot, a young man of 21, named Tom, whom I had not met before. He looked even younger than his age, and his hands shook peculiarly on takeoff. Was I worried? – Not. Until two of the girls produced joints, which they immediately lit up and passed around. Charlie, ever the genial host, had stocked the plane with champagne, which was also opened, and passed around. The cabin of an MU-2 is about the size of a stretch limo, and the marijuana smoke was affecting everyone, including the pilot. Was I worried? – I was beginning to be. Tom wondered why the cigarettes the girls were smoking smelled so funny. It was obvious this was new to him. Great.

All that champagne quickly got to everyone's bladder during the four-hour trip to Salt Lake, and the jump seat became everyone's best friend. In such close quarters, with six gorgeous women peeing right next to me, we all naturally became very good friends. As much as I tried to hold it in, I couldn't, and thanks to the razzing I got from the girls, it was my turn. Naturally, I had to stand up. I told Tom to hold it steady, as there was no room to spare. I had received compliments before, but never until that moment, did I experience such complete approval from six women who knew what they were talking about. Life was good.

We reached Salt Lake airport, somehow, and the girls dashed off to a proper restroom, while Tom oversaw the fueling and checked the tire pressure, the oil pressure and the rest of the checklist. The girls and I ate breakfast in the airport coffee shop, and brought a sandwich and coffee out to Tom, who looked like he needed the coffee.

An hour later, we were airborne again, and while crossing the mountains of Utah, Tom suddenly said, "What the hell…." "What's the problem?" I asked him, since I was now seated in the co-pilot seat. "We're out of gas," he said. "How could that be?" I asked, "We just gassed up." "I don't know," he said. Of course the girls heard this, since we were as jammed in the cabin as we would have been in a car, and all of a sudden, everyone sobered up real fast.

"What are we going to do," I inquired? "I don't know," said Tom, "probably look for a place to set down." "Set down," I asked? "Where?" We were past the mountains now, crossing over the corner where Idaho and Wyoming touch, and approaching Montana, which luckily is pretty flat in that area. The gas gauge read empty and one engine was coughing, but not as badly as I was from the pot and from fear. Tom selected a long, flat, empty ranch road, and we glided down on one engine and made a perfect 3-point landing. The fuel had been sucked out by the wind because the service people at the Salt Lake airport had not fastened the fuel cap securely, and Tom had not personally checked it. I guess it was the grass we had smoked. There I was, in the middle of nowhere, before cell phones had been invented, with six beautiful girls in various states of consciousness. What to do.

We had seen a couple of farmhouses on our way down so, devilishly, I thought, I dispatched three teams of two Playboy models each up and down the road, with instructions to obtain a telephone and call in our problem and location. Tom and I chuckled, imagining some rural farmers answering their doorbell and seeing an apparition from another world. The girls all scored and were warmly received by their hosts, some of which were youngish men who didn't want them to go. Charlie sent his bus for us and we took off for Kalispell with no further adventures. Boy, were we glad to get there.

INDIANS IN AMERICA

One of the scenes in "*Winterhawk*" called for a "rendezvous," a yearly meeting of all the local trappers, mountain men, adventurers, and Indian tribes in the area, where trading took place over the space of a couple of weeks in the spring.

David Powell, our set designer, was part Cherokee, and designed and hand made for us copies of authentic 100 year-old tribal costumes and weapons from originals and from drawings and paintings of the time. We constructed some thirty teepees, using lodge pole pines we harvested from nearby forests under the supervision of the Forest Service. A tribal consultant, Leonard White Dog, from the Blackfeet Nation, the local tribe, had been hired to act as our ambassador.

From the time that white men first entered Indian Territory, misunderstandings based on language and intent has created suspicion. White greed led to hostilities, resulting in the Indians, as a whole, being nearly eliminated by superior war technology, European diseases, and outright theft of their lands, customs, and rights available to any other citizen of the U.S. As a result, American Native people still regard whites, in general, as potential enemies. And I found that wherever reservations abut white development, there is inevitable conflict, sometimes ending in the taking of lives. More than once, some of the young Indian men we hired as extras would go from the location into town to drink and would inevitably get into fights with the local whites. Our make-up people had to become very creative in hiding black eyes and facial scrapes. And, of course, it was axiomatic that whites were taking their lives in their hands to enter the reservation without proper advance notice and without an Indian guide.

Leonard brought David Powell and me onto the reservation to look at ancient clothing and jewelry, and go house to house, passing out leaflets asking the people to come to the meadow we had prepared for the rendezvous, to be in the scenes as background, acting as though they were their own ancestors, 200 years ago. Almost everyone we met was very enthusiastic, and dug in their home chests for carefully-wrapped moccasins, buckskin dresses, bone breastplates, shields, even a few lances and arrows, to contribute to the scene.

As we traveled over the vast, barren landscape, it was difficult not to see and be struck by the extreme poverty everywhere. Broken-down cars, ill-dressed children playing in the dirt, adults sitting on the steps of their hogans, as they called their small houses, and, inescapably, the many inebriated people. I had never imagined what penury Native Americans lived in, for the most part. Coming from California, I was familiar with the Agua Caliente Indians, who owned the land under Palm Springs, and were rich. I also knew about some tribes that benefited from oil found on their lands. But for Indians without such luck, life was very hard. That experience changed me, and I now rejoice for those Indians who have managed to cash in on the gambling now allowed on many of their reservations. Nothing can make up for the past, but perhaps their future in America will be brighter.

The rendezvous sequence coming up the next week was very complicated. We flew in two more cameras, walkie-talkies and hired additional crew. Leonard introduced me to the chief, Earl Old Person, a courtly, college-educated administrator, whom I liked instantly, and who was very helpful to us. We agreed we would provide the tribe a new school bus, and we would purchase a buffalo from the Interior Department, to roast and serve as lunch for the 3,000 Indian people we expected to show up. All was set and, I thought, ready to go.

I returned to my office in the late afternoon before the big scene to find a note on my desk from Leonard, saying the shoot was off. Panic doesn't come easily to me, but this was the time to drown in it. I knew just where to look for Leonard and, although it is a rotten cliché, it's accurate in Montana to say that if you want to find an Indian, find the nearest bar. And that's where he was. And he was mad – at me. "Leonard," I said, "We're friends, what's wrong, what happened?" If this shoot didn't come off, it would cost us at least $100,000 and worse, it was mainly an outdoor picture and we didn't have a cover set available. I had about twelve hours to fix this.

"I didn't know you were a racist man, you fooled me," he said. "Racist, what the fuck are you talking about?" I said. You know I'm a Jew, from New York, a Democrat, no-one's more liberal than me!" "I saw your phone list, man," he retorted. "Phone list?" I was frantically running that over in my mind – what was he talking about? "What about it, Leonard?" I stammered. "LW, man," he said, "next to every name." "Yeah, so?" I demanded. "I know what that means, 'Looks white,'" he spit at me. 'Looks white,' I thought to myself. Nothing, apparently, had changed in 300 years with regard to communication between Indians and the white man. "You idiot," I blasted him, "LW means 'left word'. Get the fuck up from that chair; we're going out to the reservation."

We got in my car and sped out, spending the next six hours, until well past midnight, going door to door, since most didn't even have telephones, telling the people the shoot was back on. That was a very close call and from what I know about making films on distant locations, especially period pieces, not all that far from normal.

The sequence went beautifully and Charlie had a film very much like what Kevin Costner was able to accomplish with "*Dances with Wolves*" twenty years later with the invaluable assistance of another $60 million.

Being able to think fast is mandatory in filmmaking, especially when you're far from base. In this case, we were up at 6,000 feet, in the snow, and it was cold. Most of the actors we were using were in their 70s, since the story revolved around a 12 year-old white boy abducted by a Blackfeet chief, whose tracking and rescue is in the hands of a group of elderly, retired trappers. All films have paramedics or nurses assigned to the set, as accidents can and do happen. One of the old guys from town we hired as background passed out. Our paramedic couldn't bring him around, and we called for an ambulance to take him down the mountain. While we were waiting, he died. As the ambulance pulled up and the crew was preparing to put him on a stretcher, I called out, "Hold it a minute." They looked at me oddly while I ran over to our prop guy and called the make-up girl over. "Put an arrow in him," I said to the prop guy. "Blood," I commanded the make-up girl. Our second unit cameraman was nearby and I signaled him over and told him to get about a minute of film of our recently alive actor. Some of the cast and crew were aghast, but others, especially Charlie, beamed. Our actor died with his boots on. You never knew whether you could use a scene like that in the editing room, and we didn't use it, but that's forward thinking, man.

When the film was completed, we had a wrap party at the Outlaw Inn, attended by half the town, it seemed. All of our actors, including the Indians, were there and, as a special added attraction, the paramount chief of the Blackfeet, Earl Old Person, honored us with his presence. My contribution to the tribe's welfare was recognized when Chief Old Person made me an honorary member of the tribe, naming me, "Eagle Child." He sealed it by taking from around his neck a necklace of ancient coral interspersed with 1936 dimes that had been hammered into the shape of globes, and fastened it around mine. I thought that was pretty amazing, since 1936 was the year of my birth. What are the odds of that happening? I was told by several dealers in Indian artifacts they wouldn't consider making an offer to buy it from me because it's priceless.

THE REAL REASON FILMS ARE MADE ON LOCATION

Making films on distant locations is my favorite memory of the more than 50 years I have spent in the entertainment business. Typically, Charlie and I would select a small town in a right-to-work state and I, as the producer would go there a month in advance to make arrangements for the crew, cast, actual production, accommodations, and to hire locals for such jobs as driving, truck and car rental, storage, carpentry, wardrobe and make-up, and extra acting roles.

The first thing I would do is scout the town, in this case, Kalispell, Montana, and pick out the most likely motels that could handle up to 60 people, which turned out to be The Outlaw Inn. Then I would visit the local newspaper, ask to speak to the editor, and give him the story that we were seeking people to hire, that would, the next day, be on the front page. After that, I'd find city hall, and ask to see the mayor. Usually in those towns, the mayor works part-time, and is busy with his job or business, but it didn't take the mayor long to come and meet me. Movie-making is not only a clean enterprise, making no demands on the environment, but drops a huge load of money on the community in a short time, and if the movie is good, works to bring tourists to the area. A good example of this is the impact *"Lord of the Rings"* has made on the New Zealand tourist industry. Everyone I spoke to was usually very enthusiastic, as very little happened from day to day, other than crop or beef prices, and the weather.

I would normally check in by late afternoon, and find myself in the motel restaurant-bar by about six. By then, quite a few people had heard about the coming movie shoot, and that its representative was in town. I usually ended up not buying my own drinks. The next day, when the local paper hit the street, my phone was ringing off the hook. I'd commandeer the meeting room and start interviewing. The awe which with townsfolk regarded me was palpable. They all wanted to know whom I actually knew, had shaken hands with, and was it true that so-and-so was pregnant. Or Gay? All the usual stuff. They didn't believe me when I said I didn't know, and winked that they'd get it out of me some time during the next eight weeks or so that we'd be there.

By the time Charlie arrived a couple of weeks later, I had pretty much lined up all the local help we needed, had made contact with the sheriff, town and county police, booked the entire motel, obtained permission to shoot on various public and private property, made credit arrangements with dry cleaners, lumberyards, car and truck rental, furniture and stationery stores, seamstresses, construction guys, drivers, hairdressers, and make-up people.

Then the real fun began. I'd write a special half-page ad to run in the local paper saying we had written a special role in the film for a beautiful young girl, 18 to 25 and would be seeing candidates the next day at the motel. We normally would attract at least a hundred of the surrounding area's young hopefuls, taking their names, measurements, and photos. Of course we would eventually hire one, but the real purpose was to select temporary mistresses, with whom we would live for the duration of filming. We never missed.

For "*Winterhawk,*" I ended up with governor Tom Judge's secretary, Andrea ("Andy") Sinclair, a stunning 21 year-old redhead, who promptly moved in with me in my room at the motel and, when I left for Los Angeles, was bereft. We stayed in touch and I brought her to L.A. to see what a big city looked like. She was awed and terrified by the tall buildings – nothing over three stories existed in her hometown. I took her to a Hollywood New Year's Eve party populated by slinky women in slinky black dresses, and Iranian men on the make and it freaked her out. She couldn't wait to go home to Big Sky country. She later married a carpet installer and probably has a dozen children by now.

By now, Charlie was approaching establishment status and I made a deal with American International Pictures, headed by the legendary, cigar smoking, Sam Arkoff, for international distribution. Over the next two years, Charlie directed, and I line-produced "*The Norseman,*" in Tampa, Florida, and "*Grey Eagle,*" and "*The Winds of Autumn,*" in Helena, the capital of Montana, and directed second unit on the latter film.

THE SIX MILLION DOLLAR MAN & A CHARLIE'S ANGEL

Acting also as Charlie's press agent, I got him some serious media attention, particularly an interview with Joyce Haber, the show biz columnist for the Los Angeles Times, an old friend of mine. Respectability conferred by this and other notices allowed me to supply Charlie with better actors, especially for "The Norseman," such as Lee Majors, the "*Six-Million Dollar Man,*" as the lead character. Other big names included Cornell Wilde and Mel Ferrer. Using our tried and true method for casting the usual beautiful young thing role, I noticed a magazine cover featuring the perfect face. Inquiring, I tracked the model to her agency in Los Angeles, and found out it was Susie Cohello, who was then married to Sonny Bono, of Sonny & Cher fame. I promptly hired her without a screen test because her role didn't involve a great deal of speaking, and her part as an Indian required more face and figure than anything else.

We made the film in Tampa, Florida. Lee Majors was married at the time to Farrah Fawcett, still young and spectacular. He arrived on location with an entourage that included three muscle-bound, weight-lifter types who surrounded him at all times. Instead of staying at the motel we had commandeered for cast and crew, he chose to pay for his own lodging in a condo, in a private development, on a golf course 60 miles away. That made for some interesting arrival and departure times as it related to our shooting schedule, and provided a source of constant friction.

He traveled to and fro in a convoy of three black-windowed SUV's, and in a different one every day, or exactly as the president of the United States travels by helicopter. I know this, because for the past 30 years, I have lived in a penthouse directly across from the playing field of Beverly Hills high school, and when President Ronald Reagan would arrive for his L.A. visits, Secret Service sharpshooters would wake me early in the morning by stomping around on my roof and setting up their sniper rifles. I would wave to them and go out on my patio to watch the intricate and highly choreographed arrival. There would always be three Marine Corp. helicopters and Reagan could be in any one of the three. That Lee Majors thought he needed the same protection was hilarious to me. Reagan could be and was a target of assassination, but who could possibly harm the "*Six-Million Dollar Man*?" And who would want to?

As an aside, one very early Sunday morning, the familiar noises on my roof woke me to tip me off that the president was on his way in. The night before, I had celebrated my birthday with a new female friend – in actuality a girl I had known for some years. She had dated my client, Andy Prine, for a while, and was working as the secretary to one of my oldest friends, a TV producer. I had always admired her and let her know it. She just hadn't been available – until that night. She took us out to The Odyssey, a plush hilltop restaurant overlooking the San Fernando Valley, following which we returned to my place - for dessert. We had ingested the usual chemicals and I don't think we fell asleep, exhausted, until after 4 a.m. Two hours later, I jumped out of bed to watch the show, which if you haven't seen it, is pretty spectacular. There were at least 40 vehicles lined up on the circular track, from the presidential limos (three), to secret service war wagons, to Highway Patrol cars, unmarked LAPD cars, an ambulance, a fire truck, a press bus, at least twenty Highway Patrol motorcycle officers, whose job it was to stop traffic at intersections, allowing the convoy to speed to its destination uninterrupted, and more.

My new girlfriend, somewhat bleary and hearing the commotion, also left the bed and joined me on the patio. I had, as usual, put on sweats, but it hadn't occurred to her that there might be three blue-jump suited young guys with huge scoped guns staring down at her luscious, nude figure. They didn't say anything. Neither did I. It wasn't until most of the drama had passed that she looked up – and screamed. For some reason, she didn't want to see me again after that. I wonder what her problem was.

Farrah made several visits to the location. In 1976, Tampa was still a small town and the airport actually closed at midnight until 6 the next morning. Farrah would arrive on Friday nights, around eleven, dressed in a mink coat, wearing a black wig, and sunglasses. Gosh, who could that be?

Her truly tragic death recently from cancer is a reminder that youth, beauty and talent, which she finally showed just a few years before her death, in "The Burning Bed," is no deterrent to fate.

Being the film historian and fan that I was, and remain, I spent quite a bit of time with Cornell Wilde and Mel Ferrer. Ferrer was married at the time to Audrey Hepburn, and had been a respected actor for all his adult life. He didn't see himself as a star, even if he was, by virtue of star billing he had received in such huge productions as "*War and Peace*," but instead maintained a low profile. He was a great raconteur, and had wonderful stories to tell at dinner, which I tried to have with him at least several times a week. He was very much in love with Audrey, but it was clear he felt his marriage was over, and seemed depressed by the thought.
Cornell Wilde, on the other hand, was the quintessence of 40's Hollywood movie star, complete with major ego. I found him interesting to talk to because not only was he a terrific actor, but also an accomplished director. His "*The Naked Prey*" is still considered an important example of independent filmmaking. Besides Ferrer, there was literally no one for poor Cornell to talk to – except me. And the possible exception of the motel manager, an Austrian expatriate of some culture, with whom, to my surprise, Cornell could converse in perfect German.

Cornell was amusing at first, but soon got on my nerves. He attempted to monopolize me for dinner every night, which created problems for me with not only Mel Ferrer, but with Charlie, with whom I had to plan the next day's shooting, and the rest of the cast and crew. He would pout and have dinner alone when I couldn't join him. And naturally, when you're playing a Viking chief, as he was, you have some serious issues about costume and make-up. This was low budget, remember, a million-and-a-half dollars, and for AIP, the cheapest studio in town, best known for Roger Corman horror pictures, and "*Beach Blanket Bingo*," Sam Arkoff's personal favorites. We could only afford two make-up people and two costumers. Cornell would purposely show up at 5:30 a.m., a half-hour before his call so he could monopolize these hard-working and inexperienced local ladies and gave them a very hard time. When the other actors filtered in, they had to wait until Cornell was satisfied he had his wig just right, every wrinkle in his costume ironed out, his face hue perfect.

We had constructed a simulated Viking ship, face and half-deck only, and anchored it about 20 yards from the beach, from which we would row our actors out for long shots. Cornell wouldn't share a boat with anyone else and insisted on waiting until the wind had died down before stepping into the boat. He stood ramrod straight, so that his costume wouldn't wrinkle and if you've ever tried to row a boat with someone standing in it, while the waves are coming in, you have an idea how difficult Cornell made my life. He looked like Washington crossing the Delaware. Naturally, when he finally boarded the ship, or half ship, as it were, he'd call for the hairdresser to row out and tape down his wig.

The assistant manager of the hotel, Kathy, a large-boned, attractive, redheaded lady of 35, was very helpful to me in locating services I needed as line producer, and giving me credibility in her home town as I ordered materials and hired help. Sundays were our day off, and everyone took advantage of it. Tampa weather was pleasant, not like the vicious temperature changes in Montana, and even though we were doing a period costume picture, on water, at that, we could spare ourselves a few hours away from the grind. Kathy offered to show me around town and I happily accepted. She picked me up at 9 a.m. with her 14 year-old daughter in tow. We set off and drove around for a while, Kathy pointing out old Spanish gun emplacements, and other points of interest, when she turned into a road that ended up at a guarded gate. We were waved in and I was surprised to find we were in a nudist camp. "This is how Ellen and I always spend our Sundays," Kathy informed me. We spent almost every Sunday there.

It wasn't the first time I had been to a nude venue, be it beach, camp, or Elysian Fields, the famous California hippie hangout with hot springs filling rock tubs carved out of the cliffs over the ocean. And certainly not the last time, either. But what has always struck me about such places is who they attract. It should be illegal for the ninety-nine percent of the "The Nude Bunch" I've encountered at these places to ever take their clothes off in public. Other evenings Kathy frittered away in my room. Why things like this always happen to me, I have no idea.

Charlie, the Baptist from Arkansas, became an authentic Hollywoodian, complete with mistress, and a drug, alcohol, and tobacco habit, zooming from being broke to having assets worth north of $20 million. In 1975 – at least five times that much in today's dollars. And in the great hubristic tradition of the film business, he lost it all because he came to believe that he, and only he, had been responsible for his success. As Bill Shakespeare once said to me, "What fools these mortals be."

TOM CRUISE CAN COOK

Tom Cruise cooked dinner for me one night. It was 1982, and I was dating Helene Shaw, a Hollywood personal manager, whose client was Rebecca De Mornay, a fast-rising young actress. She and her boyfriend, Tom Cruise, were living in a small, one-bedroom apartment on Sunset Blvd., in Brentwood. Tom and Rebecca had recently completed "*Risky Business,*" which was his breakthrough picture, but since no one had seen it up until then, he was simply thought of a comer, based on his work in "*Taps,*" a military school drama, in which he was an ensemble player. Tom played a typical middle class teenager. Joel's parents leave town for a few days and he meets Lana, a hooker, played by Rebecca, who devirginizes Tom and then convinces him to turn his home into a whorehouse for one evening. Joel agrees, and, while a gang of Rebecca's sexy hooker friends and randy guys turn Joel's house upside down, a Princeton University recruiter arrives to interview Joel. Joel loses his dad's Porsche in Lake Michigan, all his parent's furniture, and falls in love with Rebecca. Woody Allen's long time collaborator, screenwriter Paul Brickman, made his directing debut with "*Risky Business.*" As soon as the industry saw the picture, it was clear Tom Cruise was going to be a star.

Rebecca, however, was better known and, although this can become a problem for two actors living and loving under the same roof, both she and Tom seemed very happy and very much in love. One night, Rebecca invited Helene, her manager, to dinner and, of course, Helene brought me, her boyfriend. I wasn't anxious to attend, I remember, having had a lot of experience with young actors, and thinking this was going to be a boring evening, replete with bad food, rampant egos, and rivalry between the two of them for attention.

Their apartment was sparse, as befits journeymen actors, who might be lucky enough to land a role on the spur of the moment, and have to depart for a distant location the next day. They had gone to a great deal of trouble – flowers bedecked the dining room table, wine glasses and a bottle of inexpensive Italian red wine awaited us. While Rebecca poured, we nibbled on appetizers, which Rebecca said she had made, while Tom took over the kitchen, and busied himself with a red sauce-based pasta.

I'm pretty good in the kitchen myself, so I moseyed over to check on how Tom was doing. I watched him slice garlic and onion without cutting himself, opened a large can of roma tomatoes and, while sautéing the vegetables in extra virgin olive oil, mashed the tomatoes in a bowl. He added dried oregano and basil, a few dried red pepper flakes, and a little salt. So far, so good. I would have added some fennel seeds I had crushed in a mortar, a couple of anchovies, a little sugar and some splashes of vodka, soy sauce and red wine, but then I was a guest. While that cooked, Tom broke spaghetti into a pot of boiling water, stirred it, and we joined the ladies while dinner cooked.

I was pleasantly surprised. They were cute together and I noticed the lack of competitive spirit between them, which is atypical in a situation like theirs. Tom deferred to Rebecca, and she obviously adored him. I liked them both enormously. Tom talked about his strong family ties, and his growing up in the Midwest in a normal, American town.

Rebecca, though, had had a more fractious childhood. Her father, whom she had a strong dislike for, was Wally George, a failed actor, who had a late night talk show on cable television in Los Angeles. She wouldn't discuss him in public, and even on occasion, denied he was her father. Not long after she and Tom split up, Rebecca met the much older poet and songwriter, Leonard Cohen, and lived with him in great harmony until Cohen became a monk at a Zen Center on Mount Baldy, in spring 1999. Sometimes, when girls grow up either without a father, or with a father they haven't received love and acceptance from, they will gravitate towards older men for relationships.

Tom's pasta, accompanied by a shaker of Kraft parmesan cheese, was pretty good, and Rebecca's salad, which included walnuts and slices of miniature oranges over lettuce, with a citrus-olive oil dressing, was terrific. Helene and I exchanged secret smiles, watching the two young lovers at home.

BILL W.

My old friend, Harold Rand, who had rescued me from 20th Century-Fox and hired me at Paramount when I needed a new home, away from the pressure executives at Fox were putting me under to convince my new bride, Carol, to star in the sequel to "*Peyton Place*," called me in 1980 to enlist my help in getting a movie made about the founding of Alcoholics Anonymous. It had been a few years since I last saw or spoken to him and I was surprised he had become a member of AA. I never would have known. He, and his friend and sponsor, Bill Borchert, had been entrusted by the board of directors of AA to spread the word about the organization by causing a sympathetic film to be made from a newly published biography of the founders, entitled "*Bill W.*" Residing in New York, they didn't have the connections to directors, writers, and actors I did that would make the film possible.

I had thought, like many people not in the know, that AA was a self-sustaining, basically poverty-based association that helped alcoholics deal with their addiction through peer counseling, which it is. What I didn't know was that AA, at the top, was a very rich organization because of endowments left to it by grateful, wealthy members. I was placed on salary to round up a writer first, and then a director, which AA would finance, and then, when we had an acceptable script, I would approach the studios for full financing and distribution. As any agent or producer knows, the first dollars are the hardest to obtain.

I felt that with the power of AA behind me, after all they have chapters in 90 countries, from Finland to Botswana, with many millions of members; this would be an easy sale because of its built-in audience. If the movie was any good, it could attract main stream movie-goers as well and it would be a box office bonanza. Mel

Gibson, years later, proved just how viable that theory is. Marketing to affinity groups, Christians or alcoholics, is good business.

I called the usual literary agents and compiled a list of possibles. I was surprised, once again, as in the Orson Welles chapter, how many writers revealed, in their quest for the writing assignment, that they were AA members. Most of the time, their own agents hadn't known.

I thought that was both a plus and a minus. Plus because they knew the inner workings of how the AA group therapy worked, the secret handshakes, if you will. But also a minus because I had the idea they would have difficulties with objectivity. Sometimes a writer, like an actor, does better by learning his subject from the outside in.

I selected Andy Lewis for the job. Andy had written the screenplay of "*Klute*," a powerful and eerie story about a hunted prostitute, which won the Oscar for best actress for Jane Fonda in 1971. Andy had been nominated for his work. I thought he'd be perfect, and besides, he wasn't AA.

We waited patiently for his first draft. The way it works in Hollywood contracts with writers, is that they have a set amount of time to produce their work in pre-determined stages. It begins, usually, with a "treatment," a short story, due in four to six weeks, describing the setting, the action, and the characters, running anywhere from a dozen to thirty pages or so. Lewis' treatment was terrific. So far, so good.

A man named Bill Wilson, a self-described falling-down drunk, started AA with a fellow drunk, a physician named Dr. Robert Holbrook Smith, whom everyone called Dr. Bob, in the years following the stock market crash in 1929. The tradition of using only first names in their meetings protected their anonymity and allowed them to tell their most embarrassing secrets to people who remained strangers. It was, and is, very effective. Alcoholism is now recognized as a disease, but in those days it was considered a character weakness by the protestant ruling class, and drunks were persecuted in countless ways, including public humiliation.

What made the story work for me as a producer was that essentially it was a love story. Bill's wife, Lois, was and is still considered by many in the organization as a saint. Lois was a born care-giver, and her husband needed help. We call that person today in psychological terms, an enabler. She was always there, cleaning up his messes when he couldn't get to a bathroom soon enough, and hosting their first AA meetings in her home. Lois didn't drink so she maintained a superior position among the steadily enlarging groups. She seemed to enjoy the power.

As the AA doctrine was being developed by trial and error, Bill and Dr. Bob assumed leadership positions, with Bill gradually asserting number one status. As he began to realize the benefits of the therapy he and Dr. Bob had invented, he gained control of his drinking, and eventually stopped. It didn't hurt that as the founder of this bunch of social outcasts, his role gave him increasing prestige, which built up his confidence and implanted in his mind that he had value, importance, and carried a significant social message. AA was being written up in the press, and Bill was the spokesman. And then a strange thing happened.

One day, Bill woke up and decided that since he had stopped drinking, he didn't need Lois' help anymore and moved out. This came as a great shock, not only to Lois, but to the AA organization, because they were seen as the embodiment of perfection – the net result of goodness rewarded - failure turned success by way of hard work and devotion to God. I couldn't ask for a better story.

Andy Lewis' first draft, due eight weeks after we had approved the treatment, arrived and we eagerly devoured it. The first half was truly magic, and we envisioned another Oscar nomination for him, and for the lucky couple who would eventually play Bill and Lois. The second half was another matter – it was awful. Almost as though another, a different person had written it. I couldn't understand what had happened. Andy played dumb – he said he was sorry we didn't like the second half, that he liked it and had done the best he knew how. Harold, Bill Borchert and I were pretty shaken. We had spent a quarter-of-a-million of AA's dollars and had almost nothing to show for it. I suggested we hire another writer, but this time I added we should have supervision of the next draft by a director we agreed upon.

I produced a list of director possibles, and interviewed them all. I was most impressed by a former producer turned director named Stuart Millar. I liked his credits, among them some of the better movies of the 60s and 70s, such as *"Little Big Man,"* starring Dustin Hoffman, *"Paper Lion," "The Best Man,"* written by Gore Vidal, *"Birdman of Alcatraz,"* and especially Burt Lancaster's bravura performance, and *"Rooster Cogburn"* starring John Wayne and Katherine Hepburn. Millar fancied himself a writer as well and undertook his own version of the screenplay. It was soon obvious he was a better producer than a writer and we abandoned his version.

Stuart did have another idea that intrigued me. He was a friend of the legendary writer-director, Nick Ray, famous for *"Rebel without a Cause," "King of Kings,"* and my personal favorite, *"Johnny Guitar,"* starring Joan Crawford and Sterling Hayden. He called Ray and found he was available for a quick rewrite and I jumped at the opportunity. I was a big fan of Nick Ray's because, in addition to the above pictures, he had written *"They Live by Night,"* a classic 1940s film noir, *"On Dangerous Ground,"* an early 50s example of the gangster genre, and *"The Savage Innocents,"* a remarkable docudrama of the Inuit, filmed near the North Pole, starring Anthony Quinn.

Once again we eagerly awaited Ray's first draft. It was too dreadful to describe. He died soon thereafter and I found out that he had been dying of advanced cancer and that it was his girlfriend, Sandra Scoppitone, who had done the writing. She had exactly one previous credit, "*Scarecrow in a Garden of Cucumbers.*" No, I haven't heard of it either.

By now I had spent more than half-a-million dollars of AA's dough and they had had enough. We were shut down. I later found out that Andy Lewis's brother, David, had written the second half of his script. I hate being right sometimes. I told you showbiz is a rotten way of life.

"*Bill W.*" was made as a television version in 1989, and starred James Woods, as Bill Wilson, James Garner, as Dr. Bob, and JoBeth Williams, as Lois.

A PORK-A-LIPS NOW

Helene Shaw, the Hollywood talent manager I dated in the early 1980's, also represented the wife of the fast-rising character actor, Robert Duvall. Duvall had just returned from the Philippines following a grueling near yearlong co-starring role in Francis Coppola's now classic film of the Vietnam era, "*Apocalypse Now.*" If ever there was a bad luck shoot, this was it. A typhoon destroyed all their sets, a fire then burned down most of the rebuilt village, the star, Martin Sheen, had a heart attack, Marlon Brando presented his own unique problems, Francis's marriage nearly came apart, the film was wildly over budget, the distributor, United Artists, was threatening to take the film away from him, and a host of other difficulties.

Duvall, however, seemed impervious to disaster. He was by all accounts, the strong man of the cast. Nothing seemed to touch him. He had rented a house inland from Zuma Beach, some 20 miles up the coast from L.A., and made elaborate plans for a party for cast, crew, and friends. He was going to roast an entire pig – himself. Helene invited me to join her.

We drove up the coast and completely missed the hidden entrance to the isolated road that led to Duvall's house. By the time we figured out where to turn, we were a good half hour late. But Duvall had anticipated the difficulties his guests would have finding his house, so every 100 yards or so, nailed to a tree, or round a curve, we followed his hand-lettered signs with pointed arrows that promised "A Pork-A-Lips Now."

The Coppolas and their three young children were there (Sophia has now become a director, with "*Lost in Translation*," starring Bill Murray, a critical hit picture that won't earn back its production and promotion costs), the Sheens, including his two young sons, Emilio Estevez, and Charlie Sheen (Sheen's real name is Estevez), both of whom became actors, most of the cast and crew, and friends of Duvall. He was indeed roasting a full sized pig over coals, and it looked and smelled delicious. Lots of beer, potato salad, cole slaw, and baked beans were available and by the time the pig was ready to be sliced, it was so soft it fell off the bone onto your plate. I got the clear impression that the group was celebrating not only the finish of their film, but the very fact they had all survived it.

STAN & CHERYL, FREDDIE & DAVID

I left the agency to be President of Group Three, a partnership of Wells Rich Greene, the New York advertising agency, and Wakeford-Orloff, the West Coast's largest television commercial production company. Group Three produced the feature film, "*Dirty Little Billy*," distributed by Columbia Pictures, and also developed "*Bury My Heart at Wounded Knee,*" by Dee Brown, *'World Without End, Amen,"* by Jimmy Breslin, "*I, Robot,"* by Issac Asimov, and "*The Fortunate Pilgrim,*" by Mario Puzo.

I mentioned previously that I had met director Stan Dragoti when he came to me to secure Michael J. Pollard's services as the lead in the film he wanted to make about Billy the Kid. Stan, then married to supermodel Cheryl Tiegs, was a New Yorker, and a neophyte in Hollywood. When, surprisingly, he was able to get financing to do the film from his boss, Mary Wells, chairman of Wells Rich Greene, and Jack L. Warner, Fred Jacobs, Mary's chief financial officer, asked to meet me on Mary's orders. I flew to New York with Stan for a meeting with both, and was retained by the agency, essentially to guide Stan through the shark-filled waters of the movie business.

It's a tough town for newcomers, especially those with money. The reefs are replete with the wreckage of companies like Coca-Cola, Matsushita, Transamerica, PolyGram, JVC, Vivendi, Seagram's, the aforementioned Wells Rich Greene, Sony, and Mel Simon, the premiere mall builder, who left more than $600 million on the table, before quitting, following which he had his one big hit, "*Porky's*." It's no business for the faint of heart, and the sharks love a new mark. Rupert Murdoch has, so far, avoided shipwreck, and the late oil billionaire Marvin Davis actually sold out for a profit.

CEOs that have made it in their own industries think their intellects and previous successes qualify them to run any business. But they're wrong. Showbiz is inherently guesswork, not subject to any established or known business rules. Also, running a water company, or selling insurance, or soft drinks is pretty boring, and guys who crunch numbers all day yearn for something creative to do.

So they're tempted to stick their toe in the movie world by investing in a film or two. That opens them up, like the world of drugs, to a "taste." As in the case of poor Charlie Pierce, the shit kicker movie director who hit it big with "*Boggy Creek*," a taste includes beautiful young women who would do "anything" for a part, an opportunity to throw away your suits and ties, sample and become accustomed to the best cocaine, and live a life of fun, fun, and more fun. More often than not, it can and does lead to ruin.

Big time money men have always been drawn to this world. William Randolph Hearst, the up-tight, married, Catholic owner of most of America's top newspapers in the early part of the 20th Century, began just that way – investing in a few movies. He became hooked, made a loopy untalented actress named Marion Davies his mistress, and was tied to Hollywood for years through some costly and well-known scandals, including at least one murder he may have committed himself.

Joe Kennedy, the father of President Jack Kennedy, bought himself a studio, RKO, which had fallen on hard times, with the millions he made as a 1920s bootlegger in partnership with what later became known as the mafia. Another strait-laced married Catholic, he recruited married movie star Gloria Swanson as his mistress, thus diagramming to his many male children the advantages of wealthy males in the acquisition of women.

Howard Hughes bought RKO from Joe Kennedy, probably because he was very shy around women. He knew that his luck would improve vastly as a result. He is alleged to have "dated", whatever that means, such beauties as Lana Turner, Jane Russell, Rita Hayworth, and a bunch more, and actually married Jean Peters.

John Beckett, chairman of Transamerica, an insurance company, bought United Artists in 1967, telling his board he thought it a prudent buy. Although it had been a modest moneymaker for some years, *"Heaven's Gate"* brought the company down, much as *"Cleopatra"* did at 20th-Fox. Beckett couldn't get out fast enough. My own theory, however, is that his daughter, Brenda, with whom I became friendly, wanted to be in showbiz, and that's why he bought UA. Brenda, a beauty, strangely enough didn't want to be an actress, but got her kicks developing films for the studio. I suppose I'd do the same for my kid.

And when Europeans or Asians buy into Hollywood, they're really asking for trouble. It's a club they can't join because they don't know the players, can't speak the language, and are hopeless when it comes to understanding the culture. It's as though a Hollywood producer was suddenly in charge of distilling Sake, in Seoul.

Giancarlo Parretti, later exposed as a crook, bought MGM from Kirk Kirkorian, for $1.3 billion of French bank Credit Lyonnais' money, and promptly put three mistresses on the company payroll. I love Italians.

And Edgar Bronfman Jr. (the Jr. is important because his father and his uncle never would have traded six billion dollars worth of Dow Chemical stock for Universal studios) once suggested that movie theatres charge more money for higher-budgeted movies. When pigs fly (II).

Stan and Cheryl, even though Cheryl was a local girl, having grown up in Alhambra, were immediate candidates for the top tier social life. They rented a posh house on

Parkway Drive, in Beverly Hills, and we set to work. Part of my job was to introduce Stan to the industry in the same way I had Charlie Pierce, so he could gain credibility and access to the kind of professional help he would require, especially since we were doing an independent, rather than a studio film. It took only minutes for the Dragotis to be invited into the charmed and later doomed circle presided over by the Machiavellian David Begelman and Freddie Fields. That insidious group grew out of Fields and Begelman being suddenly out of a job in the New York office, when Lew Wassermann abandoned MCA for Universal Studios. Both moved to L.A., Freddie (nee Finkelstein) and his wife, Polly Bergen, and David, between marriages.

They set out as a team to be personal managers, as F/B Enterprises, and came up with a slick line, which I bought into, along with a lot of other Hollywoodians. Freddie and Polly rented a house on Tower Road, off Benedict Canyon, a street that led to Pickfair, once the home of Mary Pickford and Douglas Fairbanks. So the location was good. Freddy bought, or rented, probably, a new navy blue Bentley convertible, very rare at that time in the movie community. Most people in 1961 drove American cars, and the now ubiquitous Mercedes were still in Germany. Cadillacs and Lincolns were what the rich used to make an impression then, so Freddy's Bentley turned some heads, including mine.

I was too young and unsophisticated to see through his and David's obvious front and, introduced to them by Lennie Hirshan, a William Morris Agent, who then represented an unknown Clint Eastwood, and an equally unknown Jack Lemmon, I listened as they described their vision. They were going to take over the careers of a select group of talent – only one male and female star, one top director, one writer, one young male and female actor marked for stardom, and nurture their professional and business activities. "The agencies had too many clients, their agents had many versions of the same clients and frequently sold their favorites against the other agent's clients, and they weren't interested in long term success – only the immediate ten percent commission. After all," Freddy and David said to me, "It's not what you make, it's what you keep." It was the first time I had heard that, but not the last.

They weren't wrong in their assessment. Even though I was a good four years from becoming an agent myself, I already knew that from what my PR clients, sometimes the same ones they were angling for, told me. F/B had decided that their bet for stardom was my wife, Carol. It sounded good to me, even though they were proposing she pay them another fifteen percent on top of the ten she owed the Morris Office when she worked. Put that sum together with the IRS's demand for 50 percent, and you almost had enough to live on, considering how much it cost you to live like a movie star in those days.

The sixties in Hollywood still carried the cachet exhibited by movie stars such as Joan Crawford, Clark Gable, and Cary Grant. You didn't go out in public unless you looked like a movie star. That meant expensive clothes, a personal hairdresser and make-up person, and you chose your destinations carefully. You certainly did not go to the grocery store yourself, nor did you raise your children alone. That was what staff was for. It's amazing to me today that actors, even stars, show up in tabloids wearing torn, even dirty clothes, their hair stringy, pushing grocery carts or baby strollers. Or topless and having their toes sucked. D.W. Griffith, one of the founders of the movie business, and its first great director, once said about glamour, "If you want to see the girl next door – go next door".

The Fields-Begelman team subtly reminded me that, although Carol was their first choice in that category, they also liked Tuesday Weld, and needed to make a decision soon. I agreed to take their message home to Carol, but that she would be the one who made up her mind. At least that was the theory. That early in our marriage, Carol still trusted me and looked up to my better judgment, based on my longer experience in business. I recommended, after some discussion, that she meet them as well. So we journeyed up the hill, since we lived on the flats on Benedict Canyon, to the Field's still unfurnished abode. Polly, sweet thing that she was, made us her homemade chili. Which was pretty good, I thought, until I spotted some cans in the garbage pail in the kitchen, when I toted our plates in after we finished eating. It was "Dennison's," a local brand. It should have been a warning that not all the Fields-Begelman edifice was real. I wish I had kept that in mind.

Carol agreed to sign with them. They also nailed down Judy Garland, through Arthur Jacobs, of course, as well as Henry Fonda, and Marlene Dietrich, and they were off. They hatched a good scheme; that of hiring away from the agencies the upcoming young agents who could bring their star clients with them.
Their first hire was Mike Gruskoff, a friend of mine, my age, who had shared responsibility for Steve McQueen. Gruskoff tried valiantly to have McQueen meet Freddie and David, but Steve resisted, saying he had heard they were backed by the Mafia. I don't know where he got that impression – perhaps it was humorous and his way of staying away. This dance went on for months; a lunch was scheduled, and then cancelled, a weekend meeting away from town was thrown out. Finally, McQueen agreed to meet with Freddie and David at their offices, at eight at night, after everyone had gone home, so that they would not be spotted and could be alone.

The offices were dark, except for the one light over Freddie's desk as McQueen and Gruskoff made their way up the aisle. They arrived; hands were shook, soft and hard drinks offered and accepted, when Freddie said, "OK, let's go to work." He stood up and took off his suit jacket, revealing a shoulder-holstered pistol. McQueen cracked up and said, "OK, you got me, where do I sign?" The gun of course, was a prop, rented for the occasion from a prop house.

That worked because of the theatricality and daring they used to good effect. Getting McQueen to roll over helped them subsequently sign up Paul Newman, Barbra Streisand, Dustin Hoffman, and a bunch of other stars, and also got some of the best agents to leave what was left of the MCA dispersal, the Morris office, some personnel from Marvin Josephson's agglomeration, and others. Mike Medavoy, later to become head of United Artists, was another young agent they acquired. I think I wasn't asked to join because of what I heard years later from another personal manager, Jerry Levy, who looked after comedian Joey Bishop. Levy told me that Freddie had propositioned my wife, Carol, while she was his client. Fields allegedly told her she should leave me and that he would set her up in an apartment, and really concentrate on making her a bigger star. Levy also said he also had heard that I had set Carol up for this because if she made more money while we were still married, when we divorced, because of community property laws in California, I'd get a larger settlement. I was told by Levy that Carol believed it, but it's hard for me to accept that. Yes, she was young, but not stupid. Did Freddie actually do that? Was it true? I don't know, but I'd put nothing past Freddie Fields, given his history. I can't say I used up any Kleenex mopping my eyes when both Begelman and Fields died.

Of course, their vision of the management business dissipated because they were moving too fast, so in order to keep their clients, they had to start an agency themselves. How ironic, after spewing their unique management concept to woo their talent from their agencies, they were now in the agency business themselves. Very ballsy, but because actors are by definition insecure, they were also unable to leave because of the new contracts they had signed, and the embarrassment and possible rejection of asking their old agents to take them back.

Creative Management Agency, as F/B called it, quickly became the hot place to go, as the Morris office was by that time some 80 years old - there were no surprises to be found there, and Marvin Josephson's acquisitions were still ongoing with no clear direction yet apparent.

Both Freddie and David worked the social scene relentlessly, giving and going to parties. Cocaine, as well as marijuana was as much currency as hundred dollar bills, and in fact that was the preferred delivery system to the nose, rolled up, of course. The sixties and early seventies was sex, drugs and Rock n'Roll – literally. I, as an agent, would frequently go to pitch meetings at the studios or producer's offices, where the first order of business was to lay out lines of "snow," and after snorting and comparing each line as though it were Merlot versus Cabernet, we'd get down to talking about movies. Woody Allen didn't make it up, when in "*Annie Hall*," his party host offered him a bowl of coke, which he promptly sneezed all over the room.

Stan and Cheryl, against my advice, eased into this scene. I told Stan, especially, that this axis was bad news, and that he should stay away from Freddie and David, and instead concentrate on making movies, going out to dinner, and staying home. But the lure of big stars to a rising director is hard to resist and Stan and his wife began spending much of their spare social time in that company. Also part of this particular clique was Robert Evans, then head of Paramount Studios, and the Polish director of "*Rosemary's Baby*," Roman Polanski. Evans, even when married to the beautiful and very nearly talented "*Love Story*" star, Ali MacGraw, and Polanski, a known womanizer, while married to his pregnant wife, Sharon Tate, were major players in the dark edges of Hollywood. Sharon Tate was among the group slaughtered by Charles Manson and his gang, in 1969, in Benedict Canyon. At that moment, I lived in a house just below the murder scene.

All of the above, Dragoti, Evans, and Polanski, with the exception of Cheryl Tiegs, managed to get into major trouble over drugs and women. Polanski raped a 13 year-old girl after getting her high, and left the country minutes before the police were to arrest him and hasn't returned since. He has a long prison sentence waiting for him if he ever steps into the U.S.

Evans went bonkers also, starting with MacGraw leaving him and promptly marrying Steve McQueen after they filmed "*The Getaway*," together for director Sam Peckinpah. Evans lost his job at Paramount despite a string of critical and box-office hits, including "*Rosemary's Baby*" in 1968, "*Love Story*," made in 1970, and "*The Godfather*," in 1972,. Evans, and Francis Coppola, "Godfather" director, had very public arguments over who the real genius was in the making of this now-classic film. As mentioned previously, failure is no bar to upward movement, and Evans got a producing position at Paramount, usually the result of the conversion of an existing contract. His first production was "*Chinatown*," 1974, directed by his pal, Polanski. It was a hit. He then produced two more box office successes, "*Marathon Man*," with Gregory Peck and Dustin Hoffman, 1976, and "*Black Sunday*," in 1977. Evans also helped resuscitate John Travolta's career with "*Urban Cowboy*," in 1980.

Evans began to tumble for real when he was arrested for cocaine possession during the production of "*Popeye*," in 1980, directed by Robert Altman, which was a flop. His real disaster, however, came in the production of "*The Cotton Club*," in 1984, starring Richard Gere. Cocaine (I'm told) gives one a heroic portrait of oneself, and Evans had it in mind to direct this picture. A very bad idea, it turned out, and Evans put in an emergency call to Coppola to save the day. Instead, the movie whipped out of control as Coppola, as usual, continued to rewrite the script. The budget doubled, and Evans and Coppola again fought publicly, not to mention the fact that Evans was also implicated in the murder of a funding source. Evans beat the rap, but he couldn't beat the bad publicity or "*Cotton Club's*" awful box-office results. He produced a few lackluster films after that, and briefly married actress Catherine Oxenberg in 1998, making exactly five wives, including former Miss America, Phyllis George. A couple of years ago, Evans suffered a stroke, allegedly from a cocaine overdose.

Dragoti's first Hollywood film after "*Dirty Little Billy*" was "*Love at First Bite*," in 1979, which put George Hamilton, for the first time, into a starring role in a very successful feature film, Stan followed that up with another hit, "*Mr. Mom*," with Michael Keaton. His next three films, however, were duds; "*The Man with One Red Shoe*," a remake of a mildly popular French film, "*She's Out of Control*," in 1989, and 1991's "*Necessary Roughness*." I know Stan exceedingly well. Not only were we business partners for a number of years, we were friends also. He was depressed, and played with the idea of returning to New York to go back into the advertising business, where he was still appreciated. Cheryl, however, wanted no part of that anymore. Her modeling days were essentially over, they lived in a big house in Bel Air, and she wanted kids. Stan told her there was only room for one kid in their household, and that was him!

They were on the verge of splitting up, when Stan decided to go to the Cannes Film Festival to meet Freddie Fields. Because of bad weather, the plane was diverted from Paris to Munich. Europe had faced terrorism long before the U.S., so metal detectors were in use and the police there found cocaine packaged in cellophane, wrapped in aluminum, strapped around Stan's chest, which he was bringing to Cannes for Freddie and their friends, and off to jail he went. To Cheryl's great credit, and even though she no longer loved him, she flew to Germany and visited Stan every day, bringing him food from the best restaurants in Munich, a pretty nifty trick if you've ever eaten in Germany. It took nearly six months to get Stan out through the efforts of politically-connected Mary Wells. Cheryl put her life on hold and stayed by Stan's side until he was sprung. Back in L.A., the marriage was over, although they stayed together for a while. The great earthquake of 1994 sent Stan scurrying back to New York (the coward). He's directed TV commercials ever since. Cheryl has married several times since and she did have her child, or children. She married photographer Peter Beard from 1981 to '83, Tony Peck, son of Gregory Peck, from 1990 until 1994, and had one child with him, and then married Rod Stryker in 1998, with whom she had twin sons before divorcing him.

IF IT'S GOOD – STEAL IT

Another director who stole Stan Dragoti's style of picture-making was Michael Cimino, who directed the magnificent *"The Deer Hunter,"* perhaps the seminal Vietnam War film. He launched what was then the most costly western ever made, *"Heaven's Gate,"* which I talk about in another section, related to how expensive movies can sometimes sink a studio. The failure of Paramount's $275 million plus *"Polar Express"* is doubtless a cause of former production chief, Sherry Lansing's departure. But, back to Mike Cimino.

Cimino was originally a fashion photographer, sought after by Madison Avenue ad agencies for his eclectic and offbeat work for their commercial clients. Of course, what he really wanted to do was direct. Doesn't everyone? *"The Deer Hunter"* astounded everyone for its realistic portrayal of how an uneducated, untrained, badly-equipped guerilla force could defeat the world's greatest military power. Do I see a connection here in our present conflict with Iraq, and perhaps Afghanistan?

"Heaven's Gate" was notable for its realistic look at our legendary settlement of the West, and portrayed the white people generally as various criminals, back-shooters,

civil war deserters, Indian killers, prostitutes and religious fanatics. Which they, for the most part, were. That was the theme of "*Dirty Little Billy*." Dragoti, my former partner, always told me Cimino emulated everything he did in advertising, so he wasn't surprised when Cimino not only used Stan's story in another context, but also Stan's dark opinion of humanity, and how he had shot "*Billy*," – in shadow, in silhouette, with overtones of impending disaster.

Cimino was fanatically devoted to his western, and pulled every trick a director has to keep the studio from knowing what was actually going on during the production. He was in Montana, far from Hollywood, and ran his operation in total secrecy. His then-girlfriend functioned as "producer," (read "gatekeeper" no pun intended) and when studio executives, alarmed by the escalating costs, showed up on location, Cimino built a psychological "Potemkin Village" to defray a meaningful look inside his closed ship.

"*Heaven's Gate*" was a box office flop, and caused Transamerica to dump entertainment for the insurance business they knew. Cimino's star rapidly fell and, although he did a couple more films, costing a whole lot less, were equally unsuccessful. He disappeared for a number of years – some said in seclusion on the 10,000 acres he had bought in Montana – and some had much darker legends to relate. There were rumors he had killed himself. More rumors that he had had plastic surgery and had radically changed his looks. Sometime last year, one of the pop entertainment magazines ran a photo which, it alleged, was of Michael Cimino, now a woman.

JUDY & DAVID

Judy Garland was slipping fast personally around this time. She and Sid Luft had had it out, and they were separated. Judy was depressed, doing drugs, and the last thing she wanted to do was work. She needed help, and Freddie and David needed her income. So David Begelman took her over, literally. It was something of a shock to everyone who knew all the parties involved, and definitely demonstrated that F/B would do whatever it took to maintain their status, and their income. I can't imagine a sexual relationship between them, but it probably happened, because Judy required the closeness of a man – especially one who was strongly devoted to her.

It helped for a while, long enough for Judy's final world tour - Concert performances around the world, especially in New York, at Carnegie Hall, from which a best selling album was produced, to the Palladium, in London, where she "killed 'em," as the saying goes. But it killed her as well. She died in London from an overdose, at the young age of 47, on June 22, 1969.

Begelman was an addict – he loved to gamble and to marry rich women, in that order. No matter how much he and Freddie were able to liberate from their personal piggy bank, their agency, David was always short of money. After Judy died, David found a wealthy widow in New York, and married her, but even she couldn't keep him in pari-mutual tickets. CMA was beginning, by then, to lose its luster, and clients were catching on that they were being exploited, as compared to being ignored at their former agencies. Freddie and David, having promised their agents a vision that couldn't be sustained, were facing a revolt and they needed a new plan.

Freddie seemed to invent an innovative concept involving four of his movie star clients and him, in a stand-alone production company that would be funded by a distributor, and which would own its films equally with its members. Titling it "First Artists," the company consisted of Paul Newman, Steve McQueen, Dustin Hoffman, and Barbra Streisand, with Freddie as its president. United Artists would distribute their films.

Memories are short in Hollywood, and very few people read – history, or screenplays for that matter. In 1919, United Artists was formed by Mary Pickford, her husband, Douglas Fairbanks, Charlie Chaplin, and D.W. Griffith, for the same purposes as First Artists. Freddie's idea only seemed new.

Freddie and David decided the way to maximize their fortunes was to be buyers of talent as well as sellers, something Lew Wasserman couldn't convince the Justice Department was an honorable thing, so Begelman, on the strength of his and Freddie's client list, sought and got the open job of running Columbia Pictures. He had a string of moderately successful films, including *Shampoo*," the Warren Beatty-Julie Christy movie that first brought the word "cocksucking" onto American screens.

Running a Hollywood movie studio is the absolute top of the shuddering, constantly swaying social pyramid in this town, and it pays really well. Not as much, perhaps, as a committed gambler, needs, because it didn't take long for the downward-spiraling Begelman to destroy this last chance either. He forged a check in the name of Academy Award-winning actor, Cliff Robertson, and cashed it to pay his gambling debts. It was for a measly $35,000, or what someone in his position would spend for a party at his home. He was fired, and the studio showed mercy by not asking for David's prosecution. This sordid affair showed up in an expose' docubook in the mid 1970s, titled *"Indecent Exposure."*

Begelman wangled himself a job as President of MGM, an ailing company long past its sell-by date. He marketed himself to Kirk Kirkorian on the premise that he could deliver movie stars to the very last place they'd want to work – his studio. David didn't last long but, under the law promulgated by the late producer, Bill Dozier, a fondly-remembered raconteur and fancier of beautiful women, "Hollywood is the only place where you fall up." Failure is no obstacle, perhaps even an advantage in this town to earning even more money in a more prestigious job than the one you just got fired from. The theory being that if you managed to lose $500 million, at least you were used to handling big sums.

I once asked a veteran producer friend of mine, Sidney Beckerman, why budgets needed to be so high, my having had experience in making films for under a million dollars that made money. He replied, "You can't steal a million dollars from a picture that costs a million dollars." How true.

Begelman limped along for several years until he hooked up with Bruce McNall, a publicity-hungry coin collector, who had made pals with Wayne Gretzky, the hockey superstar, lured him from Canada to Los Angeles, and had, through a series of tricky financial maneuvers, ended up owning the Los Angeles Kings hockey team. Well, it's one thing to be a team owner, ask Jerry Buss, of the Lakers, but quite another to be a film producer. That's where the girls really are. McNall was the perfect mark for Begelman.

Round, cherubic, and anxious to please, McNall loved being the center of attention. As a child, he amused himself with his coins, but now he was being lionized. They made a few films, but Begelman was steadily looting the film company. He wasn't the only one. If Begelman thought McNall was a fool, Bruce also knew what he was buying with David.

McNall's business empire had been built on bank frauds of at least $200 million. He was caught and served four years in U. S. federal prisons. He wrote a book when he got out, called, *"Fun While It Lasted: My Rise and Fall in the Land of Fame and Fortune."* This is what he said about Begelman in his book: "That is the way things are done in Hollywood. If you are good at making movies and belong to the small club of elite insiders, even a felony does not disqualify you from the game."
McNall is back on the street - broke, he says, and owes the government $5 million. I sat next to him at a recent L.A. Clipper's basketball game, and he is a very nice man.

In August of 1995, Begelman was depressed, - abandoned finally by all those who sucked up to him when they thought he could do them some good, and even by his friend and co-conspirator, Freddie Fields. One day he completely vanished. He had gotten married again, this last time to a former actress management client of mine turned TV producer, Annabelle Weston. She tried in vain to find him, until the cops informed her he had been found dead in a room at the Century Plaza Hotel, in Century City, with a self-inflicted gunshot wound to the head.

Freddie Fields went on to produce a couple of movies, and long divorced from Polly Bergen, married a Greek former beauty contest winner. He died several years ago.

GOLDWYNISMS

When Charlie Pierce imploded, I came back to Hollywood needing a job. I had had a great time out on the road, manufacturing movies in little towns around the U.S. The work was hard, the scenery exotic, the girls cooperative, the drugs terrific, and the rewards unbeatable. But it was time to rejoin the Hollywood rat race.

A former secretary of mine, Judy, was working for Sam Goldwyn, Jr., at Goldwyn Studios, in Hollywood. She told me that Sam was looking for a knowledgeable person to scout prospective film material for him. Sam was, of course, very well known in film circles. Besides being the son of one of the authentic pioneers, he was acknowledged for his good taste, his connections, and his friendly manner. In my agent days, I had, along with every other literary material-hawking salesman, been aware that Sam had been mainly talk, that he would meet with you anytime, buy you lunch, and assiduously court you for books, screenplays, or ideas, but would never actually buy anything.

Sam and I hit it off right away, and I think it was the fact that I was a real producer, with authentic filmmaking experience, as compared to others he had interviewed, who were recent college or film school grads, or young agents at one of the many shops around town, that got me the job. He was only ten years older than me, as well, that I think assured Sam, as I came to know he valued maturity and decision-making skills highly. As for me, I was thrilled to be working with, if not an actual pioneer, as in the case of Jack L. Warner, or Spyros Skouras, at least the first-born son of one of the greatest, who had grown up at his feet. Sam, Sr., had made some of the most famous, classic movies of all time, including, *"Guys and Dolls," "Hans Christian Anderson," "The Secret Life of Walter Mitty," "The Best Years of our Lives," "Pride of the Yankees," "Wuthering Heights," "Dodsworth,"* and 95 others. Goldwyn's films had earned over a hundred Academy Awards. Sam Jr. told me he had plans to remake some of the most commercial and honored of his father's films, and that was a big lure for me. I imagined working with the greatest writers, directors and actors of our time.

Sam was always very gracious, and frequently invited me to dinner at his grand home on upper Laurel Way. There I met his kids, Tony, who wanted to be an actor, and John, who, while at Bowdoin College, hadn't yet made up his mind what he wanted to be. Tony Goldwyn is, of course, one of our better character actors today, having co-starred in the recent *"The Last Samurai,"* with Tom Cruise. And John was the president of production at Paramount Studios for 13 years.

Sitting in the legendary Goldwyn office, and inspired by posters of Danny Kaye, Merle Oberon, Laurence Olivier, Gary Cooper, Marlon Brando, and a host of others, I went to work with a passion, but soon ran into the very problem I had encountered as an agent. No one believed that Sam would ever buy anything, that he was all talk. I had, as Irving Lazar's doppelganger, met or corresponded with every major book publisher, and although they knew me and liked me, were reluctant to send anything of commercial value to me because it might interfere with their preferred targets, the seven major studios or the top eight or 10 independent producers. The same was true of my contacts in the agencies. Nevertheless, I persisted, and because of friendship, I was slipped some pretty good stuff to review – after the big guys turned it down.

I understood, and there was nothing I could do about it until I persuaded Sam to buy something – anything. A couple of prospects interested me because I was looking for something eclectic, something that would attract Sam's intellect as well as his instinct for theatricality. I'd give them to Sam with a recommendation that, even if he didn't think they would eventually become movies, we could option them to create some credibility. Option prices were low; usually $2,500 for six months, and it would help me enormously. Sam was not ever hurting for money. His trust fund, and his father's estate were in the many millions class, but I couldn't get him to move.

I caught a lucky break however, when Warner Brothers Studios, in what would become an avalanche of symbiotic moves by all the studios, created a book publishing division, Warner Books. I happened to know the new president, Patrick O'Connor, from his former post at a big time publishing house in New York, and he had moved to L.A. to run it. He too, was anxious to hit the ground running, and was pleased I was a buyer this time, instead of a seller. We went over his forthcoming list, and I noticed a manuscript by a new young writer, Tom Alibrandi, who wrote of an itinerant handball hustler. I sparked to the idea and Pat had the piece sent over. I read "*Killshot*" immediately, and said to Sam, "This is it. I've gotten a 48-hour hold on this book. You must read this over the weekend because it will get away from us and we'll see someone else win an Oscar with it." I was also getting pretty frustrated by then.

One of the reasons I leapt at Alibrandi's story, was that, as a young press agent at 20th-Century-Fox, I had been on the scene nearly every day during the filming of "*The Hustler*," starring Paul Newman, which was shot two blocks from our Westside office, at Movietone News. I had also become friendly with Robert Rosson, the director, whom I had always admired. He was one of the creative people caught up in the communist scare of the 50's and while he didn't make the status and prestige of the "Unfriendly Ten," his career had been damaged. He spilled a few names, as I understood it, and was permitted to resume his career.

"*The Hustler*" had been a big hit, and in the great tradition of Hollywood, the other studios tried to copy it. It wasn't long before MGM had a script written about another hustler, this time a card shark, and corralled Sam Peckinpah to direct it. Peckinpah was a big favorite of action stars, even though he was an obstreperous drunk and exceedingly difficult to work for. Nevertheless, he was able to persuade Steve McQueen to star in "*The Cincinnati Kid*." And of course, some years later, 20th made a sequel to "*The Hustler*," calling it "*The Color of Money*", this time with

Tom Cruise in the role Newman had played, with Newman taking the part played by George C. Scott in the original.

Sam read it, liked it, but was unsure. I developed a headache. I asked for a meeting with the author and Sam and I. Tom Alibrandi was a character straight out of his book. He played handball, had had a rough child and teenagehood, and had flirted with disaster on a grand scale. We all got along swell, and I was finally able to cajole Sam into taking an option on the book. I trumpeted it very loudly around town, even using my press agent contacts to get us some meaningful space in the Hollywood trades, and material began to flow somewhat better. Tom wanted to write the first draft of the screenplay himself, which Sam was against, but the negotiations included one pass at no extra cost, so Sam acceded.

Poor Tom. He had never been up against a world-class ditherer. Sam could not be pleased, and this went on for almost a year – version after version. Tom had quit drinking and drugs a few years earlier, and had mellowed out considerably, but he said he was about to lose some ground. Tom eventually quit, and moved back to New York, and Sam was free to hire a more experienced and better-known name among the screenwriter glitterati. But somehow, everyone Sam wanted to hire was busy. Other opportunities presented themselves to me and I soon got weary of trying make something happen.

Looking back, Sam worked at his father's desk, in his father's studio. He went home at night to his father's house, and slept in his father's bed. I have met several sons of powerful and famous fathers before and since and have invariably found that the father's dominating influence on their children, in particular their first-born son, can be debilitating. I thought that that had been the case here. Since then, however, Sam has indeed remade several of his father's films, "*Stella*," starring Bette Midler, which originally starred Barbara Stanwyck, as "*Stella Dallas*," and "*The Preacher's Wife*," with Denzel Washington and Whitney Houston, which was called "*The Bishop's Wife*," when it was released in 1947, starring Cary Grant and Loretta Young. He also announced plans to remake "*Mitty*," in 2005, and is listed as the producer of "*Master and Commander, the Far Side of the World*," starring Russell Crowe.

NAPOLEON'S RETREAT

I went back to agenting after Goldwyn, and as I was well-connected in the book publishing world through my association with Irving "Swifty" Lazar, several theatrical agencies were anxious to have me. All writers in Hollywood secretly wish they were novelists, so my presence added another level of hope to their agency's client list. Also, the possibility of snagging the film rights for sale of upcoming or previously published books meant another potential income stream. I joined the Lew Weitzman Agency, in Beverly Hills, and got lucky right away. Friends of mine at St. Martin's Press offered me a new book, "*The Murder of Napoleon*," by Ben Weider and David Hapgood. A new theory on the death of the French emperor, made possible by DNA sequencing of locks of hair known to be from Napoleon, posited that he was surreptitiously fed arsenic until enough poison had built up in his body to kill him. Good story, good movie. I read the galleys and knew immediately where to take it. Jack Nicholson was Napoleon. And, I supposed, ham that he is, that he'd love playing that pompous yet tragic figure, pussywhipped and cuckolded by his wife, Josephine, whom he had raised from a penniless divorcee to Empress of France.

I contacted his agent, Sandy Bresler, a friend of mine, and got it right over to him. He passed it on to Jack, who read it and immediately said he wanted to buy it. Jack's lawyer sent over a check for $50,000, against another $200,000 if and when the picture got made, and Jack took it to his long-time collaborator, Bob Towne, to do the screenplay. Towne had written several pictures for Jack, including *"Drive, He Said,"* Nicholson's first directing job, *"The Last Detail,"* *"Chinatown,"* and *"The Missouri Breaks,"* and had just completed producing, writing and directing *"Personal Best,"* starring Mariel Hemingway, for Warners. Towne jumped on it, saying he'd always wanted to write a period picture with big action sequences. Unfortunately, no acceptable screenplay ever emerged, and Jack lost his $50 grand. Oh well, he can afford it. Worse, recent analysis of Napoleon's DNA seems to indicate he died of stomach cancer, not arsenic.

No movie star makes more money than Jack Nicholson. I admire him perhaps more than any actor I can think of because he has kept his same agent for 40 years. Sandy Bresler was a young William Morris agent when he picked an unknown Jack Nicholson up, and Jack stayed with Sandy when he became a star. Which is rarer than a Jew in the astronaut training program. Jack got rich and saw to it that Sandy did too. Sandy, in turn, crafted Jack's standard deal, gross from dollar one, and only a very few actors can get that from a studio, which Jack frequently violates when he wants to help one of his friends out.

Like Francis Coppola, Nicholson is intensely loyal to his friends, and will do a film for them for nothing but a piece when they really need a helping hand. It's always cost him money, as in Jack's making himself available every decade or so to help out his old friend, Bob Rafelson, who hasn't made a successful movie since they made 1981's *"Postman Always Rings Twice."* Rafelson also directed Jack in the first film to get him critical attention, *"Five Easy Pieces,"* in 1970. They did *"The King of Marvin Gardens,"* a flop, two years later, and two more failures, *"Man Trouble,"* in 1992, and *"Blood and Wine,"* in '96. Look for Rafelson to get another chance from Jack around 2010.

JACK H. HARRIS

I've known Jack H. Harris, the producer of *"The Blob,"* 1958's screen debut of Steve McQueen, for over 25 years. Now 90, and in great form, Jack has always lived like a rajah and has known everyone worth knowing in his 60+ years in the film business. He has remade "*The Blob*" four times, the first time with my ex-wife, Carol Lynley, and Larry Hagman, and may just make one more version. Warner Brothers studio had an option on the material via Jon Peters, former lover made producer of Barbra Streisand. Peters, once Hollywood's premiere hairdresser, and the untitled inspiration for Warren Beatty's comedy hit, "*Shampoo*," bedded many of the town's leading actresses that Beatty missed, and lucked into a longish-relationship with Streisand. Barbra couldn't see herself in love with a hairdresser, no matter how famous, so, coinciding with Peter's desire to crash into the movies – he was a failed actor- he became her producer. But she made few films and Jon was "at liberty" lots of the time.

Jack Harris had lived on the beach in Malibu since the early 60s, and knew many of the stars and studio execs who also lived there, among them Streisand and Peters. Peters, who knew next to nothing about the actual filmmaking process, adopted Jack as his mentor and teacher. Peters also developed a father complex about him, and dogged his steps for lessons. Jack, ever the gentleman, obliged, and the two ended up as producers on "The Eyes of Laura Mars," a Columbia picture starring Faye Dunaway. It was a moderate success, at least nothing to be ashamed about, and the relationship between the two men seemed solid. But in Hollywood, nothing is as it seems.

Peters, a street fighter from childhood, battled his way up in the precarious Hollywood jungle, and via his connection to Streisand, whose cachet was platinum, and his studied charm, managed to get his own deals at various studios. He teamed up with Peter Guber, former chairman of Columbia, and they were a hot duo, eventually becoming the men in charge at Sony studios, pride and joy of the very rich Japanese electronics company. But they became such an expensive headache to Sony, they were eventually bought out of their contract for the approximate cost of a new nuclear carrier, and the subject of a derisive book entitled, "*Hit and Run--How Jon Peters and Peter Guber Took Sony for a Ride in Hollywood*", by Vicki Griffith and Kim Masters, in 1996.

Now that Peters was on top and could grant development and production deals to anyone he wanted, including his mistress, Christine, he suddenly stopped taking Jack's calls. Jack was at first unbelieving, then dismayed, then angry, then complacent, and I heard about it through all its stages. When Jack would run into him on the beach, Peters would babble on about being "so busy," and that he would definitely take his next call, etc. But no such luck. Eventually, Jack, who should have known better, finally wrote him off.

Until, two years ago, out of the blue, Jack gets a call from Peters asking if the rights to "*Blob*" were available. For the first time in a long time, they were. Jack called me for a lunch date, at which we discussed Peter's offer. I reminded Jack about the past and used Charlie Brown and the Football as an example. For those non-"Peanuts" fans, once a year, Charlie Brown, everyone's famous fall guy, falls again for the same trick by his sister, who promises him that this time, when she holds a football up for him to kick to inaugurate the new ball season, she won't pull it away just as he leaves the ground for a bone-shuddering thump.

Well, Jack, always up for a fat paycheck, and wanting to believe once more in Peters, signed a contract with Warners for a healthy down payment. And what do you know; once more Jon Peters won't return his calls. Granted, Jack got paid for an option, but his prize asset was off the market for at least two years, preventing anyone else from buying it. Jack couldn't believe it – here he and Peters had an actual production deal at a real studio, and no-one was returning Jack's call, not even the studio executives. I told Jack to make a doll, call it Jon Peters, and stick pins in it. I don't think he did, but we met regularly for lunch to discuss Jack's options, which weren't many. Nothing happened – almost two years go by, and Jack got his picture back. Jack and I had lunch again very recently to discuss what studio might be interested in the film, when he gives me one of the most classic punch lines I've ever heard. There's a caveat in his contract with the studio that specifies that if Warners declines to extend the option, Jon Peters can do so by paying Jack himself. And Jack says, "The son-of-a-bitch will probably pay me the $200,000 due just to spite me." I couldn't contain myself. Only in Hollywood.

007'S CAR

Jerry Pam, my former partner in the P.R. business has, for over 30 years, represented Roger Moore, one of most popular of the James Bonds, and has also represented Michael Caine for almost that long. On occasion, he has looked after Sean Connery, as well, and also does Miramax's academy award campaigns. So you know he's well connected.

As a result of Jerry's closeness to the Bond universe, he managed to snag the publicity account for Aston-Martin, one of the priciest car lines on the planet, and the manufacturer of several of the Bat car-like technological marvels used by the super spy to evade and overwhelm his adversaries. Aston-Martin, which began as a builder of race cars, and wanting to expose their latest model, the $300,000 Lagonda, a four-door saloon, as the Brits call it, to the Hollywood film community, offered to provide Jerry one of these glamour machines. They knew he'd drive it to parties, screenings, premieres, and get himself and some of his star clients photographed in this spiffy sports car. Aston delivered it to Jerry while he was having lunch at one of the film industry in-spots, Le Dome, on the Sunset Strip, and waited for him to emerge. A cameraman they had brought along shot Jerry taking possession of the keys, getting into those buttery leather seats, and smiling broadly as he seat-belted himself. The glittering chrome, the richness of the British Racing Green, the throaty roar of the 300 horsepower engine, was overpowering. Jerry noted that it had only ten miles on the speedometer. He waved and pulled out into traffic.

Not prepared for, and unaware of the Lagonda's powerful engine and high torque, Jerry floored it, intending to leave the crowd with a flourish. Of course it got away from him and he immediately rammed it into a tree on the median. It was a total loss. Jerry also lost the account.

A similar event happened to Dean Martin or, more accurately, to Dean's houseman. At the time, 1975, Dean was living by himself in a house in Trousdale, a high-end development built in the 60s, above Beverly Hills. Only the rich could afford to live there and look down upon the L.A. basin. Dean was on one of his periodic splits from his wife, Jeanne, and was living by himself, with only his houseman-valet for company.

Dean, like Frank Sinatra, was a car nut, and fascinated by the James Bond car, ordered himself a DB-5, the exact model Connery drove as agent 007. Aston-Martins are built when one is ordered, so it took nine months for the car to arrive. The dealer delivered the white, low-slung beauty to Dean's house. Trousdale Road is steep, at least 35 degrees, necessitating low gear both up and down. Dean took delivery, admired it, and went inside. His houseman, a Filipino, thought it would be a good idea to wash it again before his boss took it out for a spin. He got in and started it up with the intention of turning it around in the driveway, and the same thing happened to him as happened to Jerry Pam. Except the car, and houseman, flew over the hill and down a canyon. The Aston was wrecked, but Dean's houseman was only shaken up.

BEAUTY IS AS BEAUTY DOES

I know this is going to get me in trouble, but…beautiful women are (generally) not intellectuals. I'm sorry, but it's true. And it really isn't their fault. Unfortunately, in our society, beauty is all that's necessary for success.

A beautiful girl knows she's beautiful from about age three on. She is celebrated by her parents and extended family, and quickly learns that she can get anything she wants just because she is exceptional. Beautiful people usually hang out with substantially less attractive people, and treat formal learning as a temporary pain until they can cash in on their looks. This gives beautiful people a warped view of the world. Beautiful girls are usually alone on Saturday nights because boys are terrified of approaching them. Although this is a generalization, it has happened: An 18 year-old kid from Memphis, Tennessee, perhaps a local beauty contest winner, can step off a Greyhound bus in L.A. and stumble into an open call for a TV series pilot with six or eight principals – and be hired for their "look" and how they blend with the others. Experience and talent are very rarely necessary, because actors need only say one or more lines, sometimes many times, before a director is satisfied with a "take." The "look" is all.

That pilot could, and has been in the past, picked up, and that kid is suddenly making $17,500 an episode. Or more. Can it make a monster of that kid? Sure, because the investment needed to produce the pilot, and the upfront cost of thirteen episodes, or however many a network orders, is so high, that the talent is treated like superhumans. They suddenly have agents, managers, publicists, lawyers, their own hairdressers and make-up people – all of whom constantly reassure them they are special, immensely talented, and, of course, beautiful. The fact that these advisors and staff are feeding off this kid's salary, not much different than remora, the parasitic fish that attach themselves to sharks, is obscured by the praise. And because once gained, this huge financial and emotional support is impossible to contemplate losing.

But TV shows are cancelled, and one-shot successes in movies happen every day. The kid is suddenly old news. For example, Shannen Doherty, a beautiful kid, lucked into an Aaron Spelling TV show called, "*Beverly Hills, 90210.*" Spelling didn't miss a lot, and this show was a hit. Aaron fired her during the fourth season because of constant conflicts with other cast members and repeatedly late appearances on the set. Spelling was so angry at her lack of professionalism and gratitude for her break that, using edits and digital effects, he removed her entirely from the show's retrospective, an hour-long special which included virtually every other actor in the show's history. Shannen had her wages garnished by California United Bank when she was on "*90210*" because she wrote nearly $32,000 worth of bad checks. By the way, she was being paid $17,500 per episode.

Because she had a little heat from "*90210*" and from her public firing, director Billy Friedkin gave her a job in his film, "*Jailbreakers*," but she infuriated him when she failed to turn up for the first day of shooting in Hollywood. She had just returned from Italy, where she'd raised hell by turning up late for an interview on a television talk-show. Friedkin called auditions and looked at 12 other actresses to take Doherty's part, but because production had already begun, he was forced to keep her.

In 1992, Shannen was a guest on "*The Dennis Miller Show.*" Miller, a comedian, was still new to the talk-show format. She rudely asked him if he was nervous and called attention to his nervously twitching eyebrow. This made headlines the next day and Miller routinely made her the butt of his jokes from then on.

Continuing to spiral downward, she was arrested in 2001 for drunk-driving and sentenced to either ten days in jail, or twenty days of work-release duty, three years probation, and ordered to pay a $1500 fine. She was again arrested when she got into an argument with a 22 year-old actor and smashed a beer bottle on his car window as he tried to drive away from her, in 1996. She was sentenced by the Beverly Hills Municipal Court to a year's worth of anger management counseling.

In 1997, Doherty appeared in a B movie, "*Nowhere*," in which she was billed as "Valley Chick #2." "Valley Chick #1 was played by Traci Lords, the former porn star. Second billing to a porn star? Did I mention that Shannen was from Memphis, Tennessee? More recently, Shannen got another chance, playing a role on a Warner Brothers TV series called, "*Charmed*," about a bunch of teenage witches. After a series of arguments with co-star Alyssa Milano, Shannen was dumped. She continues to work fairly regularly in TV episodes and B-movies.

Rebellious? Obviously. But, in my experience, beautiful and smart do not usually go together. I have not targeted this actress – I've never met her, and I use her as an example only because it happened and it's on the public record.

Winona Ryder, another very talented actress, nominated for two Oscars, was arrested in 2001 for shoplifting from the Saks Fifth Avenue store, in Beverly Hills. I don't know what Francis Coppola paid her for his version of "*Dracula*," in 1992, but if she didn't get at least a million dollars, her agent was derelict. She was found guilty of felony grand theft and vandalism, and sentenced to three years of probation, fines and 480 hours of community service time. Beauty is as beauty does.

Albert Einstein said that as he got more famous, he got more stupid. Imagine that. From his point of view, it was true, because he did his best work in his 20s, long before his theories made him a celebrity. He was then so distracted that he never again achieved anything of real significance.

Former vice president, the good-looking Dan Quayle, said that he wished he had studied Latin more when he was in school, so that he could have conversed better with the folks he met on a tour of Latin America. And what was it that Jessica Simpson, the beautiful TV actress said about wondering if Chicken of the Sea Tuna was made from chickens?

SEXUAL ADDICTION

Beautiful women have been my obsession and my profession all my life. They both fascinate me and terrify me. Unable to ever please my overbearing and emotionally and physically violent mother, I devoted my youth and most of my adulthood to pleasing any woman I could. I dated them, married them, represented them, hired and fired them, and, in general admired them. And still do. I know a lot about what constitutes beautiful women and their behavior. After all, I was at various times, in a position to raise the status in Hollywood of any number of beautiful young women. So completely fixated was I, that I developed a nasty case of Satyriasis, which if you didn't know, is male nymphomania. Another popular name for it is sexual addiction.

There were times I was seeing as many as seven women at once. I thought then that was a glamorous version of me. But each wanted to be with me on Saturday night, or on my birthday, or on Christmas. You get the picture. Where was I when I wasn't with them, they wanted to know? I created much anger because the lies I was telling were too difficult to keep track of. I always got caught eventually, and any Freudian will assure you I wanted to be caught. Perhaps I did. But it didn't stop me, no more than a gambler can stop gambling, or an overeater can pass a Krispy Kreme stand, without serious intervention.

I thought I had graced the edge of Nirvana one afternoon, when I hosted a table of four, myself and three women at the Polo Lounge of the Beverly Hills Hotel, to celebrate the conclusion of a successful fund-raising for a major Los Angeles charity. Two of the women were married, and the other was the public relations coordinator for the event. I was having sex with all three at the time, unbeknownst to any of them. Under the table, feet were moving. I was almost delirious. I was turned on, like all power-hungry men, by knowing each's secrets, and having what I imagined was control over so many women at the same time.

The orgy circuit I occasionally traveled in the '70s was as much social and business as it was about sex. The Marshall manse in Rancho Mirage, although populated by swingers, also was, by his invitation only, open to male casting directors, producers, directors, and actors and actresses. On occasion, a female film worker who liked the action was also invited. This tended to bring him closer to the people he did business with, or wanted to draw nearer into his agency operation. After all, once you've shared certain intimacies with people, you've formed an affinity group. Although no pictures were taken (that I know of), obvious secrets were manifested, which could be kept – or not.

Orgies in Paris, Madrid, Mexico City, Acapulco, and Cuernavaca, a wealthy vacation town some fifty miles from Mexico City favored by the Jet Set, were both business and social, in that I was in those cities on business, and the people I met at grand homes were rich and occasionally famous. Sometimes these events, which would go on for several days, would lead to lucrative contracts, or financing for entertainment projects. If one were affable, polite, and educated, one invitation would lead to another. I found then, as an American, that, unlike today, we were looked up to and admired.

For years I specialized in married women. Statistically, seventy-five percent of men cheat on their spouses. No surprise there. But fifty percent of married women cheat on their husbands. And they are everywhere. I've been picked up in the produce department of supermarkets, on city streets, while driving, in the normal course of business, or, believe it or not, by referral.

Married women, in my opinion, are the best lovers. They are anxious to please, because they've been in long-term arrangements where sex has become a sometime thing, and they're certain they've lost their appeal – but they're wonderfully grateful, and it's a good feeling to know you've helped them in concrete ways. Think I'm conceited? Patronizing? Read on.

I'm a pretty good cook, so lunchtimes were always ideal. One has to eat, yes? I'd make a light but nutritious and creative meal, with a suitable wine, following which we'd explore each other's passions for a couple of hours. I'd hear all about their lives, and why marriage was so difficult, how in-laws sucked, children were ungrateful, husbands only interested in business and sports, how their illusions about life had vanished, and their youth and beauty were gone.

I, however, was delighted to remind them that their looks, their bodies, their passion, their sexuality, and their ability to please a man, were all intact. Here was the proof. And then they'd leave.

I've often heard from them that their marriages improved, that they'd become more loving not only to their husbands, but to their children, as well. There were many women, but not once did I hear from any of them that they wanted to leave their situations for me. Nor did I ever want them to. They had their homes, their positions in their communities, their charge accounts, soccer games, hair and nail appointments, and SUVs. And I was glad of it.

Some medical doctors or psychiatrists will tell you that mania can't be created by environment, but must be located in a faulty gene structure. Not true, at least in my case, because after many years of destructive behavior that cost me marriages, relationships, job, and a great deal of pain, I took serious action to beat my problem. Over the years, I had psychological counseling from psychiatrists, and psychologists, including a former nun. I thought she, as a woman, might have some special insight. But what would a nun know about a man's sexual nightmares? She might know about her own.

I learned a few things during hypnosis, from a professional hypnotherapist, a woman I was dating, who said she could cure me. But right after the session we would immediately have sex.

I even tried a 12-step program fashioned on the successful Alcoholics Anonymous model, but devoted to my particular addiction. "*Sexaholics Anonymous*" was a lot of fun. Did I get anything out of it? I got laid - a lot. Imagine a group of sex addicts, at least half of them attractive women who can't say no, and you see what was for me, Toyland. I sold it to myself as "research" for the script I was writing. The program was located in Hollywood. Imagine being able to find a sex addicts group in Hollywood?

I was told I could examine my devils better by writing about my feelings, keeping a journal of my thoughts, desires, and how I coped with them. But having been around creative people all my life, naturally I wrote a screenplay about a guy who has everything he's ever wanted, who throws it all away – over and over – for a quick orgasm. Sound familiar? Many powerfully-seen men have the same problem, and it's linked to the same kind of childhood I had. Former president, Bill Clinton, comes to mind. The most powerful man in the universe risks being fired and denigrated in the history books forever for a furtive, half-completed blow job behind a door in the Oval Office? You couldn't write that into a movie and get away with it. But of course it happened.

And what about John Edwards? Governor Mark Sanford? Nevada senator John Ensign? New York governor Elliot Spitzer? Representative David Vitter? Senator Larry Craig? Representative Mark Foley? Going back a few years, Gary Hart? And I know at least a half dozen other guys I've met over the years, in and out of the business, with the same problem. Henry Kissinger once remarked that sex and power are intertwined. He would know! What is so striking to me is that there is absolutely no way to get away with it anymore. Clinton got caught because someone talked. Twitter, Facebook, and websites like TMZ paying for tips guarantee instant outing. In the groups that I mediated, I called these people "danger junkies." Driving like a maniac, jumping off a bridge tied to a rubber band, confronting strangers who may be psychotic, or even armed – fits that description. So does infidelity for public figures. Combine that with a feeling of entitlement – because people voted for you, and it's instant career death.

Part of the reason is, of course, that power corrupts. All of us suffered through childhood feeling powerless – because we were. Parents made the rules, and we had better obey them. Our personalities are formed by the time we're five – and earlier these days, as kids are flooded with information and images I probably didn't encounter until I was teenager. Woe unto others once we get into a position where we could rule over subordinates. And that goes for both men and women!

Odd that most of these guys are Republicans. A poll came out in the last days of June 2009, which reported that the highest rates of porn subscription, teen pregnancy, and infidelity occurred in the so-called "Red" states – the seat, nay, the rump of conservatism. The highest rates of divorce happen among social conservatives. The only way to evaluate this is to blame repression of natural and normal feelings and emotions – which arises most among "religious" people. And I'm not talking here about the problems now very visible among catholic clergy – both priests and nuns, from the U.S. to Ireland, and beyond. "Family Values," which conservatives interchangeably call "Moral Values," leads to aberrant behavior because natural human desires are stifled. But like anything that is stuffed, from feelings to drainpipes, there will be an explosion.

There's a joke concerning Donald Trump – He's in an elevator going up in his Trump Tower, when it stops on a floor, and beautiful girl enters, sees it's him, and exclaims, "Donald Trump! I've dreamed of this moment. I want to suck your cock and fuck you to death." He thinks about it for a moment, and then says, "Ok, but what's in it for me?"

Was my problem dangerous? Very. But that doesn't faze addicts. After all, what's another drop of water to a drowning man? Diseases were always a possibility, but probably because of a strong immune system, I never got any. Outraged husbands or boyfriends were something to look out for, but except for the time an LAPD motorcycle cop almost pulled his gun on me, I always got away with it.

A recent not-so-funny story about a friend of mine, David Stein: A few minutes past midnight he is cruising the Internet, accessing one of several of the dating services he is registered on, which has an instant message feature, when to his surprise, a woman pops on and says "Hi." He answers back and 5 minutes of email banter later, he invites her to call him. A several-minute conversation leads to an in invitation, and believe it or not, of all the places in the Universe she could be, she lives ten minutes away from him. Fancy that.

Ten minutes later he is at her door with a bottle of champagne, and minutes after that, they are in bed. David acquits himself well and is feeling grand on his way home at 2:45 a.m., when two Newport Beach cops pull him over, saying he was crossing the white line. Cops always pull motorists over in slack time with a weak excuse just to toss the car and its inhabitants to see what they can find. Sometimes they say it's a broken taillight, or they couldn't see the license renewal tag. It's usually bogus because their sergeant will want to know what they were doing between midnight and 6 a.m. if they haven't got a caseload.

While one cop administered a roadside DUI test, the other got to work seeing what he could find. He ignored the two joints in David's ashtray because it's merely a $100 citation for under an ounce, but sparked to the large wrench with the taped handle peeking out from under David's front seat. "Ah Ha," he said, "A deadly weapon." Out come the handcuffs and David's on his way to the slammer, while his car is towed to the impound.

David is in the rag business and drives around the worst parts of downtown at all hours and kept the wrench in case he ever needed it. No matter. He is photographed, fingerprinted, outfitted in orange jumpsuit pajamas and safely locked away. Bail is $4,000. Next morning, given a yellow pages, David locates a bail bondsman who springs him. The same yellow pages produce a law firm who will gladly take the case. So, ten grand later, David is free and able to concentrate on the message here, which is: One minute David is getting laid. Next minute, David's in jail. How perfect. How expensive. And how dangerous. The woman could have been a psycho; she could have been a lure for a robbery. Anything's possible. But for a sex addict, no logic or reason applies.

I finally controlled my addiction through yoga and meditation. After I left my marriage to Linda Jones, I moved into a penthouse apartment in Beverly Hills, determined to rein in my impulses because it was costing me the things I most wanted. I dated around, of course - I hadn't died, and through one young lady, met her married friends, Leon and Barbara. There was an ideal couple if ever I saw one. He had been a serious marijuana dealer in the 60s, made a pile of dough, and got out. He invested in the stock market and did well, so even though he was in his mid-30s, he was retired. Barbara was a fabulous cook, and her friend, Jane, and I looked forward to evenings at their home.

Leon was very cultured, well read, and knew a lot about classical music. He had two Master's degrees, one in political science, and the other in philosophy. He took an interest in me, and suggested we breakfast together alone on Saturday mornings.

My father had loved classical music and it was always on in our home when I was growing up. I thought I knew quite a bit about it, but Leon taught me how to listen and broadened my taste. Although I hadn't gone to college, as a result of my father's early death, I had, from childhood, been an autodidact. I read everything I could, and still do. I'll read the labels on ketchup bottles while waiting for my lunch. Not long ago, my girlfriend, Lori, saw me reading some arcane (to her) magazine, and asked me if I read everything? "Yes," I said. To which she asked, "Why?" She's so adorable. And blonde.

Leon and I would sit in my apartment and chat about politics, relationships, music, of course, philosophy, and pretty soon I was hooked. Another addiction, but this time, a healthy one.

One day Leon asked me what I knew about Eastern religions, and specifically Yoga. I replied I thought Yoga was some sort of cult. He laughed, and said the following Saturday we'd do some. I thought he was nuts, but I was afraid to upset him because I had come to depend on our Saturdays. They had enlightened me and I was much calmer, and seeing things very differently compared to when I had met him. That next meeting, he stripped down to his underwear, and I finally figured it out – he was gay, and this had been an elaborate set-up. I felt trapped and not a little panicky. Especially when he suggested I do the same. I didn't know what else to do – so I did.

But it was just Yoga. I was so stiff I couldn't even bend forward or completely turn my head in any direction. Leon said it would be very difficult at first, that he had been doing it for some 12 years, and that it would be six months before I saw any real progress. But not to worry, that he'd be there. It was the most arduous and grueling thing I had ever attempted. The pain was intense and Leon was a hard teacher. After six months, on schedule, my muscles began to ease and pleasure replaced pain for the most part. We continued on for another year; elaborate dinners cooked by Barbara, Saturday mornings with Leon for Yoga. Jane, their friend, and I ended our relationship during that time, because she was anxious to marry, having just turned 30, and I was a long way from being ready for that again.

Yoga had become part of my life and I found myself always stretching, because it was so powerfully pleasurable – while driving, in meetings, wherever. The endorphins I was creating in my brain had become addictive; remember I have an addictive personality, and I couldn't stop. My business partner at the time told me that people thought I had some muscular disease and were worried about me. I had no idea I was presenting this way. It just felt so good.

Eventually, Leon asked me what I knew about meditation. For some reason, this question frightened me on a deep level. I said I didn't know much about it, and I didn't want to. Of course Leon said we would begin the following Saturday, but in between he wanted me to register for some classes in meditation at TM, or Transcendental Meditation, the program brought to America by the Guru to the Beatles, the Maharishi. I said I couldn't afford to go, to which Leon pulled three one hundred dollar bills from his pocket, saying, "Now you can." I had no choice.

I enrolled in classes given in a church in Hollywood and over three nights of four hours each, was introduced to the rudiments of meditation, even receiving my own, personal Sanskrit word, whispered in my ear, as my mantra. Saturdays from that time on were an hour of Yoga and another of meditation. It was a bitch – my mind raced, I became angry, and I had periods of great fear. Leon said not to worry – it would be six months. He was right again. I had begun to be able to control my mind, at least for a few seconds at first, and then a few minutes until, eventually, I had gone over the edge and was exceeding the mandated 20 minutes, and drifting along somewhere in the cosmos for half an hour or more. One time, I woke up an hour later. That made me very apprehensive. Although I knew where I was at all times, and could hear traffic on the street below, subconsciously I had literally been away from my body. That was a first. I began to meditate twice a day, and was able to exercise some control so that I awakened at 20 minutes, plus or minus a few minutes, regularly.

In my trances, I began to examine where my impulses came from, I saw myself as a young child, interacting with my mother, the strongest influence on me, and my father, and started to recognize where my habit patterns first got created – usually as a defense mechanism against my mother. I was able to recast my early life while in trance, and understood my mother's powerful need to control everything around her, because she had been orphaned at age fifteen, and married my father immediately. Worse, her father had never married her mother, so she was also illegitimate. I saw clearly how she eventually froze my dad out in favor of me, and what responsibility she had placed on me as his replacement. She literally drove me crazy, so by the time I was eighteen, I was in therapy.

My fractured relationships with women, and my need to first please and then control them, directly resulted from my inability to ever do anything right from my mother's point of view. I realized with a start that I had always been afraid of my mother, and therefore had spent my life to that moment afraid of women in general. That jolting insight made me realize very clearly that the only person I could exercise any control over was myself. I viscerally felt the fear I had harbored about being controlled by another woman literally melting away. I have had a number of relationships since, but we now enjoy each other's company as equals, and have always converted our feelings to friendship, remaining in close personal touch over the years.

Through Leon's intervention, I became a different person. He was now about 40, and one Saturday, he informed me we wouldn't be seeing each other again. Stunned, I asked why? He said he had some things to work out personally and was leaving Barbara for a while. I couldn't comprehend what he was saying. I thought they were very much in love and had the best life together. Leon moved into a small apartment near the beach and, although he asked me not to contact him, Barbara gave me what information she was able to get, because he didn't want to see her either.

Apparently, he would get up each morning, and go to a local bar, where he would sit and drink until it closed. This went on for several months, until Barbara called me and said Leon had died. Just like that.

I was truly shaken. It just didn't add up. I thought Leon was the most evolved, intelligent, and compassionate person I had ever met. I couldn't understand what had obviously been his suicide. Barbara told me that a memorial was planned for him in Santa Monica, at Poet's Corner, in the park above the ocean. I thought perhaps there'd be just a few people.

Another surprise. There were nearly a hundred people, none of whom I had ever met, and most of whom Barbara hadn't known either. One by one, people got up to talk about what Leon had meant in their lives, and by now I shouldn't have expected to be surprised, but I was again.

When, after the tenth or so person related a similar experience with him, it began to dawn on me that Leon was having, or had had the same effect on all those people there, either at the same time he was helping me change, or in the past. I couldn't stay after that, and slowly walked away, my mind reeling. I still don't know what to think about Leon's mission here on earth. He didn't believe, as a rational person, in a god, or in religion, even though he had had a thorough Jewish upbringing. He had never mentioned he had been working with other people besides me, and I was probably too self-involved – and selfish in my greed for personal recovery, to even suspect I was sharing him. Over the years, it began to occur to me he was some kind of messenger, perhaps a spiritual teacher in the mode of a Buddha, or a Jesus. But then I came back to my senses. Maybe he just liked the power he had over people.

I decided my story needed some humor, so I wrote my screenplay as a comedy. It's funny, except to the guy whose story it is, since it seems lots of people around him want to get even for the grief he's visited on them. It's been optioned three times, but so far, no producer has had the courage to make it. Oh well, perhaps we'll have a woman president one day.

Ben Franklin, our founder, had the same affliction and wrote about it. He loved women, all women. He said about older women; "Not only are they discreet, but extremely grateful. And besides, in the dark, all cats are gray." The only cure, it seems, is age. At a certain point testosterone levels drop enough so that the addiction wanes in favor of other needs that become more important. Ben wrote that he was relieved when he couldn't manage an erection anymore – it was such pressure.

I'm struck how the culture has promoted youth sex. I saw two movies in the past several years, "*Bully*," and "*Thirteen*," that openly talk about, and even show sex acts between children as young as 12. I assume the actors are 18. A good friend has a 12 year-old daughter who is making him frantic. Because I have some experience in counseling, he asked me to sit with them and try to elicit what was going on with her. I've known this little girl since she was eight, and a sweeter, brighter child, other than my own, of course, couldn't be found. I got some eye-opener from her – from the popular drugs of choice, to what sex was being done during and after school. Oral and anal sex is very popular among the pre-teen set these days, because of the avoidance of pregnancy. Clearly, I was born too early. When I was twelve, my mother was still cutting my meat.

SIC TRANSIT GLORIA

Nope, this is not about a girl named Gloria who got ill on the bus, but the Latin phrase, which translates as "Fame is fleeting." Let's see, who do we know that was hot, and is now, not? The movie, "*Gladiator*," won the Oscar for Best Picture in the year 2000. Starring in it were Russell Crowe, and Connie Neilsen. Crowe won the Oscar for Best Actor. What happened to the beautiful Danish actress that played Crowe's love interest? I thought she was terrific. Neilsen has done a couple of pictures since, but nothing special. I find that amazing. And she's not getting any younger, either.

One of my favorite films is "*Amadeus*," the story of Mozart, directed by that master director, Milos Forman, in 1984. Starring in it, as Mozart, was an unknown actor named Tom Hulse. I thought he was wonderful. The film was a critical and box office hit. Seen Tom Hulse around lately? How about Mira Sorvino, who won an Oscar in Woody Allen's "*Mighty Aphrodite?*" Or Wes Bentley, an instant success after "*American Beauty?*"

And of course, there's Jim Caveziel (rhymes with weasel). He played Jesus in Mel Gibson's, "*Passion of the Christ*," the appalling but very profitable, hysterical if nor historical, re-telling of the alleged betrayal of this most admirable figure (if indeed he ever existed) by the power structure of his tribe, the Jews. He's been in a couple of small films since then, but his intense association with that role limits his chances in the future.

If, by some chance, an actor, director or writer, does become a "star," in that they are subsequently employable, it is usually a matter of luck and timing to be able to extend that moment more or less indefinitely. For every Tom Hanks, there are most likely 100 actors who achieved a brief flash of visibility in some film or TV show, before flaming out. And another 900 who never even got a chance.

Acting is a terrible business – Of some 150,000 members of the various acting guilds, less than one percent actually earns a living at it. But the same is true of directors, producers, writers, grips, electricians, camera people, make-up and hairdressers, prop masters, and all the other crafts associated with entertaining us.

My ex-wife, Carol Lynley, early in our marriage went to an audition for some role, either in a film, or commercial, I don't remember which. When I got home from work, she was in tears. "What's wrong, honey," I asked? "I didn't get the part," she sobbed. "So? You're a professional; you know acting is 99.9% rejection, why are you taking this so hard?" And she gave me the ultimate actor's answer: "I've heard every reason I didn't get a job - that I was too short, or too tall, my nose wasn't long enough, I was too thin, or too fat." "Yeah, so what did they tell you this time?" I said. "That I wasn't neurotic enough, and then I broke down and started crying, and said, but I am neurotic…I am neurotic." I felt so bad for her.

Carol was happiest when she got a job. Then she could adopt a new personality, live in a new world, wear someone else's clothes, be called by another's name, speak words written for her and, above all, take direction. And that's what I found was the rule when I was an agent.

Actors are also their own worst enemies. I was quoted in a TV Guide article about how actors, in collusion with their agents, lawyers, accountants, managers, and press agents, regard contracts the way a baby regards diapers. I remarked how actors can get bad advice from a number of sources, telling the insecure and influencable talent that they're not being paid enough, they're being ripped off. It's a double-edged sword, however, because if you overestimate the importance of your client, they, and you, can be out of a job. An example I gave was a Desi Arnaz show called, "*The Mothers in Law*," which had as one of its four stars, an actor named Roger C. Carmel. The show didn't do well in the ratings, and was tentative for a second year. The network offered a pickup if the show could be made for the same price as year one. All the personnel agreed to forego their contractual bump. Except Carmel. He was certain audiences would revolt if at the start of the new season, if Kaye Ballard had a different husband with no explanation of what had happened to him. He wouldn't back down and he received a telegram telling him he was history. Richard Deacon showed up the following season in Carmel's part and not a single soul wrote in to ask what had happened. And how do I know this? I was Roger's agent.

Lee Rich, who headed that successful TV show factory, Lorimar, told the actors in "*Rat Patrol*," that since it was a war show, he could kill any of them off any time he wanted, so they'd better shut up and go back to work.

Carroll O'Connor walked off "*All in the Family*," and Redd Fox ankled (as they say in Variety, the showbiz bible) "*Sanford and Son*," and even Suzanne Pleshette, a veteran actor who one would think had better sense, tried to pull a strike on the producers of "*The Bob Newhart Show*," by not showing up for work the first week of production. The producers, and Newhart himself, warned her that Newhart could get a divorce, or she could get killed in a traffic accident. On the show, of course. She reported to work the next day.

I concluded my remarks in the TV Guide piece by saying that it's standard practice in show business not to live up to one's contract, and the simple reason is greed.

Actors in hit TV series, for example, will threaten to quit, or not show up, or get sick, in order to extort more money from hapless producers whose budgets are locked in the by the networks, or cable nets. The inside term for this is, "eating the jumps," or somehow swallowing their demands, and putting possible profits that much further away, if at all. A recent example of this is the terribly lucky cast of the NBC smash "*Friends*." A dozen years ago, no one had heard of this bunch of youngsters, who lucked out by having the "look" the producers wanted for their show. Only somewhat talented, and unable to generate much box-office power once their fans are asked to pay to see them, as proven by their inabilities to graduate to movie stars, with the exception of Jennifer Anniston, they are comforted, I'm sure, by their last year's salary of $1 million each for each 22- minute show. Times 22 shows. They may find occasional work again, but it's not a lock.

Jerry Seinfeld doesn't need to do anything but his stand-up act for fun, and an occasional American Express commercial, but his TV playmates, Michael Richards, and Jason Alexander, haven't been successful on their own as yet on TV. Alexander has had a couple of pilots, and has been doing stage work, which is strenuous and, I'm sure fun at times, but less people will see him in Mel Brook's "*The Producers*" in two years than would watch him in a single episode of any TV series. As for Richards, he self-destructed while performing in a comedy club by insulting several African-Americans.

Ask David Caruso if he's glad to have gotten on "*CSI*," and pay his bills again. He thought he was bigger than "*NYPD Blue*," jumping out after a couple of seasons of a show that finally quit after eleven years, and found himself out of the business after appearing in several horrible movies. He came back to TV on his hands and knees.

Rob Morrow, who put one of my favorite shows, "*Northern Exposure*," into a tailspin by his attitude and hostility to the producers and other actors of this quirky, critically acclaimed TV series, survived a near-death experience when the show was cancelled and he reached out to the community for work. Sure, he got a few minor movie jobs, but I'm certain he's thrilled his new show, "*Numbers*," is getting respectable numbers.

Another good example is James Gandolfini's demands for a five hundred percent increase in his salary to return to "*The Sopranos*," on HBO. Yep, he got it, and I'm glad, since I loved watching the show. But is it fair to the network? I don't see why they should be held up at gunpoint, as it were, after making him a household name. Gandolfini's was and is, and will always be a character actor, not a leading man. Prior to his role as "Tony Soprano," he had had a couple of co-starring parts in movies, but was usually cast as a heavy in an assembly of actors.

I understand the credo, and I used it as justification myself as an agent, to get it while you can, that the public is fickle and, as Werner Ehrhard, the founder of est was fond of saying, "When you're hot, you're hot; when you're not, you're not." But it's still armed robbery, and deleterious to the business.

The recent economic meltdown has re-ordered priorities in Hollywood, both in movies and TV. Star vehicles are not bringing asses to the seats, as Jack Warner used to say. "*Land of the Lost*," with Will Ferrell, "*Year One*," with Jack Black, "*Imagine That*," with Eddie Murphy, and the remake of "*Taking of Pelham 123*," with both Denzel Washington and Russell Crowe, "*State of Play*," also with Crowe, "*Duplicity*," with Julia Roberts, "*Lions for Lambs,*" and "*Valkyrie*," both starring Tom Cruise, and even Robert Downey, in "*The Soloist*," have all underperformed, to be kind. Worse for these actors, Ferrell, Black, Roberts, Murphy and Crowe's last several films also bombed. Films with unknown actors are doing well. "*The Hangover*," for example, made for a measly $35 million, with actors I hadn't heard of before, is a big boxoffice hit. Special effects, like "*Transformers,*" "*Star Trek,*" and animation/family films, such as Disney's "*Up,*" and "*Harry Potter*," are now what people want to see. Adults are no longer sought by movie studios – these days, its families and teenage boys who are the targets.

As a result, the star system, created almost from the day movies were made, is done for. Salaries for all talent are on an elevator ride down, and no-one knows where it will stop. The most recent example of fiction starring as script "problems," was Sony's closing down of "*Moneyball*," a movie about baseball, five days from production. This flick was to star Brad Pitt, a terrific actor who sometimes brings in the fans – and sometimes doesn't. I read the budget was some $58 million. Baseball movies, like all American sports, get mal de mere when traveling outside the U.S.

"The script" was blamed, and that statement may have some truth because Steven Soderberg, the director, wanted to shoot interviews with people who knew the protagonist of the film well enough to talk about their remembrances, according to press reports. Warren Beatty did the same thing in *"Reds,"* a wonderfully artistic film set during the Russian revolution in the early 20th Century. The studio wanted a straight narrative, so they say. The real reason, I suspect has more to with the eventual cost of making, promoting, advertising, and distributing a picture with limited appeal, I would guess, all in, $150 million – even in the U.S. Brad Pitt's deal, as a major star, calls for a gross position, wherein he gets paid before anyone, including the studio. Although *"The Curious Case of Benjamin Button,"* did OK eventually at the boxoffice, it was not a barn-burner. Neither was *"The Assassination of Jesse James,"* earlier last year, another Pitt vehicle. Is Pitt declining in popularity – or is he simply picking non-commercial stories? If only Soderberg had agreed to film it the studio's way, say the honchos at Sony, they would have been glad, nay, eager to go ahead. How come, then, when they released Soderberg and Pitt, and the script out to bids at any other studio, no one jumped at it?

The slide in paying for "names," has only been accelerating. In the last couple of years, just three of the 10 highest-grossing films – *"War of the Worlds,"* *"Charlie and the Chocolate Factory,"* and *"Mr. and Mrs. Smit*h" (Brad Pitt, with his wife, Angelina Jolie), had above-the-title stars. The rest, *"Star Wars: Episode III,"* – *"Revenge of the Sith,"* *"Harry Potter and the Goblet of Fire,"* and *"The Chronicles of Narnia,"* were star-less. My friends on the inside have been telling me for the last several years about how studios are slowly ratcheting down deals they would have killed their relatives for just two years ago. I understand Sony wouldn't make *"The Holiday"* until Cameron Diaz acceded to a "cash break-even" deal. Tom Cruise supposedly took a lower cut of the grosses than his usual 25% for Paramount to open their wallets to *"Mission Impossible 3."* *"Believe It or Not,"* a Jim Carrey starrer was cancelled by Paramount, and Fox turned down another Carrey film, *"Used Guys."* Both studios claimed the budgets were too high. But clearly, Carrey's star has lost some of its shine. The net result is that studios have discovered they can make money without stars.

I think the announcement from the Academy of Motion Picture Arts and Sciences that the best picture nomination list is being enlarged from five to ten spots is another death vector for the film business. Once again it's all about money. The last few TV Oscar shows have nose-dived in viewership. Opening the awards to teen-pop pictures might get the kids to watch.

Some years I can't think of even five that deserve a nomination. I've heard from both sides among my friends and associates. Pictures that do well at the boxoffice, like *"Spiderman,"* or *"Iron Man,"* aren't considered because they're not "art." Films with no one we've heard of, from odd countries like India, win the Oscar for Best Picture. Forget about *"Star Trek,"* or *"Transformers,"* or *"Up"* – they're popcorn/bubble gum pic for kids. But films like *"Doubt,"* or *"The Wrestler;"* that's another story. As a matter of fact they do have stories. And good acting. And good directing. Obviously they deserve to be nominated. Well, I do believe that, and it's probably because I grew up before the slick F/X, computer-generated technology had been invented. Films with stories were what Hollywood made – from *"Lassie Come Home,"* to *"The Best Years of Our Lives."*

I read a review of a new book recently – *"Management Rewired,"* by Charles Jacobs, in which Jacobs points out that as animals, and we are, human emotions pre-dated logic and reason – that we prefer stories because that's the way our minds naturally work and that's the way we evolved to make sense of the world. He goes on to insist there is no such thing as objectivity, and that we all operate from our personal versions of reality. Clearly that's true. If we see it, it's real. If we're told about it, that's faith. And that's a choice.

Special effects were clumsy in the 50s and 60s, with guys like Ray Harryhausen doing lumbering stop-motion with clay figures and puppets for potboilers like *"It came From Beneath the Sea,"* in 1955. No one took them seriously, and although kids could be frightened, it was all in good fun. Today's F/X can scare the hell out of me, and since life these days is scary enough, I don't feel the need to add more.

I went into politics, when John Plaxco, an eminent Democratic Party fundraiser offered me the position of Southern California Finance Director for our present senator, Diane Feinstein's first senate race, in 1992. I was fed up with the lying, low-down, back-stabbing Hollywood crowd, and thought, dumbly, as it turned out, that politics was on some kind of higher level of endeavor.

Ron Burkle, one of California's richest dudes, who owned most of the supermarkets in the state, was a reliable and generous supporter of the Democrats. He hosted a weekend retreat at his multi-million dollar cliff top Laguna home for Feinstein, where I got to meet candidate Bill Clinton, Missouri Congressman, Dick Gephardt, former vice president, Walter Mondale, and a gang of high roller contributors. I thought I was involved in something significant, at last. Boy, was I disappointed. I had been in lots of Hollywood meetings, where properties were stolen, profits were diverted, credits purloined, but even that paled in the light of what contributors were to have access to what politician, and who would be appointed to what ambassador's post if they wrote a check for such an amount; what would the blacks be promised, what can be thrown to the Latinos? In short, who and what could be bought?

Feinstein won. I was then hired to be campaign manager for Dennis Sinclair, a candidate in a local race - Malibu city council. I got to write, produce and direct commercials, design media ads, set up interviews, run a phone bank, and oversee volunteers. It was great fun.

One of the better-known democratic operatives in Malibu is Maryann Hamill, wife of Mark Hamill, "Luke Skywalker" in the first *"Star Wars"* movie. Maryann ran our phone bank out of her home, overlooking the Pacific. Mark was out of town. Apparently he was out of town a lot. I asked her what Mark had been doing all those years between *"Star Wars"* and then. She said Mark, after he became an overnight sensation in the George Lucas film, decided he really wanted to do theatre. And left town. What a career mistake that was. Harrison Ford stayed around, worked for Lucas' friend, Steven Spielberg, and became one of the top stars of his generation.

Mickey Spillane, the author of the *"Mike Hammer"* private detective series, and the fifth most-translated author in the world (after Lenin, Tolstoy, Gorky and Jules Verne, no kidding) says, "An actor is someone who hates himself so much he has to be someone else."

So why is show business so alluring to so many? Because it's easier than working for a living, and when you're not employed, especially in warm, sunny Los Angeles, you can hang out with others of your profession and not feel like you're a failure. But the real reason is - that to be a big success in show business, you don't need experience, ability, or even talent.

Talent cannot be taught – you either can act, or direct, or write, or you can't. As a former talent agent, independent producer, studio executive, studio producer, press agent, personal manager and more, I can assure you that when young actors talk about their acting coaches, or classes, they're being shaped and propagandized by failed actors who teach because it's all they can do. And that goes for the fabled Actor's Studio also. I think it's a shame there isn't more stringent oversight of the many scams directed at gullible young people to separate them from their scarce funds, in their quest for fame.

Film schools can and do teach aspiring directors, camera people, editors, and the like the mechanics of filmmaking, much as vocational schools can teach young people to repair cars, but better than ninety percent of film school graduates never earn a decent living after they graduate. How do I know? Because I was a regular guest speaker at UCLA and USC film classes given by such artistic luminaries as film critic Arthur Knight, of the Saturday Review, author and professor Donald Freed, TV Emmy winner, writer, Morgan Gendel, and lots of others. I have addressed seminars given by TV actor Hugh O'Brian, Founder of HOBY (Hugh O'Brian Youth Leadership), which helps recognize leadership potential in high school sophomores. The Hugh O'Brian Acting Awards Competition was developed in 1964 at UCLA with cash awards going to acting talents. I have also guest-spoken at Pepperdine University, the Westlake School, Mount St. Mary's and Loyola, in Los Angeles. I have been retained on occasion as an authoritative source on international entertainment and have been quoted in Time, Newsweek, TV Guide, and in various newspapers and books on the subjects of contracts and changing mores and social values in the media. I have also appeared on national and international television programs, commenting on Hollywood studio history, and been an expert witness in court and for various Hollywood guilds.

LYING FOR A LIVING

In Hollywood, everyone lies. I was also going to use the phrase, well known out here, "Good Morning, He Lied," but Lynda Obst beat me to it with an incisive book she wrote in 1996 about Hollywood. Hers was entitled; "*Hello, he Lied,*" but you get it.

I had a partner once who would lie to me about his morning bowel movement. I was so annoyed with him that I checked with his wife, who confirmed what I already knew. That he was constipated, and had been for days. That was also a description of him. Why does everyone lie in Hollywood? For the pleasure. For the power derived from superiority, to get a job, and to delude themselves that they matter. In fact, nobody matters. In Hollywood, you don't live long enough. In career time, I mean.

A recent public hallucination had the newly-elected leader of the Writer's Guild West, Charles Holland, inventing a career for himself that included the U.S. military's Special Forces, in conjunction with the CIA, and a mythical football scholarship to a major university. That he lied about in public, in an interview in the WGA official publication, is egregious enough, but when confronted with absolute proof that his story was a falsehood, he continued to insist it was true, citing "national security" reasons. Beyond that, as he was poised to begin negotiations on behalf of his union with the major studios, his board of directors, other writers, voted to keep him in place because, get this, "That's what writers do, they make up stories." He was fired, of course.

On the public record is a letter written by Disney CEO, Michael Eisner, to his once-best friend, former super agent, Michael Ovitz, in which he advised him to resign from the high post Eisner had given him at the studio after he had left CAA, the agency Ovitz co-founded. Eisner accused his pal of "exaggerating the truth, not telling the truth, deception and dishonesty." Eisner also said he and his executives never knew when Ovitz was telling them things as they were, and that the truth was often hard to decipher. Now really, when you give your best friend $140,000,000 and a roof over your business head, isn't it a bit much to expect him to always tell the truth?

I have hired actors on the basis of their résumés and their in-my-face assertion that they could ski, skydive, bronc ride, conduct an exorcism, and drive a motorcycle, whatever. One actor, shown his motorcycle, got on and promptly drove it into a wall, breaking his leg. No actor's résumé can be believed; they are always filled with local plays from their hometown, or commercials that can't be traced; or work in Europe, or China, or movies never released, etc. One of the best actor-lying incidents came in 1998, when 32 year-old Riley Weston passed as an 18 year-old to land the job as "*Felicity,*" on TV. We can admire that one. Height, weight, hair and eye color are unreliable, even when they are sitting in front of you. Head shots are either so old, or airbrushed that, sometimes you're looking from them to the photo and wondering which is real.

This has gone on since the beginning of the movie business. From *"Bronco Billy"* Anderson, in the very first movie, 1908's *"The Great Train Robbery,"* when, supposedly a cowboy, he mounted on the wrong side and fell off. Nevertheless, he went on to star in hundreds of films, eventually directing some. Tom Mix, the first big western star, lied about his war record. The studios have always lied to the public about everything, from the origins of their stars, such as Errol Flynn, an Aussie, presented as an Irishman, and an Olympic boxer, to boot, to Merle Oberon, of Indian ancestry, who, we were told, was born in Tasmania, to how much films cost, or how much they've made. The term "creative bookkeeping" was invented here.

The movie industry lies. "It's only entertainment, it doesn't influence people." "We only reflect reality." "We give the public what it wants. If people don't like it, they can always turn it off."

Really? I go to movies a lot, more than I should because today's movies really don't interest me the way they did when movies were better. Violence in films is the chief attraction in American movies. Conditioning, as any sociobiologist will tell you, becomes ingrained behavior. And Darwin proved that behavior is adapted and passed on through genes and, being a higher form of monkey, we see, and we do. In speaking to college and film school classes on the subject of movies, I always make sure to include some time for my rant on violence in films. One college class was asked to write term papers based on my visit, and obviously, I impressed them, for I kept all 31 for future reference.

Violence in films continues to expand. The respected critic, Michael Medved, shares my concern, and in a talk he gave some years ago, quoted statistics that have stayed with me. He said that some 350 characters appear nightly on TV, and that average of seven are murdered. Transposed on our population, in fifty days, the entire population of the U.S. would have been killed off. Medved says he has never seen a murder, and that most of us haven't, except in the movies or on TV. He points out that the real ghetto isn't in South Central L.A., or around Washington, D.C., but nightly, on our TVs, and from a seat at the local movie theatre.

As for audiences turning off the TV, or reducing movie attendance, what alternatives are there? We are acclimated, accustomed to flickering, colorful, action images, combined with loud, confusing sounds that feed our addiction. It's not like it hasn't been predicted, from George Orwell's *"1984"* to Stanley Kubrick's *"Clockwork Orange."*

By now, the vast majority of our impressionable children won't support a film or a TV show unless it pushes the envelope. The more violent the better. As Medved says, popular culture is everywhere, like the air we breathe. That's why the messages of pop culture are an environmental issue.

I'm concerned that it's only a matter of time until our society spins out of control and into an irretrievable condition we may not be able to pull ourselves out of. The fastest-growing business I know of is not war, technology, medicine, or even entertainment. It's the domestic violence counseling business. It's up 35 percent every year, say Dr. Jim Gordon, of the Beverly Hills Counseling Center, who should know – it's what he does every day.

The average studio production chief gets about a year and a half to show what they can do. It takes, on average, eighteen months from the moment one decides to "greenlight" (I hate that phrase) a movie, to its being completed and ready for exhibition. While that's happening, you're buying film rights to novels, plays, ideas, pitches, screenplays, magazine stories, and, occasionally, a bright idea from yourself, assigning writers and commissioning screenplays, taking meetings with directors, perhaps actors, with whom the studio has a "put" deal – meaning a contractual obligation to make a film or films within a specified timeline, dispelling rumors that you've already been fired, meeting with agents to insist you still have your job, working eighteen hours, including two or three breakfast dates, one or more lunch dates, cocktails, or two, and dinner meetings. Oh, and "greenlighting" a few more movies you pray will keep you at your choice table at Spago a few months longer.

There is barely time to have an affair with the many female (or male, if that's your preference) lawyers, producers, personal managers, and agents anxious to let you know how "special" you are to them, or to take a multi-million dollar bribe to "greenlight" a movie. Yes, it happens.

Only alpha lions have a rougher life. All they have to do is have sex about sixty times a day (no kidding) with up to eight lionesses for about five years, until they're worn out, and kicked out by the pride in favor of a new, younger lion. I want to come back as an alpha lion.

In eighteen months or so, you've made six films, more or less, and four have been released, with two completed and ready to go out. At least half of them didn't turn out the way you thought, probably because you played it safe and followed the trends of what the other studios were putting out, but when asked, you lie, and say all of your children are beautiful. You had better have had at least one hit, meaning if you've spent $100 million of your allowance, your worldwide gross has to be $300 million. Two of your babies must be breakeven, and you can absorb a near-miss and one and a half disasters. That might get you picked up for another six months to a year.

As an aside, having spent more than 40 years representing writers, hiring and firing writers as a producer, and then becoming one myself, I learned that when a studio, or a producer, turns down your submission with a letter that says, "Thanks, but we've got something similar in the works," watch out. It usually means they like your idea and, as in the clothing business, they intend to change a few buttons, or a seam, copy your idea and do it themselves. How do I know? Because as a producer, in partnership with the former president of CBS Films, when we started our own production company with offices on both the 20th-Fox and MGM lots, we occasionally did the same. And so did every one else. Including the studio executives themselves.

This has always been the case in Hollywood and is behind the mechanism created by the Writers Guild of America, whereby any writer, member or not, can register their property for $20 for a period of five years, and obtain a registration number for their screenplay's cover sheet. Does this deter rapacious producers or studios? Not a bit. It's been quite common over the years for lawyers to sue on behalf of writers whose ideas were ripped off. Even the world famous satirist and International Herald-Tribune columnist, the late Art Buchwald, another Lazar client, by the way, sued, and won, when his idea for an Eddie Murphy movie, "*Coming to America*," was proven to have been stolen by Paramount and credited to Murphy as the writer.
A flap involving writing credit for the Tom Cruise hit, "*The Last Samurai*" also made headlines. A French children's author sued Walt Disney Pictures and Pixar, claiming the cartoon fish in the blockbuster "*Finding Nemo*" was plagiarized from his 1995 creation "*Pierrot Le Poisson Clown*".

An "independent" producer lives or dies on lies. A producer must first own, or at least control a "property," meaning a book, screenplay, notion, idea, comment, cartoon – something from which to build a movie idea around. Some producers might say they own a possible object of affection, but may not actually have it in writing. Said producer could take that lie to an agency with the goal of "attaching" a talent – actor, director, or writer, and then take it to a funder, typically a studio, or a more important independent producer, perhaps with a "put" deal somewhere. That other producer, operating on a lie, takes the package to his funder, and extends the lie, unwittingly perhaps. And so on.

Studio executives lie. As a partner in an independent company with a "first-look" deal at 20th-Fox, with a subsequent same situation at MGM, I sometimes was guilty of informing my executive, meaning the particular functionary responsible for our "housekeeping" deal, that I had an exclusive "hold" on a particular package or talent, until I could scramble enough credit or favors to actually have such a hold. That executive could always check me out independently and find, to his or her dismay, that my information wasn't exactly what I had represented. That would usually be after that executive's Monday morning staff meeting, where my good news had been transmitted. OK, not their fault.

But what about a studio exec who told me and another producer on the same lot about a book or screenplay the studio wanted without letting either of us know about the other, telling both of us we were the only one going after the project? The embarrassment and lack of veracity ensuing with the agents involved, and the agents for the book, or screenplay could be very damaging.

Agents also lie. As a talent agent, I was frequently approached by a producer or would-be producer, for a commitment for one of my clients. Let's see, what would be in it for me? OK, ten percent for the client. But that's surely not enough. I might have a director, or writer that I thought could also be part of the package. That way I could justify a "package" fee, or ten percent of the entire bundle – including the producer. What else…? If the package was strong enough, I might offer it to two studios, or more, at the same time, generating a bidding war. Or I might have designs to become a producer myself; in which case, I'd make sure the studio that accepted me in that role got the deal. I might or might not have informed the original producer of my plans to take over his job. Oh, he'd get paid and maybe even get a small piece of the profits. But we all know there aren't any profits.

Then I could go to the talent; my clients, actor or director, or writer, and tell them about the project. The better way might be to lie to the producer and to the designated studios and say so-and-so loved it and was committed to do it. I could then possibly elicit an offer – meaning pay-or-play, should the client really decide to do it.

All along, I'd be lying – to the producer, to the studio(s), and to my own client(s). One could rationalize it by having made money for a bunch of people, me included. But of course I never did that.

Press agents always lie. I gave an example earlier about myself while working for the two biggest PR firms in Hollywood. But that's excusable, as we all know that what we read in "The Globe," or "The Star," or newspaper columns, or hear as gossip, or see on "Entertainment Tonight" is hype. We expect it. Nay, we crave it. How pathetic we are.

Writers lie. See my chapter on "*Bill W.*," the Alcoholics Anonymous story. Also journalists lie. My friend, Richard Warren Lewis, worked for Playboy magazine, where he was the "editor" of Playboy Forum, the column where "readers" supposedly wrote in for advice on solving their sexual difficulties and received cogent and, of course, droll answers to their problems. Well, Richard was both "reader" and advice giver. And the same is true in all magazines where similar columns appear. Do you really think the harassed, worried, itinerant, security-obsessed consumer really sits down to write a letter to some magazine they picked up on a grocery check-out line, asking for life guidance?

Rap impresarios lie. Russell Simmons, one of the progenitors of the Rap movement, branched out into fashions with a line he called, "Phat." He used an interview to claim his company had made $350 million in its first year of sales. When it was discovered that the actual figure was $14.3 million, he explained, "It's how you develop an image for companies. You give out false statements to mislead the public so that they will increase in their mind the value of your company."

Lawyers lie. Yes, they do, I'm sorry to report. An attorney in showbiz operates much like an agent and a producer. Their clients usually trust their legal advisors more than they trust their spouses, but they shouldn't. Lawyers start out as bookish people. Don't believe that the actors on TV playing lawyers represent what real lawyers look like. They are usually not the best-looking high schoolers, or they'd be sports stars or playboys. When a lawyer gets power, stand back. They've got a lot of getting even to do. Many lawyers and I've seen it in action, gain power for themselves by acting on their client's ignorance and trust. Attorneys have wrecked the careers and even lives of unsuspecting performers because their self-images have exceeded even the gigantic egos of their clients.

In Hollywood, as a representative, you are as influential as who you represent. I've watched clients on the set, under pressure, sign documents messengered to them by their attorneys with instructions to sign it immediately and send it back with the waiting messenger. They don't have the time, inclination, desire or even knowledge to understand what they've just authorized. And on occasion, it's been harmful, even deadly.

A lawyer and financial advisor to the stars, Reed Slatkin, for instance, who was trusted by Scientologists, a few years ago, scammed at least $593 million from his fellow constituents who also belonged to his organization. Among them were many important entertainment figures, including Fox News' Greta Van Susteren, Armyan Bernstein, the producer of *"Air Force One"*, and the actors Giovanni Ribisi of *"Cold Mountain,"* and Jeffrey Tambor, of *"How the Grinch Stole Christmas."*

In my opinion, all religions are cults. Scientology is a combative cult, although they refer to it as a religion. Many celebrities belong to it, including, most famously, Tom Cruise. Others are Nicole Kidman, Kirstie Alley, John Travolta, Cathy Lee Crosby, Juliette Lewis, Peggy Lipton, Cher, Lisa Marie Presley, who briefly brought in Michael Jackson, Sharon Stone, at one time, Shirley MacLaine, Linda Blair, Mimi Rogers, Anne Archer, Valerie Harper, the late Sonny Bono, Lee Purcell (my former management client), Karen Black, Barbara Carrera, Brad Pitt (while dating Juliette Lewis), Christopher Reeve, Rock Hudson, Ernest Lehman, screenwriter of "*The Sound of Music,*" Jeffrey Scott, a script writer, and the grandson of Moe Howard of *"The Three Stooges,"* the late producer Don Simpson, musicians John Denver, Lou Rawls, Edgar Winter, Ron Wood of the Rolling Stones, Isaac Hayes, and Van Morrison, Yoko Ono, and others. They claim the training helps them to be "clear."

What is clear is that actors become actors because they have no sense of self identification. Actors have, in general, an inner void that yearns to be filled by authority. Actors want to be told what to do, which is why strong directors, like Elia Kazan, or coaches, like Lee Strasberg, grow into giant mythic celebrated figures.

Cruise has been damaged by this association. Having fired Pat Kingsley, his press agent for 20-some years, who did a magnificent job of keeping his hot-headed religious passion under control, Cruise's sister, as virulent as he, now is in charge. Since then, he's made a fool of himself on TV and in public, creating a new journalistic campaign centered on "What's Wrong with Tom Cruise?" Among his more outlandish claims, in an interview he gave to Entertainment Weekly in 2005, was that the drug methadone, used to wean addicts off heroin, was originally called "Adolophine," because it "was named after Adolph Hitler." Not good for a career. My guess is that the ruling cadre at Scientology has advised him they need more members and contributions, so he should raise its visibility. It's been widely reported that on the last two of Cruise's films, he had a tent set up staffed with Scientology "Auditors," who 'introduced' its tenets to cast and crew – those, of course, who wanted to be hired for the next Cruise-produced movie. I somehow doubt Steven Spielberg set foot inside. The head guy at Scientology recently was quoted as saying that Tom Cruise is the new Jesus.

According to Michael Shermer, publisher of Skeptic magazine, in an article written for the February 18, 2008 edition of the Los Angeles Times, the "bible" of Scientology centers on Xenu the galactic warlord, who 75 million years ago was in charge of 76 overpopulated planets. Xenu brought trillions of these alien beings to Earth (called Teegeeack) on spaceships that resembled DC-9 planes and placed them in secret volcanoes. He then vaporized them with hydrogen bombs, scattering to the winds their souls, called thetans, which were then rounded up in electronic traps and implanted with false ideas, These corrupted thetans attach themselves to people today, leading to drug and alcohol abuse, addiction, depression and other psychological and social ailments that only Scientology classes and "auditing" employing "e-meters" can cure – for a stiff price.

Another famous "celebrity" involved with Scientology is Charles Manson. Scientology has denied that he was a member, but in the FBI raid on Scientology's headquarters, the F.B.I. found Scientology internal intelligence information regarding Manson's involvement with Scientology. The New York Times stated that Manson first got interested in Scientology while he was incarcerated in the McNeil Island Penitentiary in Washington (Scientology has recruiting programs for prisons). Manson received about 150 hours of Scientology counseling in prison by three of his cell mates. One of them, Lanier Palmer, was a "Doctor of Scientology."

After his release from prison, The New York Times reported, he went to Los Angeles where he was said to have met local Scientologists and attended several parties for movie stars. Scientology literature was also said to be found at the ranch when Manson and his family were captured. There were hints that he later joined the Process, the sex and Satan group which originally broke away from Scientology.

Interestingly, Scientology has an officially secret agreement, as of 1993, with the Internal Revenue Service, allowing Scientologists to deduct the cost of religious education as a charitable gift! How about that? The federal government has never before or since granted such a favor to any other religion. Talk about moles infiltrating an organization.

Charities lie. Forever, it seems to me, charities have paid performers to appear at events, telling their supporters and the public that said performers were contributing their services. Win-win for both, as the charity appears to be so important that so-and-so would take time out of their busy schedules to appear, thus increasing their contributions. The performers look like generous, caring, benevolent souls to their fans, and the media gets to celebrate both. Both as a publicist and as an agent, I was constantly besieged by recruiters for charities begging me to allow my clients to appear. Not only were my clients offered cash and gifts, I was too.

But times have changed, thank goodness. There's nowhere to hide from a rapacious media anymore. In fact, Bill Cosby was caught in a media expose' some months ago with his hand in the cookie jar, and the vaunted Jerry Lewis Telethon for Jerry's Kids with Muscular Dystrophy has always rewarded certain favored singers, and actors for showing up. I wonder how Jerry supported himself in these many years away from the cameras, or spotlight? Royalties, must be.

And the people running such charities live exceedingly well. As one example I pulled from the Internet: Aaron Tonken, known as "fund-raiser to the stars" was indicted, co-operated with federal authorities, and was sentenced to 63 months in prison and ordered to pay $3.8 million in restitution for mail and wire fraud. According to the U.S. Department of Justice, "Tonken falsely represented to donors and underwriters that their contributions would pay event expenses or would benefit charities. In fact, Tonken used the contributions for his personal benefit, including payment of personal loans and the purchase of luxury items. In a scheme reminiscent of the 'Producers,' he routinely promised more than 100% of the net proceeds from the events to multiple charities. He also falsely solicited contributions for events he never produced, such as 'Celebrating Diana,' a supposed tribute to Diana Ross." He also was investigated in connection with a fundraiser he staged for Bill and Hillary Clinton, and for defrauding former president Gerald Ford, Paula Abdul, TV producer David E. Kelley, and Roseanne Barr, among others. Tonken diverted the donations to bank accounts with names such as "Performing Arts Foundation" and "Giving Back Fund," which were not charity funds. Tonken is also being sued by the California attorney general for allegedly defrauding $1.5 million from several charities, including the Betty Ford Center and City of Hope. And, naturally, Tonken wrote a book about his "life," which was published.

His lawyer said Tonken received less than 5 percent of the money raised, and that Tonken "feels extraordinary remorse for his conduct in this case." Uh huh.

Even governors lie. Did Arnold lie when he denied groping, or worse, of multiple helpless females in his glorious acting career? Did former Governor Ronnie Reagan lie when he sent in the National Guard to suppress the Berkeley Free Speech Movement on the basis that it presented a clear and present danger to the people of California? Remember, it was an actor that shot Lincoln.

HOW MUCH DOES IT COST TO LEARN TO LIE?

And then there was est. In 1971, est, or Ehrhard Seminar Training, hit the west coast. Naturally, legions of Hollywood actors signed up. A Jewish car salesman named John Rosenberg, who had run out on his wife and two small children in Philadelphia a couple years earlier, and was bumming around San Francisco during the tail end of the hippie movement, got into Scientology and saw so much money being separated from the wallets of the emotionally needy, he decided to hang out his own shingle. He also changed his name to Werner Ehrhard. Imagine a Jew reinventing himself with such a forcefully German name so close after the end of World War II and the Holocaust?

L. Ron Hubbard, Scientology's founder, became an important influence on Ehrhard. Scientologists accuse Erhard of having stolen his ideas for est from Hubbard. Erhard says Scientology, a notoriously litigious group, hounded him, including siccing the IRS on his organization, and promulgating rumors of incest with his children. Erhard sued the IRS and won, and has since made the incest accusations a minor point by claiming they were based on false memories encouraged by therapists. Erhard also said that Scientologists hired hit men to kill him.

est is a mélange' of philosophical excerpts assembled from existential philosophy, motivational psychology, psycho-cybernetics, Zen Buddhism, the writings of Alan Watts, Freud, L. Ron Hubbard, Napoleon Hill, Hinduism, Dale Carnegie, Norman Vincent Peale, P.T. Barnum, and whatever else, including "The Farmer's Almanac," Erhard thought he could throw in to impress and access the budding Human Potential market.

Erhard promised those who paid thousands of dollars for his programs he would "blow their minds" and raise them to a new level of consciousness, because their consciousness was screwed up and needed to be "rewired." And of course, his program would do the rewiring. Once their consciousness was organized, life would be splendid. They would be strong, confident, and successful because they would be independent and in control. They would see things very differently. est would make them free to be born again. Since all problems and limitations are in the mind, simply rewire the mind, reconstruct your personality, dump all negativity, stop blaming others, and learn to accept things.

Naturally, I signed up. Everyone I knew was talking about the incredible changes they were experiencing, and how positively it impacted their lives and careers. I became an early "est-hole," as we were later called by Scientologists and, eventually, the media. Good negative catch phrase, even I must admit.

I wasn't personally trained by Werner – he was too busy madly dashing off to other cities to cash in the buzz and open new centers. But the trainer I had was his brother, Harry Rosenberg. Why Harry didn't bother changing his name, even though he had no problem identifying himself, was a mystery.

We were taught that we should always think and talk positive, even if this means lying. If you're a flop, put on a positive front and tell everyone that business couldn't be better. If you have no idea where your next meal is coming from, lie and tell yourself that you are doing great. Try harder, have more faith, and be positive. Maybe you need to take advanced courses to help you succeed. The advanced courses became increasingly expensive – just like Scientology.

Erhard studied hypnotism, but decided a better way to go would be to focus on "programming" and "reprogramming." He said that bad habits are programmed into us - that we have been "hypnotized" during normal consciousness by television, our parents, and our teachers. Hence our problems. Therefore, unconsciously, we're lugging around heavy and painful habits and beliefs. est would erase them, replacing them with positive, life-enhancing beliefs. The Human Potential Movement was mushrooming and Erhard would be in on the ground floor.

est did their own hypnotizing – the training used some of the same techniques the CIA used to interrogate "enemy combatants." You were packed 300 into a room that held half that, for an entire day. You were not allowed to leave the room for any purpose, including bathroom breaks. Until the trainer said you could. Doors were sealed and monitored. You sat upright until your back was breaking. Sleep deprivation was practiced. And you were bullied, insulted, yelled at, belittled, and embarrassed. This went on for two weekends and two Wednesday nights. You could always quit, but a quitter was what you were when you signed up, so you couldn't admit they were right. Also, your friends who were doing the course with you would never let you forget it. And besides, you had paid your three hundred dollars upfront and there were no refunds. And you were desperate, weren't you – or you wouldn't be there in the first place.

So what did I get from est? When you "graduated," you got a little brown book of aphorisms, which I still have. You were supposed to keep its contents secret and show them to no one. It was special – information from beyond our galaxy. So here are some samples: "*It's easier to ride the horse in the direction he's going.*" Not bad. I agree.

Here's another: *"If you could really accept that you weren't OK, you could stop proving you were OK. If you could stop proving that you were OK, you could get that it was OK not to be OK. If you could get that it was OK not to be OK, you could get that you are OK the way you are. You're OK. Get it?"*

As Danny Kaye said in *"The Jester,"* "Get it? Got it! Good!"

One more? *"If God told you exactly what it was you were to do, you would be happy doing it, no matter what it was. What you're doing is what God wants you to do. Be Happy."* He forgot to say "Don't worry." And how does he know what God wants? Oh, I forgot, he was God.

Some 700,000 people, among them many, many actors, directors, and writers, took the course before the seminars closed down, in 1991, when Erhard hurriedly left the country. Some say the law was after him, others claim he was frightened by death threats from Scientology – still others said he had finally gone 'round the bend', and was totally nuts. I think he had all the money he needed and went someplace far away, changed his name, and is enjoying the best wine, cigars and hookers money can buy.

Other, similar programs sprung up to fill the void, including Landmark Forum, which is run by Werner's brother, Harry Rosenberg, Lifesprings, Tony Robbins, and many more.

A friend of mine told me recently she had hired a salesperson who, for the last seven years, has spent most of her income on Tony Robbins. She goes to his seminars four times a year, wherever they may be held, "firewalks," buys his books and tapes and, incredulously, pays $5,000 to speak to the Master himself by telephone for five minutes. I wonder if Tony needs a partner.

SPEAKING OF LYING TO ONE'S SELF

It wasn't long before Neuro-linguistic Programming (NLP) made its appearance. Tony Robbins is without question the most successful "graduate" of NLP. Anybody who can manipulate the public like he does is a master. Founded by Richard Bandler, a mathematician, and John Grinder, a linguist, NLP assures individuals, groups, and corporations the ability to achieve their maximum potential and great success. Practitioners also offer individual psychotherapy for phobias, schizophrenia, and probably hangnails.

I signed up in 1975 and took training for six months in the Beverly Hills office of Dr. Donald Dossey. I liked Don, and became friends with him even though I came to believe he was selling snake oil, just like Werner. Just not as expensively.

NLP claims to help people change by teaching them to program their brains, creating a change in the way we see life.

We were given brains, I was told, but no instruction manual, which NLP provides as "software for the brain." NLP says the unconscious mind constantly influences conscious thought and action and by using self-hypnosis it's possible to motivate and change oneself. Don Dossey said he could teach me when a person is lying. Actually, I've always known when a person is lying. And so do you.

NLP says to watch people's behavior and teaches you how to read "body language." From that, you "model" your behavior on your subjects in a subtle way, thereby communicating to their unconscious that you are not a threat – that you can be trusted, that you, in fact, are a friend.

For instance, if someone you are trying to sell something to is sitting cross-legged at a meeting, without attracting their attention you slowly assume a similar position. You watch their breathing and subtly time yours to match. When they change position, so do you. Just don't let them catch you at it. But try not to read too much into it. Legs apart may not be an invitation to sex.

Dossey claimed that NLP identifies the Primary Representational System (PRS). This unconscious system thinks for us in specific modes: visual, auditory, kinesthetic, olfactory or gustatory. A person's PRS can be determined by words the person uses or by the direction of one's eye movements.

He gave me an example; two elderly men had been partners in a furniture store for over 40 years and now wanted to sell out and retire. But they couldn't agree on how and when. He said they had never gotten along – that they had squabbled like two angry roosters the entire time they had been in business, and each said the other hated him. Dossey was called in and he told me he had solved their problem in one session by the way they spoke about each other. The first man said, "I scream my fool head off at him, but he doesn't see what I'm saying." The second man then jumped up and yelled, "I show him the books, I point to the competition, he doesn't hear a word I say."

Obviously, Dossey said, they communicated in two different languages. One of the men received his information visually, i.e.; "see what I'm saying." The other gets his knowledge aurally, i.e.; "hear a word I say." When he showed them what their problem was, he said they jumped up and kissed him. They sold out and became friends.

So does NLP work? I had some negative thoughts that had bothered me for years. Don had me hypnotize myself into a seat in an empty movie theatre. When I was ready, I visualized those thoughts as a movie and watched it onscreen. Then he had me run it backwards. He suggested I become the projectionist in the booth, take the film off the projector, and chop it into many pieces, then glue it back together and put in back onscreen. I had now become the viewer in the theatre seat again, watching a jumbled, unintelligible film that bore only a slight resemblance to my former negative thought. That mess was then run backwards. The process was repeated many times, until I could no longer recognize the thought that had given me such difficulty over time. Did NLP work for me? I have to say that part of it did.

Werner Erhard is not mentioned by Grinder and Bandler in their writings, but I'd bet he was the model for NLP. Bandler and Grinder were located in Santa Cruz, and Ehrhard started est a few miles north in San Francisco, just a couple of years before they started their NLP training business.

HUBRIS

Agents, managers, lawyers, press agents, even doctors, have enormous power to make or break a career, a studio, even lives. Dr. Neal Ellatrache, doctor to the stars at the celebrated Kerlan-Jobe Clinic, in Beverly Hills, my orthopedist, was interrupted in a consultation with me to take a very important phone call. On his return, he told me that at that moment he had the power to stop or delay a $100 million movie. Of course he would never reveal any confidential information, but it is an example of clout wielded in the unlikeliest of circumstances.

A couple of years ago, Dr. Ellatrache, who looked after many of the L.A. Dodgers and Lakers players, operated on my knee, repairing a torn meniscus. I shared a stationary bike for several months in his rehab unit with Helen Hunt, who suffered the same injury while she was shooting *"Twister."*

Doris Day, one of America's greatest pop singers and actresses, made a fortune, over $50 million, in the forty years she entertained the world. She was married to her third husband, Marty Melcher, who had managed her business affairs for 17 years, and when he died in 1968, Day found to her horror that he had lost or embezzled her entire career's earnings. She was left broke, and suffered a nervous breakdown.

The same thing happened to the famous producer, Ross Hunter who, coincidentally produced many of Doris Day's hit movies during the 60s, like "Pillow Talk," some of which she starred in with Rock Hudson, prior to public knowledge of his gayness. Hunter was too busy and had no interest in what his attorney and business manager sent him to sign. He was one of the people I had in mind when I said I had witnessed the signing of unread documents. He had made 46 movies and amassed a great deal of assets, but died virtually broke. He had the same lawyer and business manager as Doris Day.

My last father-in-law, Spike Jones, also became rich in the entertainment business. The first comic bandleader, his group, the City Slickers created anarchy on stage, parodying popular songs. He reached his greatest movie success during the WWII years, and had co-starring roles in films with Lucille Ball, Veronica Lake, Humphrey Bogart, Eddie Cantor, Dick Powell and Bette Davis, to name only a few. His musical hits included, *"Der Fuehrer's Face,"* and *"All I Want for Christmas Is My Two Front Teeth,"* a number one hit in 1948. He was married to his former band singer, Helen Grayco, when I wed his daughter, Linda, by his first wife. Spike, too, trusted his business manager and lawyer, and when he died, after earning some $25 million, Helen and his children were shocked to learn they were broke – all his money had disappeared. Helen had to come out of retirement and go back to work.

Later, Helen dated Johnny Roselli, a known Mafia operative in Hollywood. I met him several times at Helen's home, when she would make one of her fabulous Italian feasts. I liked him enormously. Not only was he tall and handsome, with a graying full head of hair, he had charm and wit. I always looked forward to seeing him. Roselli also dated Marilyn Monroe, who told friends that Johnny was angry at the Kennedys for giving the Mafia a hard time and bragged about "friends in high places" who were going to knock Kennedy off. It's said she tried frantically to warn Jack and Bobby, but was obviously thwarted. In the late 1960's, Roselli cooperated with the authorities and testified before Congress about CIA-Mob ops to promote the claim that Castro was responsible for the Kennedy assassination. Columnist Jack Anderson reported that Roselli told him that mob leaders had ordered Jack Ruby to kill Lee Harvey Oswald because they were afraid he might crack and reveal their part in the conspiracy to kill President Kennedy. In July 1976, shortly before Roselli was to be questioned by the Senate Intelligence Committee, his body was discovered floating in Dumfoundling Bay in Miami. He had been strangled and stabbed; his legs had been sawed off and stuffed into an empty oil drum along with the rest of his body.

Speaking of hubris, I'm just as guilty. I was approached by a well known Hollywood producer, Harold Hecht, once Burt Lancaster's production partner, but then a Columbia Pictures producer, who wanted Michael J. Pollard for a remake of the Lee Marvin western comedy hit, *"Cat Ballou,"* playing Marvin's son. I turned him down, as Pollard's agent, because, after starring in *"Frenchy King,"* and *"Little Fauss & Big Halsey,"* with Robert Redford, I thought he should pursue romantic roles. Do you know what Pollard looks like?

ULTIMATE HUBRIS

The Golden Globes are a phony organization. The show is a scam. You heard it from me. When I was a press agent, we were begged to provide some names, any names, to their pathetic attempt to gain some notoriety in Hollywood. This was prior to their being on TV. Their membership of less than twenty consisted then of a bunch of "stringers" for publications we had never heard of and which were impossible to trace. These "journalists" were immigrants who worked as salespeople, a barber, a security guard, a taxi driver, etc., and those were just the ones I knew from the free screenings we let them go to. We would agree to deliver some clients who needed publicity – if, and only if, they got a prize that we chose. Absolutely no problem. We would pose our clients with whoever they appointed as "President," and the pictures would be serviced by us to U.S. publications, which we could check. Somehow we never saw any clippings from their "foreign press" outlets.

Of course today we live in a celebrity-obsessed culture connected by the Internet, and the worldwide public is, if possible, even more gullible now than it was when P.T Barnum coined the phrase, "There's a sucker born every minute." Today's Golden Globes have slightly more credibility and about 80 "journalists," some of whom may actually be, and work for an expanded media devoted to celebrities. The show is very professional because it's produced by the Dick Clark company in association with the major studios, but the awards are still stage-managed by the people who control the movie business – the studios, which have movies they want the Globes to act as a trailer for before the Oscars, held the following month, the press agents, who hope to sway the Academy voters, and the agents, who plan on huge salary increases based on their client's popularity. And the awards are given to those who guarantee they will show up for the show. Yes, it's all about money. Variety's January 23, 2004 edition noted the Hollywood Foreign Press Association, which owns the GG, netted over three-and-a-half million dollars from their 2003 show, up 68% from 2002. Not bad for a scam.

The profusion of "awards" shows are, in my opinion, a celebration of out of control sycophancy. Like the real estate market of the early 2000s, it's a bubble that's going to burst. Just some of the movie awards, and forgive me if I've left any out; are the American Film Institute (AFI), Golden Reel Awards (sound & music editors), People's Choice Awards, Screen Actor's Guild (SAG) awards, Producer's Guild Awards, ACE Eddie Awards, (film editors), Director's Guild Awards, National Board of Review (whoever they are), Writer's Guild Awards WGA, and Scripter's Awards. Throw in the ad nauseum number of awards shows for the music business, and the TV business.

As Jimmy Durante, the beloved former vaudeville comic, who became a movie and TV star, once said: "Everybody wants to get into 'da act."

THEN THERE'S MEL BROOKS HUBRIS

In the late 80s, I had an office in the producer's building on the 20th-Fox lot. It was on the third, or top floor. Status is everything in Hollywood, from what you drive, to where you live, to what table you get in the hip restaurant of the moment, to whom your yoga, Pilates, personal trainer, massage therapist, kinesiologist, or drug dealer is, and who their other clients are. The third floor was the place to be. In the next office was Mel Brooks. If you had such a neighbor in your apartment building, you'd either be calling the cops, or complaining to your tenant group about the commotion next door.

In this case, being next to Mel was pure joy. A nicer man does not exist. When it became too raucous, I'd go next door to see what was going on, and it was usually Mel and some of his crew acting out scenes from some movie they were dreaming up, or from past films they made – or liked. I'd lean against the wall for a while and be treated to moments of madness that civilians, or people not in showbiz, would have to pay $450 a ticket for, and did down the road.

For some reason, we were still dressing up, which happily has become extinct. I wore a suit and tie every day to the office. Mel of course, being "creative," didn't. One day, I was sitting at my desk, on the phone with some agent or other, when Mel rushed in and stared tearing at my clothes.

I started laughing, but he soon was sitting in my lap, pushing my jacket back over my shoulders, pulling up my shirt collar, unknotting my tie and, finally, whipping it off me and dashing back to his office. I became flustered, sputtering into the phone about what was happening. My secretary Wilma, a solemn, older lady who had been a pool secretary in the movie business for 40 years, the last twenty at Fox, shook her head gravely at such goings on. Wilma had seen a lot - It was hard to shock Wilma, but she was speechless.

I pulled myself together, hung up and went next door to Mel's office to see what in the hell was going on. There was Mel, sitting behind his desk, beaming, wearing my tie and a borrowed sports jacket, being interviewed for Japanese television for the upcoming release of his next film, a remake of the Ernst Lubitsch classic, "*To Be or Not to Be.*" Some of his interview was done in Mel's famous Japanese accent. I'm sure every word was understood by his intended audience. Every day, or almost every day thereafter, either Mel would stick his head into my office to see what tie I was wearing, or I'd go next door and coyly wave my tie at him from behind a door.

GREED

Greed used to be exclusive to the studios in the days when contract players and writer and directors were literally enslaved, sometimes for their entire careers. The studios owned their services, made money by loaning them to other studios, and kept all the proceeds from their films. As I mentioned, this began to slowly change when Jimmy Stewart got a percentage of the gross, and when Shirley MacLaine and Bette Davis took on Warner Brothers in the courts – and won. Well, the pendulum has swung, as it always does, and this time, greed is squarely in the hands of the talent – and their agents.

Around the beginning of the 1980s, it became apparent that only a couple of actors could "open" a film, meaning that a certain percentage of the audience could be counted on to turn out for the first weekend, justifying a second weekend and its attendant high costs of advertising. Clint Eastwood and Barbra Streisand, among them. Their salaries, coincident with ballooning costs in line with inflation, caused film budgets to shoot out of sight, and those actors (and later certain directors), began to demand conditions for their employment that would have turned Mayer and Zanuck purple with rage. But because the "stars" had the hot hand, the studio structure gave in. It was modest – at first. Separate trailers were the beginning, and lots of torrid tales about what went on in some of those trailers between shots or after work are some of the best inside stories. Trailers originally made it easier for movies to shoot on location and make many moves in a day. Since then, these wheeled five-star resorts have grown so huge that they can actually reduce rather than expand the options for location shooting. When you have a single star asking for three trailers — one for himself, one for his gym equipment, one for his entourage — moving all these vehicles is like mounting a military campaign.

Trailers led to make-up people and hair dressers, who usually work for union minimums on a film or TV show being put on the studio's payrolls. When a star insists on them for a publicity campaign or magazine photo shoot, they can and do charge thousands of dollars a day and get first-class airfare and luxury hotel rooms. A personal stylist, whose job it is to go shopping, can make as much as $7,000 a day.

Then there's the private jet syndrome. OK, given the current difficulties of flying commercial, plus the need for security, a major face or name needs a certain level of protection. But a round-trip in a private jet from New York City to Los Angeles exceeds $60,000, and even if a star owns his own plane, the studio gets charged thousands of dollars a day for fuel and crew time.

The assassination of John Lennon threw a chill into celebrities. Then when John Hinckley shot President Reagan on March 30, 1981 to impress Jody Foster, and a Hollywood starlet named Rebecca Schaeffer was killed when she answered her doorbell, by a crazed fan who had gotten her address from the Department of Motor Vehicles, 24-hour security became an authentic issue. And the paparazzi, in addition to being annoying, can get you killed – as in Princess Diana's deadly attempt to escape them in Paris. And thin is always in, so $3,000 a day personal chefs are required to maintain their meticulously calibrated diets, so you know why greed is necessary. The better schools for celeb's kids cost $25,000 a year. And let's not forget the entourage. An agent friend of mine told me one of his clients installed two kitchens in his Beverly Hills house, one for his family, one for the band, just like Victorian society, upstairs and downstairs. Some actors have enough hangers-on in their entourages to populate a small city. A lawyer I know tells me an A-list movie star's contract typically includes as many as 30 to 40 "comfort zones." TV actors get no more than 10, but then they don't move around a lot. Each 'zone' costs the studio or network heavily. Nanny's charge $1,500 a week (one star actually asks for three for her baby), $3,000 a week for a private chef, $1,000 a week for a trainer, $10,000 a week for a personal assistant, $3,500 a week for incidental expenses, etc. An actress I know once demanded a Feng Shui expert to adjust the chi in her trailer and insisted on an astrologer to forecast the most cosmically favorable days to work.

Today's most unashamed example of celebrity greed is the gift-bag. It's no longer enough to win an Oscar, an Emmy, or a Grammy — now stars are "gifted" with luxury freebies just for showing up. In the past few years, the value of the official Oscar presenter's thank-you basket has risen from around $20,000 to an estimated $150,000 (including $500 cashmere pajama bottoms and $3,500 spa packages). The competition to pursue celebrities with free stuff in exchange for publicity has become so intense that some stars are on the payroll of upscale fashion houses for six-figures to wear their clothes and jewelry. A studio executive told me five years ago, (imagine what is it is now) giveaways to stars most likely cost them 5 percent of a film's budget. The average studio film now costs $100 million to produce and market, If Hollywood produces 40 "A" movies each year, that means $200 million is thrown away by the studios to placate and entice a bunch of overgrown children to play in their sandbox. And who eventually pays? The ticket buyer now shelling out an incredible $10 or more for a movie ticket. Attendance is actually down these past few years, even though the yearly gross goes up. I read where one action star has to have a basketball court wherever he's shooting, even if the studio has to build one for him, for $35,000. This is having a dangerous effect on the below-the-line people, who are being squeezed by the normal inflation of life in the U.S., and the constant runaway production now centered in Eastern Europe. Resentment toward the stars is building among the camera people, grips, editors, and so on. The re-ordering of financial conditions, which are affecting the entertainment business as well as the general economy, will, I believe, level out this greed. Until the next boom, of course.

DIRECT THIS

There is an apocryphal story I have heard for years about the Hungarian director of the 30s and 40s, Michael Curtiz, who was something of a sex addict. He made some of the era's finest films, including *"Casablanca,"* and *"Mildred Pierce,"* Curtiz never properly learned English and, like Samuel Goldwyn, Sr., was known for his malapropisms. During filming of *"The Charge of the Light Brigade,"* in 1936, he wanted riderless horses in the background during the final charge. His instructions were, "*Bring on the empty horses.*" David Niven, the suave British actor used that phrase as the title of Niven's first autobiography.

Curtiz once bawled out an assistant for the way he was not following the director's orders, and yelled, "The next time I want an idiot to do this, I'll do it myself!"

In the days that Curtiz worked in Hollywood, most films were made on the back lots, and lunch was an important part of the business day. That was when contract directors and producers could eye each other's costumes, sets and actors, and imagine what they could steal for their next production. It was also a good opportunity to get to know actors from other studios who had been borrowed for one picture or another.

Social matters too, could be attended to, and although the agent business had just begun, with David O. Selznick's brother, Myron, setting up his own agency, agents began filtering onto the lots to woo prospective clients. It was so when I was an agent during the 60s, and 70s, but sadly, those days have passed.

The computer has caught up to the most intense of personal businesses and today's agents e-mail résumés and photos to casting directors and rarely, if ever, visit the lots anymore. The commissaries, which once were the hub of studio life, with Louis B. Mayer's mother's recipe for chicken soup the highlight of the MGM lunchroom, most in-studio eating places have become fast-food outlets in the relentless drive by multi-national corporations, which control the movie studios today, to push cost figures down to intersect with management projections. It'll never be the same, and it's one of the reasons I was happy to drift away.

Michael Curtiz, however, would usually skip lunch, or at least the ritual appearance in the commissary, in favor of a blow job in his office by some prostitute or other, followed by a sandwich. His secretary would bring him his lunch before she too went to eat. One day, Curtiz didn't lock his door securely and his secretary, thinking his ritual had been completed, opened the door to check with her boss about the shots they needed to make that afternoon, and came upon her boss, legs spread, with a naked woman between them. Curtiz, it's said, surprised and shocked, leaped up, throwing the woman to the floor, and yelled at her, "Who are you…how did you get past the guard?" Have you guessed by now who Curtiz's secretary was?

MORE RUMORS

A movie was made in 1970 called *"Dinah East,"* which was little seen and, apparently, is not much remembered either. The story purported to tell the real story, however disguised, of the world famous entertainer, actress, writer, producer and director, Mae West. Gene Nash, the writer-director was brought to my attention by Bobby Mirisch, who was now an attorney in Hollywood. Although Bobby had some major clients in the above ground movie colony, and had served as in-house lawyer for First Artists, the four-star movie company, he also had wide contacts elsewhere. He suggested I look at the script and see if I could be helpful in raising some of the production costs.

"Dinah" was a not very thinly disguised story of a man in 1919, who upon arriving in Hollywood and seeking work as an actor, is reduced to extreme poverty attempting to break into the film business. In those days, before agents, or media, casting offices

were street-floor and open to the public. The day's job openings were posted on a blackboard and casting directors would assess the crowd outside and, much like longshoreman bosses, point to applicants they liked, or thought the director needed. This particular actor got a few day work opportunities as background, or extra, at the royal pay of 25 cents for BG, or as much as half a dollar for extra, but even in those days, when a steak dinner went for 60 cents, you had trouble living on movie extra wages.

The story goes that one day, a film company was looking for women. Our man went home, dressed appropriately, did his make-up, returned to the casting office, and was hired. It seems he/she stood out, and the die was cast. He/she got other roles, steadily increasing his/her status among the film recruiters, until he/she caught the eye of a particular director. That can sometimes be a ticket to the top in this town. He/she was a talented writer, as Mae West was, and brought his/her script to the director's attention. It was filmed with him/her in the lead, and a star was born.

In the film, "*Dinah East*," the elderly lady, well into her eighties, is being driven home to her grand, entire floor, apartment in Hollywood, when her chauffer, who had been drinking, loses control of her Cadillac limousine and runs into a tree. Dinah is dead. Her body is transported to the morgue, where an autopsy is done, and her secret is out.

In the movie, which closely replicates many of the peculiar characteristics of Mae West, Dinah never marries, but is sure to keep up a heavily-sex inflected dialogue and, in later years surrounds herself with at least a half-dozen muscle men, as she called them, or body builders, as they later became known as.

Some reviews compared the film to a very early "*Tootsie*," made in 1982, in which Dustin Hoffman dresses in drag to obtain an acting role in a TV soap. One reviewer said, ""Dinah was totally before its time. A great adaptation of what Hollywood was like way back then, when there were limited acting parts for men."

So, was Mae West a man?

"I've seen Mae West without a stitch and she's all woman. No hermaphrodite could have bosoms... well, like two large melons," said Edith Head, Oscar-winning costume designer, debunking the rumor that Mae was actually a man. On the other hand, cosmetic and plastic surgery is a high art in Hollywood.

CAREER SUICIDE IS

Mel Gibson making an anti-Semitic movie – and then in a drunken rage spouting that the Jews are in league with the devil, or some such, in a business founded and controlled by Jews. Good thing for him he doesn't need money because it's gonna' be a long time, if ever, when any Hollywood studio bankrolls him again. Of course I could be wrong.

TRUTH REVEALED: GOD IS A TV CRITIC

My friend for 30 years, Peter Engel, has a direct connection to God. He actually met Jesus at the foot of his bed in the middle of the night some 20 years ago, when he awoke, sweating and in a panic, thinking he was suffering a heart attack induced by years of drug abuse, moral malaise, a failed marriage, unemployment, and economic dread. Jesus told him he loved him.

Immediately, Peter straightened up, and in no time, became very successful in all areas of his life. He insists these two events are intimately connected. It sure looks like it.

Peter and I, and a group of other young agents and would-be producers on the rise in the turbulent 70s in Hollywood, were all from New York, were Democrats, and had all been born into the Jewish culture – although none of us had ever taken that seriously. Still, it was a club, and as everyone in business knows, affinity groups are easier to do business in – and very useful for keeping other people out. Marijuana, cocaine, alcohol, was the currency underlining the creative fabric of the entertainment industry, and you couldn't play if you couldn't pay. Peter, like myself, had a wife and a couple of kids, which also, like me, and most of our cohort, went by the wayside under the onslaught of distorted values offered by chemicals, and the availability of the most beautiful young girls in America flocking to town to become stars in those days of "free love" permissiveness.

Peter's awakening in such a fright was not uncommon or even unusual – it happened to me, and to most of our friends. Showbiz is an itinerant profession – executives lose their jobs over disappointing boxoffice or ratings, performers wink out like so many fireflies at dawn, and agents, lawyers and press agents are measured by their client lists. Naturally, we all saw psychiatrists several times a week, but Peter also consulted his psychic and astrologer. He was perfectly prepared for a visitation. Always a man of over-the-top enthusiasm, when it came, he was swallowed up. Dropping drugs, sex, booze and uncertainty, he was hired by a well-known TV production outfit, where he soon regained his stride. I was happy for him.

The first signs of concern came when letters and inter-office communications from Peter came plastered with "Jesus Loves You" stickers. Then phone messages ending with the same or similar phrases such as "Have You Been Saved?" I was worried. But then, Peter called me and asked me to be best man at his wedding – I hadn't been aware he had met someone. His wife-to-be, a Christian he had met at a local evangelical gathering, was a recent divorcee from a crazed record producer, who left her with a million dollar house in Westwood, two small kids, and an alimony package that would choke Kevin Federline. The wedding was nice, the bride was beautiful, actually – a former model, and crosses were in evidence everywhere. Alice couldn't have felt more out of place at the Red Queen's palace than I did that afternoon.

Very soon after, Peter soon became the greatly successful TV producer of "*Saved by the Bell*" for NBC, and produced another NBC hit show, "*Last Comic Standing.*" "Bell," stressing moral principals to a teenage Saturday morning audience, and syndicated in 85 countries, made Peter very rich indeed. Shortly after he got the "Bell" job at NBC, I got lunch invitations to join him at the NBC commissary, where I was regularly prostelized. I indulged him – for a while, but then it became annoying. I wasn't alone. Pretty soon, I was ducking him, and so were most of his former friends. His new crew was all evangelicals who spoke in tongues. He showed me one day – it freaked me out.

Several years ago, saying the Lord told him it was time to leave Hollywood, he became the dean of the School of Communication & the Arts at Regent University, in Sally Beach, VA, a Christian school run under the direction of Pat Robertson, the dean of the religious Right Wing in America. Peter has been clean and straight all these years, with a beautiful wife and two handsome teenage children.

The point of this story, to me, is all about addiction. I've spoken of mine previously, and I begrudge no one theirs. Some addictions are better than others and Peter's works for him. But it's still a mental aberration as far as I'm concerned. Trading cocaine for Jesus is not new; convicts in prison do it all the time. Occasionally it results in early release, but I'm sure it's not their motive. What intrigues me, however, is the seemingly direct connection with the type of programming Peter specialized in and the immense rewards he has reaped from it. Is God guiding Peter's hand? Does God want to see more moral programs on TV? Peter says he was "saved so he could serve." As dean, Peter is preparing his students to take leading positions in the fields of communication and the arts and begin to change the world for Jesus. Oh, Lord.

JAY BERNSTEIN, GUNMAN

No, I don't mean hired gun. Jay Bernstein, whom I've known for 45 years, and worked with at Rogers & Cowan in the 60s, and who recently died of a stroke at age 68, was very ambitious. Jay was best known for his management of Farrah Fawcett, whom he boosted to stardom after the original "*Charlie's Angels*" TV series. Using Farrah as a lever, Jay self-publicized himself into the first "super manager." He advertised in out of town newspapers, inviting young female hopefuls to Hollywood for "auditions," slyly reminding respondents that if he did it for Farrah, he could do it for them. Once in town, Jay had a currency he could spend with producers, directors and studio execs. If you know what I mean.

Jay liked to portray himself as a cocksman, and to prove it, he always had a new young beauty on his arm. They had usually arrived that afternoon on a bus from some Midwest cattle auction center. In reality, women I knew well told me Jay was, at best, ambivalent about sex and, in some cases acted very inappropriately around the subject. For example, I was Joanna Moore's agent, remember her? Joanna played a sexy call girl in "*Walk on the Wild Side*," in 1962, but is probably best remembered as Andy Griffith's girlfriend in the "*Andy Griffith Show*," on TV. Joanna was a Southern beauty with a seductive Lauren Bacall type voice. I liked her a lot and felt sorry for her because she couldn't seem to hold herself together after she and Ryan O' Neal, her husband, and father of her two children, Tatum, and Griffith split. Tatum, at age nine, co-starred with her dad in "*Paper Moon*," a fun and entertaining movie about a father-daughter confidence team, directed by Peter Bogdanovich, in 1973.

She dated around a lot, like other young unattached actresses around town, and one night, ended up in Jay's rented Bel Air mansion. Jay liked to pretend he was rich and grand – even adopting a chauffer-driven Cadillac for a time, driven by one or another of his young "under management" beauties, sort of the poor man's Hugh Hefner. He later adopted walking sticks, and had a different one for each day of the year – or so it seemed.

Joanna woke up the next morning, in Jay's bed, with clear evidence she had had sex – unbeknownst to her. She told me she put up a big scene, and when she got home, she called Ryan, who blew up. Ryan went over to Jay's house and beat the excrement out of him. Jay denied everything, including Ryan's mopping up the driveway with Jay's head, claiming he had had an auto accident.

During one of my ex-wife Linda's periodic estrangements from Swifty Lazar, she took a job as Jay's executive assistant, working from his home. Jay's affectations had become so extreme that he stayed in bed all day, commanding his legions from there. Only when the sun went down would he rise, dress, select a walking stick and a young beauty for the night, and make his rounds of the in-restaurants, debarking from his Cadillac for his entrance. Only Count Dracula did it better.

As with all great men, Jay was prone to volcanic anger when he imagined he had been slighted, or one of his employees didn't immediately respond to his slightest whim. In fact, he was known to carry a holstered gun. One day, in his darkened bedroom, Jay lost it with Linda. She had told me she couldn't take his insanity any longer and was quitting. He probably knew it, and when she turned away from him to leave the room, and refused to return, he pulled out a pistol from under his quilt and pegged a shot into the door, above her head. She continued out and was gone. I begged her to let me call the cops, but she wouldn't let me. Just before he died, I saw a picture of him wearing a new blonde hairpiece. And he still had his walking stick.

DONALD T.

No, not that Donald T., as in Trump. This is the West Coast version, Donald T. Sterling, whom I've mentioned before. I don't know what it feels like to be super-rich, even though I've consorted with many in that class. But here's an example, and apparently it's something of a headache.

When I was working for him, circa 1990, as his voice to the media, I received a call one day from a man in New York who said he represented Barney's department store. Growing up in New York, I recalled Barney's as a lower East Side, low rent emporium similar to Filene's in Boston, where middle class people went for bargains in clothes. How times have changed. They had moved uptown and so had their prices. The man told me that Barney's had decided to open a branch in Beverly Hills and had been scoping the area for a while. Sterling owned a building on the corner of Wilshire Blvd. and Beverly Drive, obviously a prime piece of real estate. It had been built in 1927 by Louis B. Mayer, the legendary chief of MGM, as an investment. There were few autos in L.A. then, so the building didn't have below ground parking – the only such building of 12 floors in Beverly Hills. Because of that, and its creaking elevators and musty smell in the hallways, it was mainly unoccupied, except for a few struggling theatrical agencies, cheap jewelers, and a tailor or two. The Donald of the West Coast had for some years been officed in the penthouse suite of the Bank of America building across the street from his own building. It simply wasn't grand enough for him

Sterling's real estate philosophy is that you buy but never sell – that over time, everything of value goes up, not down. He's right of course, but it goes against the human desire to take action in our daily lives, whether it's problem solving in our businesses or homes, or day-trading in the stock market – anything to remind us we're alive, and in charge of our own destiny. For many years, he bought the building in 1975, real estate values, even in Beverly Hills, were stagnant. But when Barney's expressed a desire to me to purchase the building from Don and asked me how much he wanted, the light must have gone on in his head. He told me to tell them he wasn't interested.

But Barney's, obviously, hadn't become a prominent success by not persisting, so we negotiated – and negotiated. Finally, the offer was a clear $15 million profit to Sterling. The entire cost to Barney's would have been some $50 million, which would have entailed completely rehabbing the building, which was loaded with asbestos, and providing parking for those occasional rainy days. Still, it was preferable to them to avoid starting the city approval process from scratch, finding another site, and constructing, which would have delayed them by a year or two.

I walked into Don's office and told him Barney's final offer – fifteen million. Cash. He looked up at me and said, "What would I do with another fifteen million dollars?

I'd have to find some place to put it. I'd need to protect it. It's too much trouble. Tell them to forget it."

So that's what it's like to be super-rich. It's a problem. And a burden. Barney's did build their own edifice on Wilshire Blvd. I assume they're happy. Don, however, decided to upgrade his building – probably because someone else wanted it, and spent a few million himself, bringing it up to code. Painting the outside brilliant white, with gold accents, and so brilliantly lit at night, it's probably an aviation hazard, he named it Sterling Plaza. Old Louis Mayer, that suspected pederast, had installed a penthouse on the top floor, probably to get away from his wife, whom he loathed, and Don made a Caliph's palace out of it – for himself. He subsequently moved his offices there and occupies the two top floors. The rest of the building is empty. I'm reminded of Jimmy Cagney's last words in his famous gangster movie, "White Heat,".... "Top of the world, ma, I made it."

BEAUTY SECRETS

Besides Mae West's daily enema, which she swore was what kept her skin so beautiful until she died, Preparation H, applied generously to the skin at bedtime, is what many Hollywood actresses use to keep the wrinkles at bay. Yeah, the very same Preparation H sold in drugstores meant to reduce hemorrhoids. Try it, you'll like it.

And in Beverly Hills, you can get a Butt Facial. No kidding, in fact BH is known as the home of the famous Butt Facial. Think about it.

HENRY MILLER DIED HAPPY

When Charlie Pierce and I made "*Winterhawk*," in Montana, in 1975, I had hired a tall, statuesque and very striking actress named Brenda Venus to play the wife of the film's star, Michael Dante. Dante, of course, was the Indian chief, Winterhawk, so his wife needed to look Indian. And she did. Long black hair, luscious body, hawkish nose, and she even claimed she was half-Apache. She worked out well; the movie was finished, and like most film personnel after the wrap party, went her separate way.

That same year, I moved into my present apartment and, to my surprise, ran into Brenda on my street five years later. She was my neighbor in the condo building right next door. We had a nice reunion and she asked me to visit her the next afternoon. I did, and after showing me in, took me into her bedroom, where she introduced me to the legendary author, Henry Miller, in her bed. Although he was 89, and obviously ill, he was very cordial, and had a twinkle about him. Miller had written a novel, "*Tropic of Cancer,*" published in 1934, that rocked the literary world. He wrote two more books based on his growing notoriety, called "*Black Spring,*" in 1936, and "*Tropic of Capricorn,*" in 1939. All were banned in the U.S. on grounds of obscenity, but were being smuggled in, making Miller famous. Much like a later Hugh Hefner, his anti-puritanical books helped determine from both legal and social aspects the future of sexual subjects in American writing. The publication of "*Tropic of Cancer*" in the United States in 1964 led to a series of obscenity trials that codified American laws on pornography. That same year the Supreme Court overruled the State Court findings of obscenity, which led to what we now call as the sexual revolution.

Miller was a celebrated cocksman – all you needed to do was read one of his books, or see the 1990 movie, directed by Phil Kaufman, made about a portion of his life in Paris in 1931, entitled, "*Henry and June,*" which loosely portrayed him with his wife, acting out the scenarios he would later write about. This one was where Miller, played by Fred Ward, and June, portrayed by Uma Thurman, meet soon-to-be-famous, Anais Nin. Imagine the possibilities. See the movie, it's pretty good.
I forget how, exactly, Brenda met Miller, but she was taking care of him near the end of his life, and, as we chatted, snuggled up to him in bed, which only made him twinkle even more. I understood perfectly. It's how I want to go as well. He didn't die there, however, but in New York, in June of 1980. Brenda moved away and I haven't seen her since.

HOW FAR WOULD YOU GO TO GET AN AGENT?

Let's just say I nearly died. I mentioned previously I had become a screenwriter – which I've always referred to as the last refuge of a scoundrel. No longer an agent myself, and because of the Billy Wilder law, I now needed an agent to send my material to the studios. The Billy Wilder law is not really a law, but is an agreement among the studios to protect themselves from lawsuits, and concerned a screenplay sent to him when he was in residence at Paramount Pictures in the 40's. Wilder's secretary received it and confirmed to the writer it had arrived and that she would speak to the great man himself about it. Several days later, when the writer called again, Billy's secretary said she had discussed it with her boss, and he wasn't interested. She returned the script to the writer by mail.

Several years later, Wilder wrote, produced and directed "*Ace in the Hole,*" the story of a miner trapped in a mine shaft. Despite heroic rescue efforts by the entire town, the miner dies. Key to the story is the role played by Kirk Douglas, as a fiercely ambitious reporter out to make a name for himself. Douglas drops all pretence at morality or good taste while exploiting the terrified family, the police, state officials and everyone else he comes into contact with. Sort of sounds like today's cable news coverage, doesn't it? The movie bore more than a striking resemblance to the script the writer had submitted several years earlier. He sued, and won. Ever since then, no civilians are able to submit material directly to a studio. Hence the agent's unassailable position in Hollywood.

Lee Gabler, a tall, distinguished New Yorker, had moved to L.A., to work for International Creative Management Agency in the early 80s, because he didn't want to have to tough out another winter on the east coast. He knew a friend of mine, a TV producer named Barry Weitz, who introduced me to Lee on several occasions. I decided Lee was going to represent me. At first, to be kind to me and to his friend Barry, Gabler was pleasant but non-committal. I had no credits as a writer, had not sold even an option to anyone, and besides, Lee was busy meeting his west coast agent colleagues, producers, and his new client list. I persisted though, and pretty soon, Lee was not being so nice in turning me down.

Barry always considered himself a sportsman, an outdoorsman, and an expert in the manly art of slaying barnyard animals with large caliber guns. He was a hunter and also a fisherman. He justified his activities by always eating what he slew – from a wild pig, to a deer, to a trout. In fact, as Barry's specialty, Movies of the Week, diminished, and then disappeared entirely, Barry spent most of his time in the woods or standing hip deep in freezing water. One day, Barry said he had invited Gabler to join him on a three-day deer hunt in the mountains above Mammoth Lakes, in the High Sierra, and wanted to know if I'd like to join them. I figured this was the perfect opportunity to win Lee over through sheer force of my personality. That, and being trapped in the mountains with no one else to talk to. I accepted, and set about assembling all the elements I'd need for the event. Barry lent me one of his many rifles, and I scrounged, or bought long underwear, waterproof pants, down jacket, wool watch cap, insulated gloves and socks, etc. We were to have a guide and, I found out half way between Beverly Hills and Mammoth, we would be on horseback between camps. I've never been much of a horse person. I like them, I think they're beautiful animals, but I also think they're pretty stupid, untrustworthy, unreliable, and probably hate whoever's dumb enough to climb onto their back. I know I would.

Barry assured me the horses were essentially pack horses that worked the very trails we would take most of the year, bearing supplies to scattered communities high up in the Sierra, and working with our guide and his clients on missions such as the one we were committed to. He said the horses were smarter than we were. At this point, I was beginning to think he was right. Probably because as we rose steadily into the mountains, the temperature dropped sharply, and it began to rain. We spent the first night in a Motel 6, which, as it turned out, might have been the Beverly Hills Hotel, compared to what was coming up next.

We piled out of bed at 4:30 a.m. the next morning, drank some awful hot liquid the motel insisted was coffee, and drove to the pack station to meet our guide. It had stopped raining, but it was still dark and cold at 6,500 feet above sea level. Frank, our man in the wilderness, looked like a more sinister version of Ben Johnson, the movie western heavy who menaced Marlon Brando in "*One-Eyed Jacks*," Brando's only directorial effort. He was affable, however, and had already selected our horses. Mine was a plug. Obviously, Frank had gotten the message. We saddled up, mounted up, and were off – straight up. Besides we four humans and our nags, Frank led four loaded pack mules, and as we climbed ever higher around switchbacks, on trails no wider than our horses, where the drop-off on either side was sheer and straight down, I began to wonder just how important it was to have an agent anyway.

We reached the first camp site around noon. We knew it was noon because our watches told us so. Just as we arrived it had begun to snow. We helped Frank unload the mules and struggled to erect our tents in the swirling, wet snow-rain. Shivering helped, Frank said, because it kept you from hypothermia. It was the body's way of protecting you. Swell. Frank said a-hunting we would go around dusk, when the deer were moving. We munched on cold, damp bologna sandwiches and colder coffee, and retired to our tents to build up anticipation for the hunt. So far, Lee and I had had a few interesting words and I felt I was making progress, but nothing like the male bonding over the still-warm body of our quarry to come.

The day was fading when Frank spurred us to action. We saddled up again and hit the trail. I hoped Barry was truly right about the animals being smarter than us, because the snow had completely obliterated the trail, and the horses kept tripping on loose rocks and shale. Frank signaled to stop. We all froze. Except for Lee's horse in front of me, who decided to take a hot, steaming dump. Apparently that scared the target off, and Frank motioned us to start up again. A few minutes later, he signaled us to stop and dismount. Whispering, he said there was a group of deer up ahead, and who wanted the first shot? Not me, I assured him, as Barry tactfully pushed Lee forward for the honor.

Lee Gabler, a nice Jewish boy from Manhattan, was as at home in these circumstances as Woody Allen would have been. I knew what he was thinking, because I was thinking it too. But it was too late – we were there, and no turning back. Frank and Lee stole stealthily forward, with Barry and me bringing up the rear. The falling snow muffled our footsteps. Frank held up his hand - up ahead was a large buck with several does. They were motionless looking right at us. Damn deer were to dumb to flee. Frank pointed, Lee aimed, pulled the trigger – and missed. Now the deer took off. Frank looked annoyed, this probably happened to him more often than not. If each of us had scored that first day, we would have headed back down the mountain and home, and Frank would have been paid and off duty in front of his fireplace, scratching his dog's head. Or his balls, if he didn't have a dog.

Frank whispered we'd catch up with them shortly, and Barry said he'd take the next shot. Fine with me. The snow had let up and true to Frank's prediction, there was the deer family again. Not out in the open as before, but partially hidden in a snow-covered thicket. You could see the buck's head, which is all you needed for a shot. Barry aimed – and missed. Frank was pretty pissed, he couldn't hide it. The deer lit out and I said, well that's it, let's go back to camp. I was freezing, wet, hungry and cursing my ambition. Frank agreed, and as we turned to trudge back to the horses, the deer appeared on a far ridge to our right. Frank motioned to me to take the next shot. I demurred, saying it was too far, even with my telescopic sight. Frank's face darkened, and I didn't want to be starring in the sequel to *"Deliverance,"* so I purposely aimed high and pulled the trigger. Now, let's go home, I said. "I think you got him," Frank said. Shit, no, I thought. No chance, not at this distance, in the near dark. "We gotta' go see," Frank said, "We can't leave a wounded animal." Wounded animal, I thought, this guy's got more than coffee in his thermos.

We slipped, and slid, and climbed, and scrambled through brush, and up the hill and to my shock, there was the buck, down, mortally wounded, and looking right up at me with enormous black eyes that seemed to say, "Now are you happy, you dumb shit?" I was mortified and sick to my stomach.

Frank went behind the animal, drew his buck knife, and slipped it into the back of the buck's neck, snipping its spinal cord and instantly dispatching the poor thing. Barry and Lee were pounding me on the back, congratulating me on my marksmanship. Frank began to gut the animal so we could carry it out and back to camp, when Barry knelt down, dipped his fingers in the deer's blood and suddenly wiped it on my face. Yuck! What was that for, I asked? It's a ritual - first blood. Oh. I'll be sure to tell Sylvester Stallone when I see him. Frank took a large plastic bag from his pocket and slipped the deer's liver inside. He cut down a sapling with his knife, tied the deer's legs, we hefted the 100 pound animal and walked out to the horses. Frank tied the deer over his horse, behind the saddle, and we rode back to camp. When we got there, Frank strung the deer up, head down, from a tree limb, to bleed out, of course, while we unsaddled the horses and put feed bags on them. Frank then built a fire, fished out a frying pan from his gear, slapped that liver in it and fried it up for us, saying that too, was part of the ritual. And if it was a hundred years ago, we'd be eating it raw. I thought I'd throw up.

Later, Frank regaled us with mountain man stories while we drank good scotch. Frank seemed to drink quite a bit more than we, but then he was a mountain man, while we were pansy-assed pussies from Beverly Hills, wherever that was. I passed out not long after, in my tent, and was rudely awakened by Frank kicking me at 4:30 the next morning. It was hell leaving my down-filled sleeping bag, but at least his coffee was better than Motel 6's. So were his eggs and bacon. At least it wasn't raining or snowing – just really cold.

We saddled up and set off, and that day neither Lee nor Barry got their deer. They were both pretty glum, not to mention Frank, who was beginning to mutter, and I was feeling a little like Humphrey Bogart in *"The Treasure of Sierra Madre,"* having a stash of gold, while Jim Huston and Tim Holt, both my former buddies, glare at me enviously across a campfire. Bogie tried not to sleep that night, fearing he'd be robbed and killed. Hell, they could have my deer, I wasn't going to do anything with it, anyway.

The next day, the last day, we hunted in the morning, but no luck. Frank said he'd go on ahead back to camp and pack up while we hunted some more, but to be back by noon for the six-hour trip down the mountain. When we arrived back at camp, Frank was gone. So were his mules, with all our supplies, tents and all. This was a fine kettle of fish. Lee, Barry and I looked at each other. It had begun to snow again. We checked what we had on us. I had a candy bar; Lee had a package of trail mix. Barry had an apple.

Well, it was all downhill, we told ourselves, and Barry broke out his 35mm Leica to memorialize the adventure. Nothing but the best for ol' Barry. I would have brought a disposable. And besides, the horses were anxious to get back to their warm barn and knew the way, even though we didn't. And of course, they were smarter than us. We headed down the trail, which at least we could see, as the rain had melted most of the snow.

Not an hour into our descent, it began to snow again, lightly at first, then heavier, until it became a fully fledged blizzard. The trail disappeared once more. Barry, Mr. Outdoorsman, who himself came from the Bronx, assured us we were fine. I wasn't so sure. But Lee started to worry out loud. I chuckled, remembering some recent modern painting in which some beautiful girl about to be blown up says, "Oh, no, I forgot to have kids." Lee was openly mouthing off about dying on this Godforsaken mountain, miles from anywhere, and how our bodies wouldn't be found until spring melt, some six months away. I was beginning to detest him for his cowardice, vowing not to have this pussy as my agent even if he begged me. But I was also scared.

The first rule when lost in the wilderness is to wish you had never…no, that's not it. The real rule is always to head down, following a stream if possible, because the less stupid people always lived in the valleys. We were doing fine going downhill on slipping, sliding, defecating horses, until mine fell into Lee's, which bumped into Barry's, and we were all sliding downhill in a lump until we reached a dead end. Whew. We were all OK, but it was obvious we had lost the trail. What to do? The snow was now approaching whiteout conditions, and even Barry was whimpering. We were in serious trouble. No one, not even our cowardly guide, knew where we were. And he didn't care. We had on warm clothes, but were getting increasingly wet. We had no food and only a pack of paper matches between us. We debated whether to try to reach the top of the hill where we had veered off the trail and try to locate it again, or to stay where we were until the blizzard was over and then make our way. We thought a nice fire would help us make our decision, so we used up all our matches on the wet wood. I suggested, since we still had guns and ammo, that we shoot the horses, hollow them out and climb inside to keep from freezing. Lee looked at me the way Walter Huston looked at Bogie, asking me where the hell I got that idea. From *"Jeremiah Johnson,"* I replied, citing the Robert Redford movie about a mountain man named "Liver-eating Johnson," who survived a similar experience in just that way some one hundred years earlier. "That was in the goddam movies," Gabler shouted at me. "So? It worked," I shouted back. I was and remain truly a child of the movies. That's how I relate to most situations. I even dream in color, occasionally with credits. My plan to secure an agent was now in shambles. Survival was the object. We decided we had no choice but to lead the horses back up the hill and let them find the way home. After all, they were……

By the time we struggled back up, it was near four p.m., and growing dark. We had sweated heavily, and forgot to dry the saddles before mounting, plopping down on wet seats. I remembered, in doing due diligence for this trip, reading somewhere that you weren't really in danger of hypothermia, which can be fatal, until your core got cold, and that the warmest place in your body was between your legs. That explains the population explosion. And the reason we were now really shivering. Which was good, according to Frank. But I don't think he meant to be shivering hard enough to knock your fillings loose. I thought it was all over and mentally said goodbye to my kids, caviar, sex, good red wine, 77% dark chocolate, all the things I liked about life on planet earth. We let go of the reins and abandoned ourselves to the superior instincts of our mounts. We didn't fall into any more dead ends, but going down a curving, winding, narrow mountain trail, at night, on a horse, in a blizzard, is not recommended for the faint of heart. Barry had a few more shots left in his camera but it didn't seem important.

I feel differently about horses now. Just before midnight, 12 full hours after we left our camp at 7,500 feet in the wilderness, we emerged on flat land. We were exhausted, our legs cramped from standing backwards in the saddle to compensate for the horse's downward lean, nearly numb from the cold, and almost faint from lack of food, water, sleep and fear. The horses, smelling their barn, began to gallop, throwing all of us off onto the hard ground.

Frank was nowhere to be found. We unsaddled our trusty heroes, rubbed them down, fed them some hay and piled into Barry's jeep. We took turns driving the six hours back to Los Angeles, speaking only when we had to. Around three a.m., Lee was the first to say how grateful we should be having survived. No argument there. Barry, who was married, as was Lee, said how glad he was to be able to go home and see his kids. Lee agreed. Then Barry said he would have missed the world of women, having reliably cheated on his wife, Beth, for many years. Lee agreed again, saying he was wowed by the amount of beautiful, available women he had found since moving to L.A., and couldn't wait himself for the opportunity to get to know some of them better. Lee then said how delicious he found Barry's secretary, Joan, and how he'd like a shot at her. "Me too," said Barry, "but she won't shit where she eats," he said mournfully, "so she won't do you either." Lee looked hurt. I couldn't resist. "Then no one minds if I try?" I piped up from the back seat. Barry and Lee looked disdainfully back at me, as if I was Quasimodo. "Yeah, go ahead, you got as much chance as a sperm," said Barry. Very original, I thought. By now I was getting pretty annoyed – first at myself for even having considered going on this near-fatal quest for something as dim-witted as my desire for an agent, then at Lee for his constant rejection of me, and now certain that I didn't want him even if he wanted me, and at Barry for his supercilious dismissal of my vaunted appeal to women.

Barry, another sufferer of satyriasis, thought he was successful with women, and he was, to a certain extent. As a TV producer, he had access to any number of actresses who would "do anything" to get a part. But he was boastful and dismissive of women, and once with him, they were not anxious for a repeat. He did have some longish affairs with a couple of neurotic actresses and they invariably ended when they called Beth, Barry's wife, or even, one time, showed up at his front door. I had no respect for his efforts, and considered his conquests like "shooting fish in a barrel," in that the result was pre-ordained, and that his subjects were brain-damaged, if not brain-dead, to begin with. So I said in an unruffled voice from the back seat; "I've already had Joan." That nearly caused an accident, as Barry shot a look backwards at me, hurriedly gaining control of the car before running off the long, straight, pitch-dark highway. What do you mean, both wanted to know, and when? Men love the details. Two weeks before, I told them. Joan had taken me out for my birthday. Dinner at the Odyssey, with dessert at my place. I left out the part about President Reagan's helicopter landing and the Secret Service guys on the roof.

Silence from then on. I was dropped off, and didn't speak to Barry again for twelve years. Never did get Lee Gabler to represent me, either. And I have never again mistreated an animal.

L.A. IS A FACTORY TOWN

And in a factory town, everybody works in the factory. And I mean everybody. In Beverly Hills, there is a beggar on practically every street corner. Some have had the same location for years. I don't know whether they have a lottery system, or what, but passersby eventually get so used to seeing the same person there day after day, they eventually get to know them and, after dropping some change in their Starbucks (!) cup, exchange a few pleasantries.

There was this beggar named Dick….no, this isn't a limerick, who sat sprawled out in a wheelchair on South Beverly Drive, bundled up against the cold, when it was 80 degrees, baseball hat jammed down over his face, with what looked like a heavily-infected foot on view. You couldn't avoid him, which was the point. He parked himself near Al's Newsstand, so he'd have a high volume of traffic, and from I could see, did very well for himself. One day, while perusing the latest Town & Country, which everyone knows has the best horoscopes, I heard Dick conversing with what looked like a young movie or TV executive. You can always tell by their cell phone, razor cut, and gold necklace. And Dick was saying, "My agent at the Morris agency really likes my script and says he'll get it to Tom Cruise, but first I have to fix the third act." I swear.

THE CULT OF CELEBRITY

We hear a lot about that, but I think it's always been part of human culture. Frightened as we are by life itself; losing a job, losing a spouse, a kid, getting old, getting sick, dying, we look out for more "successful" people whom we can endow with qualities we wish we had; whose lives seem golden. In reality, those folks get old and die, and sometimes have even worse catastrophes happen to them than ever occur in our lives. It was probably that way from the moment we dropped from branches and began walking upright. It's certainly true among most animal species, especially chimps, with which we share better than 98% of our genes. So leaders matter. In fact, the worse our lives seem to be, the more we yearn for a strong image to follow. Sometimes it's a good thing, sometimes not. Roosevelt saved the U.S., in my opinion, in the 30s and 40s. Hitler sunk the Germans, not to mention Hirohito, of Japan, and Mussolini, ditto for the Italians. I'm sure you can think of dozens more examples.

The same goes for show biz figures. People who can make us laugh, or cry, or otherwise capture our imagination for a couple of hours, distracting us from the drudgery of our usual lives, earn big rewards for their talent. I was a waiter for several summers at hotels in the Catskills, or the Jewish Alps, or the Borscht Belt, if you like, when I was a teenager, and the "talent" that would appear on weekends was truly awful; not as terrible as the acts that Woody Allen, as *"Broadway Danny Rose,"* booked in that movie, but close. And bad as they were, they made us laugh, or forced us to dance, and made fools of us with stupid stage tricks. And we were grateful. Some of them became big names; Henny Youngman, Milton Berle, Rodney Dangerfield, Danny Kaye, Buddy Hackett, Lenny Bruce, Danny Kaye, Mel Brooks and Sid Ceasar. Five-year-old Jerry Lewis. But they were the exception.

And that kind of adulation was harmless. Today's celebrity mania is poisonous to our society, I believe. It's "bread and circuses," much as the Roman Emperors put on, to keep the populous quiecsent. We divert ourselves by focusing on the trials and tribulations of people in the spotlight temporarily. First we create them and then we tear them to shreds. *We* are the tigers and lions of today's Coliseum. The crocodile tears shed over Michael Jackson's death appall me. Is it because he was a great talent ingloriously torn from our hearts before his time? Or do we simply don't have him around any more to point to as a freak. I'm guessing the latter. "Alas, poor Yorick, I knew him well," says Hamlet, in Shakespeare's eponymous play. He was referring to the skull he found of the court jester who befriended and amused him as a child. Do we need to humiliate and frighten and make more painful the death of Farrah Fawcett? How has that enriched us? So Heath Ledger died of an overdose. So do thousands of people every day in our drug-ridden societies around the world. He wasn't a great actor, a good one, sure, but an Oscar for playing the Joker in "Batman"? And the same goes for sports.

The political structure, which includes the media, as its employees, encourages and endorses the cult, and there's no other word for it, of celebrity, because it keeps the rabble from focusing on their rage at not being able to control any aspect of their lives, from being stolen blind by the wealthy and the corporations, to having their children killed in unessessary political wars, and keeps the mob from revolting.

PHILOSOPHICALLY SPEAKING

I was going to title this remembrance, "The Man Who Got What He Wanted," because it occurred to me, rather late in life that I always got exactly what I wanted. After all, when I was 18, I wished the girl on the cover of "Seventeen" magazine would come into my life – that we'd be married, have a child, and live happily ever after. Well, four years later, exactly that happened. The only part that didn't work was the "happily ever after." Whether it was happiness or unhappiness, health or illness, wealth or poverty, success or failure, that's what I got - it was always, and remains, my choice. And then, looking around at others I knew, and those I studied from the media, it was obvious that all of us get exactly what we really want from this short existence, even though logic and reason, exclusive, it seems, to our species, would argue against it. Apparently, we are hard-wired by evolution to not be satisfied where we are – to force ourselves to reach for what we don't have, in order to be "happy." It stems from the dual nature of our continuously-evolving minds. One would think that rationally we would want health, wealth, long life, perfect children, world peace, etc. Strange, however, that as we rummage through the crowded closet of our lives, and those around us, we discover that usually we possess only some, or perhaps none of those. And then only temporarily. After all, in the long run, we're all dead.

My theory is that we evolved biologically to be unable to achieve happiness. All science, medicine, music, the arts, literature come from our deep desire to satisfy some ephemeral need to improve our unhappy lives. After all, before we fell out of the trees three million years ago, we had everything – protection from all the fearsome predators with big teeth roaming the ground, and all the fruit and nuts we could eat. But we descended, small and defenseless, with urgent needs to find ways to survive. And that meant solving constant life-or-death problems. No room for humor here. Since then, we have become the top predator on the planet by reaching for solutions that were always just beyond our grasp – always struggling, forcing our brains to enlarge, improving our longevity by out-populating the other predators, and then eating all our competition. If, at any time during our journey to today, *including* today, we decided we had enough, we needed no more, we would have had contentment. Our inability to be satisfied, I am convinced, is the source of war.

I wasn't exposed, except in a general way, to religion as a child, but my parents, wanting to do the "right thing," sent me to Hebrew school to prepare for Bar Mitzvah. It took me all of two weeks to get expelled. Once I saw the trading in fear and the essentially capitalist show that was going on, I was out of there. I was eleven.

Religion, in my opinion, is essentially what U.S. law calls a RICO Act, or an organized criminal enterprise, springing from fear of the unknown, especially death, among illiterate and superstitious people only minutes removed from the jungle (in anthropologic time), and has its roots in a small group divining (and I use that word purposefully) that assuaging fear was a foolproof business plan to separate the larger group from their clamshells, or shekels, or whatever they were using before credit cards. Come to this special cave every Sunday, we'll put on a show, mumble some words you've never heard before, and we'll introduce you to the big guy (guy?) upstairs. Kind of how the William Morris Agency operates.

Religion, in my belief system, not money, is the root of all evil. Pick up any newspaper and read the front page if you need proof.

But looking around, it's impossible to deny that all we see and experience is brilliantly designed, and integrated, which bespeaks a higher intelligence. Sure, we can design a computer, which is after all, based on the human brain – input information, store it, and retrieve at will – and the automobile, a mechanical replica of our bodies – infuse fuel (food), produce energy, while expelling waste (tailpipe), but try as we might, we can't make a tree. Our former president tried to open the door to ID, or Intelligent Design as an option to teaching evolution in the U.S. school system. Although his motive was to extend the influence of evangelical theorizing, there could be some scientific correlation to be discerned. We definitely are the highest intelligence at the moment on this planet, but proof exists there have been at least five complete extinctions of most, if not all life on Earth, from which new forms, the latest being mammals (including us), have risen. Take the ant, for example. Ants pre-date us by about 100 million years and what do they know about us? Do you think that an ant can even imagine that we exist? And that we're prepared to exterminate them anytime they get in our way? My favorite Gahan Wilson cartoon puts two ants sitting on a blade of grass, looking up at the moon. One ant says to the other, "Kind of makes you feel insignificant, doesn't it?"

Well, why not a vaster intelligence viewing the evolving Earth the way a human scientist views cellular life evolving in a Petri dish? Can we imagine, the way an ant cannot, that we exist at the pleasure, and peril, of a much greater force that can and will do away with us if we become a threat to it, or if we're no longer useful evolutionarily, or just for fun?

And if there is an intelligent designer, what can we say about such an entity that is busy, apparently, designing a super virus that just might reduce our population by many millions. Malevolence toward us, its adoring throngs? Or compassion, perhaps, for all the other life forms our burgeoning population threatens?

Perhaps the oldest story in literature is Jekyll & Hyde (or Cain & Abel) or (Martin & Lewis). OK, strike that last one. It is about the dual nature of our still developing minds - in which we struggle every moment of every day (and night, as represented in our dreams) between wanting to be moral and upright, and wanting to experience the thrill of being bad - very bad. Aren't we both, sometimes?

Our worst enemy (and paradoxically our best friend) is our ego. On the one hand, it's enabled us to go from living in the trees to standing on the moon in milliseconds of evolutionary time. On the other, it's terrified us by allowing us to realize, unlike any other animal on the planet, that we will die one day - a fact that has, as a species, driven us insane.

Which explains our aberrant behavior and our darker side that permits our frantic and cruel behavior to ourselves, our loved ones, and all the other strangers, animals and plants we share this space with (and don't forget the poor ants). So we set up elaborate defenses against our fear that beyond this life, there is….*nothing*.

What are some of those? We pass the buck. We create great edifices to assure us that past this existence are other, more pleasant ones; a place to go, where we'll meet up with our friends, families, perhaps golfing buddies. We actually pay people to intercede on our behalf with a mysterious, unknowable, seemingly contradicting higher power, and we believe! We have faith that beyond this struggle, if we're lucky, that ends up with us old, sick, and enfeebled, there is a better life somewhere. Or lives, if you're a Buddhist. What religion is actually very good at is entrapping people in mystery, superstition, and addiction - in other words, the dark.

Or, we alter our consciousness. Some people gamble, shop, overeat, others have non-stop sex (hello?). Drugs may work for a time. So does booze. So does making tons of money (I'm told). But as we get older, don't we sometimes wake up in the middle of the night with the cold hand of terror on our throats? I don't believe that anyone, religious zealots, included, does not secretly dread the end. John O'Hara's lead character, in "*Appointment in Samara*," thought he saw death approaching him in the town he lived in, so he hurriedly packed and fled across the desert to Samara - where, guess who he met?

Old Bill Shakespeare was right when he said we start our lives terrified and in diapers, and we end it the same way. Perhaps one day, if we don't extinct ourselves, we will look back on religion as just another bad idea in human history, like slavery, or witch burnings (hey, that's religion).

We are, generally, sociopathic, in that our consciousness is limited. Socially, we have not progressed very far from our survival mode of only 6,000 or so years ago.

Certainly we're cleaner, we live longer, we have structured societies - but we're also managing to continue slaughtering each other (and everything else) much more efficiently and in much greater numbers. And the benchmark of us humans is that we're afraid, very afraid.

Well, fortunately we grow up - bent and fractured sometimes, but now able to make our own decisions. We are every bit as determined to pursue happiness as we were as children, but we just don't know how. We seek assistance - from peers, wives, husbands, ministers, therapists; and everyone, in their way, has something to teach us. But the only real teacher is the one inside us - the one we don't believe - because we were taught not to.

At what point do we turn inward for guidance? When we've tried everything else and can't take any more pain. And will wonders ever cease – there are the answers! All along we've instinctively known what we should do. But how could we disobey our authority figures, beginning with our moms and dads. Bless them, but they didn't have a clue what they were doing, did they? *It would be disrespectful -it would be wrong. What would other people think of us?*

But of course there's hope. That the knowledge we are born with and acquire through experience (or light, as some term it) within us is capable of overcoming the darkness (meaning the fear), the way it does when you enter a black room, (afraid of who might be waiting for us) and switch on the light. There! Feel better?

We would be better off employing our unique ability to reason and to logic to stimulate, preserve, encourage and grow the light (or knowledge) within ourselves and, where you receive permission, within others.

GO HAVE KIDS

I never wanted my two girls to go into showbiz, and I always told them so. I insisted that today a woman can achieve anything, can be anything. Except president of the U.S., of course, although that may change, and that I didn't want them growing up feeling they needed a man to make their way for them. I suggested medicine, science, even law, although I didn't want them, in the latter case, to someday be chased by peasants with torches.

So both are in show business. Jill, by Carol, is a music industry journalist and TV producer, living in London since her beloved boss, Andy Warhol, died tragically from a medical mistake. Alexandra, from Linda, after graduation from the Rhode Island School of Design, went to work in Boston as the sweater designer for Victoria's Secret catalogue, and is now a successful film and TV costume designer in Hollywood.

I began this remembrance with a phrase from the Bible and end it with the title of one of William Shakespeare's comedies: "All's Well That Ends Well." And Bill has never lied to me.

Lightning Source UK Ltd.
Milton Keynes UK
UKOW031825190513

210903UK00006B/100/P